RADIO
OKAPI
KINDU

The Station That Helped
Bring Peace to the Congo

RADIO OKAPI KINDU

JENNIFER BAKODY

Figure 1
Vancouver / Berkeley

Cataloguing data available from Library and Archives Canada
ISBN 978-1-927958-97-1 (pbk.)

This work depicts actual events as truthfully as recollection permits and/or can be verified by research. Some names and identifying details have been changed to protect the privacy of the people involved.

Editing by Scott Steedman
Copy editing by Shirarose Wilensky
Proofreading by Lucy Kenward
Maps by Eric Leinberger
Design by Natalie Olsen
Author photo by Jean Claude Bisiliabo
Printed and bound in Canada by Friesens
Distributed in the U.S. by Publishers Group West

Figure 1 Publishing Inc.
Vancouver BC Canada
www.figure1pub.com

To Benoît, my best editor;

to Anne and David, my pillars of strength;

and to the soldiers of peace whose reporting
has brought forth great honour.

Prologue

IN 2004, JUST BEFORE my thirtieth birthday, I was offered a job as a public information officer with the United Nations Mission in the Democratic Republic of the Congo (MONUC). Six years of civil war (famously called Africa's "first world war" by former U.S. Secretary of State Madeleine Albright) were trickling to an end. The war had involved three main factions: the Congolese government (Kabilists, or PPRD, supported by Zimbabwe, Angola and Namibia); the Rally for Congolese Democracy (RCD-Goma, supported by Rwanda); and the Movement for the Liberation of the Congo (MLC, supported by Uganda). The hostilities had given rise to the assassination of Congolese president Laurent-Désiré Kabila and the creation of the United Nations (UN) peacekeeping mission I would work for.

My job would be to manage a small radio station that was part of a larger national network backed by the UN and a Swiss non-governmental organization (NGO). Radio Okapi had become known as "the frequency of peace," because its programming aimed to build consensus by putting high journalistic standards above all else. The idea struck me as pure genius. Radio Okapi offered people a much-needed source of hope and, more than that, the solid grounding that comes with having a public record. Unlike during the war years—when long drawn-out battles had cut off all classes of people, when at times even the arrogant who thought the say-so of their money could control what was happening had found themselves sorely mistaken—the vast distances between the cities of Matadi and Goma, Mbandaka and Lubumbashi were now being bridged. By airwaves.

With droves of young fighters laying down their arms and daring to believe in the promise of free and fair elections, our job was to provide evenhanded information. And so, during the nine months we were together, eight Congolese journalists and I worked like dogs to demystify the intangible impetus that left so many people disposed to conspiracy theories, Biblical hexes and general highfalutin mumbo-jumbo. We knew we had to have our facts straight, if nothing else. Our listeners judged us by one simple measure: *Was Okapi's reporting balanced and impartial?* In the end, that's all people cared about. Every other thing we got right—presentation, storytelling, entertainment—would fall like a coconut to the ground if ever we allowed for bias. Simply put, information was too precious to treat like "breaking news"—it had to be verified.

The place was called Kindu. Five, six hundred years ago, Arab traders called it Kindo, meaning "footstep." The Belgians renamed it Port Empain, after an industrialist who'd built electric tramlines in Cairo and the Paris metro. The Congo was a Belgian colony then, and Kindu–Port Empain was a carousel some three hundred kilometres south of the equator that linked the country's resource-rich southern and western provinces by rail and the upper reaches of the world's second-largest river.

Nine months. It isn't long in a lifetime. One day, years after the fact, my husband brought up the subject of my fortieth birthday. He had taken on the task of making our plans. We called him the master planner, because he loved to make personal projects come together and revelled in a sense of achievement when things went smoothly.

In a slight French accent my ears no longer heard, he said, "Promise me you won't be disappointed if what I organize has nothing to do with Africa."

"I know, I know, I know," I said. "I won't be. I promise."

He paused to give me an accusatory look.

"I know there are other places in the world. I know. I get it."

The conversation was left there, on the kitchen counter, next to a pile of junk mail, my husband's unopened bills and my *New Practical Chinese Reader*. I turned towards the stairs, my mind narrowing things down to one of two possibilities: Either my husband had plans to make a liar out of me. Or we were going to Africa.

THE DAY I DISCOVERED that Mamy was on Facebook, her cover photo showed a panorama of twenty-one people, including a uniformed white man whose head was out of the frame. They were gathered outside a thatched-roof hut – Mamy, the only woman. She was holding a blue-socked microphone shaped like a pineapple on its stem, under the chin of a man who was talking. I saw that 24 of her 274 Facebook friends were mutual, and her "likes" included the 2003 movie *Aki na Ukwa* – a Nigerian comedy about two brothers who were constantly getting into trouble. Her page linked to the American television series *24*, which we all used to watch at the cafeteria on movie night.

Mamy doesn't write to me very often, which is just as well, because a message from Mamy coming out of the blue usually means bad news. When I'd recently checked in with her, she responded straight away.

"Waouuuuuuuuuuuuuuuuuuuu," she'd typed. "Back to school, learning Chinese… Jennifa, you don't just sit around."

Jennifa! Having my name purposely misspelled *à la congo-laise* felt like the ultimate compliment; I laughed when I thought about what this said about me.

Mamy went on to say that she admired what she called my courage and she was trying to follow my example. I read her message several times and at last understood it was possible to possess both confidence and self-esteem and still not realize the distinction of one's own life.

After logging out of my email, I remained at the computer to read the news on radiookapi.net. Recalling the past, I bemoaned the future: the Congo's problems were so severe, so deep-rooted and convoluted, when, *how,* would anything ever change? All of a sudden, my mind turned to Sadala's old yellow Volkswagen Beetle. Was it still parked where he'd left it? That car would have been worth something to someone, which is why, somewhere along the way, someone who knew must've taken a machete to hack at the vines constantly threatening to engulf it. Because that's how it works: After the whole is gone, the parts take on a life of their own. Things break. Erode. People go. Others forget, or never knew.

THE RISING SUN WAS turning the sky a purple shade of grey when a white, large and lumbering UN-marked bus grunted to a stop outside the main entrance of Kinshasa's Grand Hotel, eighteen-odd floors and soaring over a cacophony of hubbub — the cardinal condition of things, tired and beaten down, even before the coming day's swelter. Inside the lobby, a set of steel elevator doors parted with a high-pitched *ding!* Rushing out was a sandy-haired woman on the pretty side of attractive. Sparkling green eyes and a still-young smile eclipsed her face at their will, softening the sharp lines of her body, nose and triangular chin.

Two black-suited doormen looked up to see the woman struggling to wheel a nubby black Samsonite over the gap between the elevator and the floor. The two men had paused their conversation and were considering taking steps to assist her during the time she hurried by, smiled at them and sang out hello.

This woman was me. Some two weeks after arriving in the Congolese capital off flights from Halifax, Montreal and Paris, I was continuing my course to wherever it was I was going: from here to Timbuktu.

At my back towered a high-ceilinged, luminous and surprisingly modern hotel, if slightly outdated inside the rooms. Of the hotel's two wings, I'd been staying in what was called the Grande

Tour, away from the casino and closest to the tennis courts and long-term residences. What had I been expecting? Certainly not to be eating wood-fired pizza under a straw cabana by the pool as two Congolese men in sombreros went from table to table singing "Guantanamera" on the guitar. Some foreigners, including me, would throw back their heads and giggle—perhaps even to their faces. And the two (whom we called Juan and Carlos for some unknown reason) would laugh back garrulously, all for the show, so that a person never would have guessed that armed rebels and soldiers had taken over the place not six months earlier.

The war had been rooted in generations of mass pillaging and crimes against humanity. In the 1880s, Belgian king Leopold II had turned the territory into a personal capitalist venture; after which, in 1908, the Belgian Congo practised indigenous forced labour. Then, five years after independence, in 1965, former colonel Joseph-Désiré Mobutu ousted the country's president and prime minister before spending thirty-two years enriching himself and his allies with the Congo's vast mineral wealth. This was some of the history I'd read on the plane ride here. The book, called *King Leopold's Ghost,* topped the suggested reading list for all new international staff of the United Nations Mission in the Democratic Republic of the Congo. The mission was known by its French acronym, MONUC—with a *u* and not an *i,* despite the way most Congolese people pronounced it. "Monique," they said.

Racing up the steps of the bus as if I'd been holding everyone up, I collapsed my suitcase's long handle and bent at the knees to hoist it onto a pile of others spilling over the bus's front seats. My shoulders dropped in relief when the driver sprang up to help.

"Hello, *Maman*," he said. The white of his teeth popped against a crescent of black cherry lips.

I smiled back and said, *"Bonjour,"* and thought, *Hey, wait—* "Mother"? *Don't they call everyone "Sister"?* The thought alone made me feel inexplicably guilty—enough to ensure I ignored the strong tang of body odour caught up in the bus's air conditioning.

We stopped several times to pick up more people and their luggage, accompanied by the fat big-band bass of Papa Wemba's "Show Me the Way." Its final notes faded into a succinct three-tone jingle: first *O-ka-pi* rang out in falling tones; then the same three syllables rose speedily anew, as if to pare the losses. Next thing I knew, the playlist had moved on, as did we, lurching down the same road for an hour.

Down the same road, for an hour—it bears repeating. And it wasn't a highway—I wouldn't have called it that. It was more like a wide, flat free-for-all on which everyone was competing for the space to keep moving. There were no lines or lanes, but after a while organization sprang forth from the bedlam. The rustiest, slowest-moving vans—the ones with welded-out windows overflowing with passengers—tended to drive closest to the shoulder, whereas the newer-model suvs—those with tinted windows—appeared to be driving head-on into opposing traffic. Our bus drove somewhere in the middle, and as it advanced at a steady clip over potholes, chunks of gravel, pooled sewage and litter, it squeaked, as if powered by a team of racing mice rather than plain old gasoline.

I'd already figured out Kinshasa was like this: sprawling, overgrown. The city had presented itself in a similar fashion when I'd arrived off my Air France flight. It had been nighttime then, pitch black but for lanterns and candles glowing like giant fireflies along the main road into Kinshasa's administrative and diplomatic centre—Gombe, the municipality was called. Someone I knew from home—someone who worked here and had put me onto the job in the first place—had accompanied the UN protocol officer whose job it was to fetch me and the other UN arrivals, be they new to the mission or back from leave. There'd been about a dozen of us, all flocking to the protocol officer's bobbing white MONUC sign like sheep among wolves. In fairness, public pandemonium at that level went beyond the scope of my imagination: people sitting, people standing, people grabbing... This was an international airport, yet there were no screens, no announcements, no Customs to speak of—at least I never passed through any. There was plenty of waiting around by the defunct baggage carousel, holding your ground at the expense of kisses and hugs. You just grabbed your bag and pushed your way out as quickly as possible.

Suddenly, our bus sharply tilted, turning my head around. Probably half the passengers were Congolese. Pockets of people leaned into each other, as if it were natural for them to sit together. Their ages seemed to range from around twenty to forty-five, everyone in the prime of their lives. I wasn't privy to anyone's specific situation but knew that I, for one, had a plane to catch. After two weeks in Kinshasa, I was about to travel 1,200 kilometres eastward to a small city called Kindu, the capital of the province of Maniema.

Expatriates and Congolese alike had been irrefutably clear: Kindu was broke and broken down. They made Kindu out to be some malaria haven and said the place mattered little to the Congolese state, and even less to its neighbours, which, paradoxically, had at least spared it the hardship of harbouring wanted natural resources. Apart from the town of Kasongo's famously juicy pineapples, which were said to be as big as pumpkins, the whole of the province scarcely produced food or goods. To be well and truly cynical, the mother of all Maniema exports was disease. Cholera. Malaria. Tuberculosis. Even monkey pox.

And if the region didn't produce it, it simply didn't have it. In the absence of road, river or operational rail infrastructure, the population was hard-pressed to access potable water or up-to-date pharmaceuticals. Local salt had no iodine.

It was the jungle, they said.

Nationwide, the war was meant to be over. There was meant to be a nation. I'd covered the Congo from Paris during the two years I'd worked there as a journalist for Radio France Internationale, so I knew a bit about recent developments: the Global and All Inclusive Agreement recently signed by Congolese belligerents and political groups in Sun City, South Africa, had ushered in a transitional government that saw President Joseph Kabila Kabange—"Kabila *fils*" the Congolese called him, as the son of the previous president—share power with four vice-presidents. One of these was Azarias Ruberwa, a man I'd actually interviewed once over the phone. Ruberwa, Kabila and the other three vice-presidents were all implicated to varying degrees in the fighting that was stubbornly soldiering on throughout the east and the northeast and, to a lesser extent, in pockets of the west.

In this context, the context of conflict, Kindu was more central than east. Having been posted to Kindu some time back, another *chef d'antenne,* as we were called (which even then I knew was just a fancy French way of saying "regional station manager"), had gone over the ins and outs of the job before me. This guy, Étienne, had passed on a gamut of local contacts, which I ought to have written down but didn't, owing to what a more organized person might have considered reckless abandon. Étienne had also told me the names of the station's journalists and technician: in all, one woman and seven men (though one of the men had been suspended indefinitely for a reason that hadn't been clearly explained; I'd understood it had something to do with substance abuse). A second man was on a short assignment in the warring city of Bunia, in the country's northeast, where the Hema were fighting the Lendu. Or the Lendu were fighting the Hema.

"It's too dangerous for Okapi to keep reporters in Bunia," said Étienne, unembellished, before going on to say that to keep the Bunia station up and running, the network used a rotation system. "Every three weeks, we take journalists from the regions and bring them in. In and out. We have to."

"Because it's dangerous."

"Because time puts them at risk. You know, there can be fall-out from news coverage. People—authorities, the elite—can get threatened. The justice system… There's no deterrent. There's nothing stopping them."

From doing what? I said to myself—before on second thought answering my own question.

The fighting that had taken place in Maniema wasn't about the Hema or the Lendu, or any one ethnic group against another. In Kindu, a hodgepodge of local militants known as the Mai-Mais had banded together to defend their land against Rwandan-backed rebels who'd besieged the place. I was told the situation had lasted about two years. Now, with the peace deal inked, the rebels had stood down, their leaders preparing for the elections. And with no one to fight against, the Mai-Mais were disbanding.

Seen this way, it felt as if Kindu were yesterday's news. At the same time, I reminded myself that the causes behind each clash were as diverse as the country's peoples, their struggles and fears. In the Congo, where factions had tussled with splinter factions, and six neighbouring countries had been sucked in, conflict was proving to be as incomprehensible as it was intractable. Even in so-called peaceful pockets such as Kindu, hastily brokered disarmament deals had laid a giant bandage over cavernous problems, such as injustice and corruption and impunity. All the same, the transitional process underway called for national elections to be held in eighteen months. If the country was to get there, ample rebuilding would have to be carried out, and swiftly. All state institutions were forsaken, and any point outside Kinshasa was still waiting for its state representatives to be named.

As far as Kindu's journalists were concerned, Sadala, what was her name—*Miffy?* and a man with the very strange name of Rigobert were said to be the station's strongest, whereas Matthieu and the technician were said to be... otherwise. Standard UN procedure required Radio Okapi to hire locally, which meant that at the time of recruitment in early 2002, any candidate living in Kindu who had a university degree and could speak proper French and Swahili—the two languages in which Radio Okapi Kindu broadcast—saw his or her resumé rise to the top of the pile.

The lack of formal training didn't particularly worry me. Long had I said, "Reporting isn't rocket science"; anyone with the slightest intelligence and curiosity could learn to collect and relay facts. To be honest, it suited me to think they didn't know much. I liked the idea of teaching. I thought I'd be good at it; I liked people and liked to lead, and figured I had skills to share. I was, however, worried: Wouldn't a crew of mostly men resent the authority of a woman flown in from Canada (and one young enough in some cases to be their daughter)? In their shoes, I would have.

Coming up on the left, the words of a small inconspicuous sign were becoming increasingly legible through the crisscrossed bars of the bus's grated windows: *Mon... uc term... inal.* MONUC's air operations (or AirOps, yet another new "word" to learn) had agreed on terms with the Congolese government, allowing it exclusive use of a secured section of Kinshasa's N'Djili Airport as one of its hubs. All domestic UN travel used the mission's eponymous network of flights. There were only three hundred kilometres of paved roads throughout all of the Congo—*Could that really be right?* At any rate, UN policy strictly forbade staff from any form of domestic travel other than the ones it had created. (Forbade *international* staff, surely? You wouldn't think it could stop Congolese people from using their own forms of transport in their own country.) It didn't make sense, now that I was thinking about it.

The bus slowed. Its wheels cut sharply as we turned down an uneven dirt path, bumping along to a checkpoint. A local guard rose indolently, securing his gun but tipping over an orange plastic chair that had been leaning on a slant on a hummock of flat, dead, straw-coloured grass. He lifted a wooden bar, and then moved to sit back down. As my window passed him by, a trickle of sweat ran down his cheek like a tear.

The bus's final squeak came to naught in front of a prefabri-cated container. Moments later, I was half in, half out of the compound, in a lineup of UN staffers, Blue Helmet peacekeep-ers and accidental tourists—all of us loafing around, fiddling with cellphones and such. The humidity made standing in line back-breaking. At some point, I had to lean against the long handlebar of my suitcase, for there was nothing else to do, short of sitting in the gravel. Some people were off to the side, leaning against a container wall, smoke rising from cigarettes between their fingers.

Given our lassitude, merely reaching the front of the lineup felt merciful.

"So… Jennifer?" read the UN worker behind the counter ani-matedly. "You're off to Kindu. Is that really as rough as they say?"

His hand made a gesture that I promptly answered by placing my suitcase on a large tottery scale that jingled following a heavy thump. A whiff of cologne made my eyes water.

"Is it rough?" I thought aloud. "I don't know. Beats me. I've never been. I've just arrived in the mission. It's where I've been deployed."

"It's the jungle, you know."

"So I've heard."

The man — brown-eyed, broad-shouldered and strikingly handsome — looked me up and down with neither shame nor intent. "You a UNV?"

By most accounts, two weeks in the UN was only about a third of the time needed to achieve organizational fluency; still, by this point I knew enough to know that his *V* stood for volunteer — and that I was getting paid, thank you.

"No," I countered, with a modicum of pride. "I'm the new station manager for Radio Okapi Kindu." (This was half true; in fact, I'd be wearing two hats — one: running the radio, and two: assuming all local MONUC public information tasks.)

"Eh!" said the man, throwing out his hand and walloping my shoulder. "Radio Okapi! That's good, that is! *En tout cas…* That's very good."

THE ANTICIPATION OF our plane's descent lodged itself in my stomach. I leaned forward, then back a hair, to secure a clear view out the window located one seat over. Wide-eyed, I watched as we passed through cottony clouds, gradually sinking lower, until one tip of the plane's wings parted the clouds to reveal splendour and deficiency.

They say the human eye can distinguish more shades of green than any other colour. Mine saw more than they'd ever seen before: densely clustered banana and palm groves, which, from above, looked like broccoli tops. Not grass but sun-whitened patches of brown filled the clearings, upon which sprouted dunes of weeds, bamboo and coconut trees. The corrugated tin roofs of straw huts and cement and iron-red clay brick homes glistened in the sunshine. The roads were dirt, perhaps even silt. Many were beige with a distinct titian hue. They had no structure and appeared to start from nothing and lead nowhere. Surprisingly for such a rural outpost, there was no sign of farming or agriculture. No sign of kempt growth on the land.

The plane fell a couple hundred metres, shifting the perspective fractionally. The mighty Congo River branded a muddy-watered *S* across the land.

Out of the dirt, asphalt was rising.

IT WAS NOON IN KINDU — Tuesday, and the cold foggy mist of Nova Scotia in early March was a faraway memory in the scorching yellow sun. At first sight, everything was awash in bright sunlight, casting a white lens over the rudimentary tarmac with its blinding fool's gold. Rocks. Dirt. To the sides, reedy trees with young shoots held unimpeachable posture. There certainly were a lot of trees — but enough to qualify as the jungle?

Straight ahead in the middle distance, the airport's white-painted terminal appeared as simple as Lego. Every banana tree, every bird that flew by looked too animated to be real. It was hard to think of anything but the heat, and by the last pressed-steel stair, I, who rarely sweated, had to peel my handbag off my arm. It took work to breathe.

We proceeded across the tarmac single file as local ground staff, all of a boy's age and wearing neon yellow–striped pina-fores, mingled at our edges. A stocky man in a short-sleeved suit, who seemed to know everyone by name, kept blocking my view.

"Excuse me," I said to him at one point, in a friendly tone, as if he hadn't nearly clocked me in the face by whipping around to say hello to someone loudly in my ear.

"Eh! Sorry," he said, and patted me on the shoulder. Two seconds later, seeing someone else, he suddenly stopped altogether. *Ohh!* I teetered awkwardly as I banged into him. He laughed—more apologies traded. And I laughed, too.

In the entire city, I knew one person, vaguely. Not she but someone else had come to fetch me. One of MONUC's twenty or so expatriate public information officers had been sent from his regular base in Kinshasa sometime ahead of me, because the previous officer—a Lebanese woman; Eliane was her name—had had to run off urgently to the east, to the city of Bukavu, where tension was building, and someone had to smooth the transition of my coming. The man who'd come was more seasoned than I was; no one had said so, but I could tell because in Kinshasa people who knew him put an "ah" before his name with an air of assurance (as in "ah, Mamadou"), and I'd heard someone say he'd once worked for the French magazine *Jeune Afrique*. I hoped in at least one way he was not like me and was the sort to keep to the shadows.

Through the door, Mamadou spotted me at once. We stood exchanging pleasantries while the pinafored men carried in the plane's luggage piece by piece. Mamadou jangled keys while fanning his shirt for air. With the room emptying, the thuds echoed louder and louder: so many black suitcases and not one nubby Samsonite! Mamadou said nothing would change until people's mentalities changed, and having the right mentality was half the battle won.

Finally, my suitcase showed up. Mamadou took it. "That's it?"

"It is." I'd had another two boxes sent separately through MONUC's Movement Control section. MovCon, I called it.

We went out to the car. Only two vehicles were parked along the gravel row. Both were white and UN branded. Ours was a Toyota SUV. The other was a pickup.

Although it was dead quiet, a herd of elephants tramped through my head. I'd never seen… never felt… anything like this. I looked and saw a few random people in a panorama of partially cleared land, most of it wild grass, dirt and broad-leaved trees. There was only one path in sight. The… *vastness* —was that the right word?—of it all reminded me of American suburbia, if you were to take away all the houses and roads, the buildings and strip malls—and turn it into a campsite. And make it tropical.

So, really, not the same at all.

I reached for the car door handle as Mamadou began talking to a South African soldier in a blue beret. A Congolese woman who'd been lingering near the asphalt's edge straightened her spine. She approached and reached a hand to her head to thrust a wicker tray of shelled nuts under my chin.

I smiled and said, *"Non, merci."* (They would have been safe enough to eat, I supposed—how wrong can you go with nuts in a shell? But the smallest bill I had was five U.S. dollars—and I didn't want to get into some song and dance, not with Mamadou and the other guy standing there.)

The transaction failed, the *marchande* sniffed then loosened the *pagne* draped over her hips—red, black and yellow cloth unfurling—before scattily rewrapping it and tucking the corners in place. I wondered how a wrap so rudimentary could possibly hold; there must be some trick. As it turned out, the woman would give me at least two more chances to figure out her secret before Mamadou and the soldier parted ways.

Just a few hundred metres down the lumpy ginger road, as at last the car vents moved cooled air, it became apparent that almost everyone in Kindu travelled by foot. The first person we drove past was a woman my age transporting a load of cut bamboo in a basket strapped to her back. Each time we came up alongside someone, Mamadou would brake until the speedometer's needle dropped to thirty kilometres an hour; even then, men would reach into their pockets for a rag or a square scrap of cloth to shield their faces from the fine particles of dust our vehicle stirred up. We passed a child, who cupped her hands. Mamadou said the man he had just been speaking with was UN military police.

"They hand out speeding tickets. They don't mess around."

He asked if I'd gone to MONUC's Iveco Base garage in Kinshasa before coming to pick up my UN licence. I told him I had.

The road was wide and twisty; I realized just how wide when a ten-tonne UN truck passed us in the other direction with room to spare. Low shapes of constructions on my side of the window were juxtaposed with luxuriant trees that branched at eye level as if they'd been planted. Along the flatter plains, a dug well or muddy stream was constellated with box-shaped shanties that looked as simple, as unfussy, as a child's drawing. Portly pigs snuffled their snouts here and there in what should have been someone's front lawn but instead was a pigsty gone to seed. Washed garments lay at the hearth of many houses like paper dolls under the sun.

"That's Camp Makuta up there, the local Congolese army base," said Mamadou at a bend in the road. He motioned towards a hill, noticeable at once because its green grass looked tended to. His head pivoted. "And that's your house. You're living with Bérénice?"

"With Bérénice."

I could see nothing of the house, for its plot of land was fenced by bamboo columns and a rusted-red metal gate, above which the tendrils of a rubber tree hung like corn braids.

"It's big," said Mamadou.

The car slowed as we approached a *T* in the road. Just then, a chicken clucking every which way, as if it had never been cooped up a day in its life, jolted out of nowhere.

I laughed and cried out, "Whoa!"

Mamadou said all roadside pigs and goats belonged to someone somewhere, and if you were ever to accidentally run over a chicken, it would cost you a hundred dollars.

Turning right, we arrived at the main drag. This was easy to tell because there was more activity — still not a lot of cars (and only UN ones), but more people were scrambling about, without necessarily being weighed down by a load on their back or head. That said, I saw one man pushing a wheelbarrow with sheets of something (scrap metal? tin?) as shiny as his chest. Also, the trees had thinned out. In their place, a number of large orange, beige and blue parasols lined the streets. Lampposts and exposed power lines at least twice the height of the structures behind them stole the light like a rainforest canopy. I didn't think to ask if there was electricity.

Sparsity. That was the word I'd been looking for earlier.

"*This*," said Mamadou, with a detectable note of affection, "is Kindu."

I laughed, almost giddily.

On the left-hand side of the road, out Mamadou's side, you could see the river through the gaps between the street's mud-walled shops, kiosks and pillars.

"The Congo River? The part of it that's here — the… ah? Lua… laba?"

Mamadou glanced in its direction. "Hmm."

It appeared as if it was just a small walk to get there.

"Annnnd…" he said, with finality. "We're here."

"What? Already?"

We'd stopped at a four-way intersection in front of the big-gest building I'd seen here yet. It was square, boxlike—at least, a square on three sides, because the side facing away from us was a blue kind of half-moon balcony. On closer inspection, it was actually two separate structures connected by a passage-way, all of it concrete brick and painted white with cyan-blue trimmings, though the white paint was visibly streaked with grime. Yes, this was my first time in sub-Saharan Africa—and my first time in any place with an active peacekeeping mission —but the structure stood out as obviously UN (never mind the big Mission des Nations Unies en République Démocratique du Congo sign) given the short brick fence wrapped all the way around, topped by a coil of barbed wire.

The metal gates parted. The opening widened and a young, slight worker slipped through. He threw his weight against one gate. Then the other.

There was an old man standing in the middle of the inter-section. How could I have not noticed? Perhaps I simply hadn't seen him over the front of our vehicle; he was that short. He was wearing the tatters of a navy uniform and, strangely, white gloves. Now, suddenly, there appeared a whistle between his lips. His arms came up over his head with purpose.

He was directing traffic.

"Is that a… Congolese police officer?"

Mamadou released the brake. "Yeah." He didn't laugh but sounded amused, though not by me necessarily. Whatever it was gave me the feeling that he liked his job.

We drove through the gates and parked, and just the act of doing so—having made it here, *My goodness, in the Congo!*— brought a rush to my head.

It had all happened so fast. I'd been back in Canada for about a year since Paris, back in Toronto at the corner of Front and John, working at the CBC Broadcasting Centre between the green and pink elevators on the third floor. Although I'd hoped otherwise, the fit between me and Canada's public broadcaster had been worse than ever; after years away, my professional contacts felt stale. There were occasions when some press conference or event would come up and I'd raise my hand to go just because it seemed easy and self-contained. My heart wasn't in it.

At the same time, that... something else... that something other than ambition that I could never quite put my finger on — the impetus that had seen me first leave home at age eighteen — re-emerged in a surprising way. Two things happened, both within the space of months, if not weeks.

"Don't you feel like... like... we've been given everything, and... it's our... *responsibility* to achieve something? Useful?"

At the time, I'd said it to someone else, though I'd actually just been thinking aloud. But it was significant because it marked the first time I'd ever articulated the ideas floating around my head about the notion of service.

Not long after that, someone I knew growing up sent me an email. Last I'd heard, this guy had been working with the UN in Africa. It turned out he'd just changed peacekeeping missions — this one in the Congo. He'd said his bosses were desperate to recruit regional managers for the mission's radio network. Which was funny, because I was desperate, too.

RADIO OKAPI KINDU LIVED UPSTAIRS, on the first floor as Mamadou called it. We were speaking English, but Mamadou was from France.

"After you," he said, with smiling impish eyes. And because I didn't know where I was going, he swept his pinstriped arm to indicate the direction. The staircase was to the left of the imperfect square at the foot of MONUC Transport's garage. I glanced in. A UN-branded SUV like the one we'd just parked was jacked up on a hydraulic car lift. Several young Congolese guys in steel-toed boots and navy zip-up coveralls—so, mechanics—were busy doing something. They had tools. Mamadou caught the eye of a balding, slightly pot-bellied white man who appeared from around a corner.

"Hey, (*Somebody*)"—he said the man's name—"new PIO." (That I caught: public information officer.) "We'll be back down."

The man said, "Sure, no problem," in a heavy Québécois accent.

From what I could tell, about twenty-five international civilians worked for MONUC Kindu. Plus, there was the military—five contingents: the Swedish, the Bolivians, the South Africans, the Uruguayans and the Chinese. And there were military observers from all over. Some military officers… and

Congolese staff (national staff, as we called them). Basically, all the civilians worked here, in this building, and the soldiers had their bases... somewhere else. I wasn't exactly sure where.

Mamadou and I continued up the stairs, which were narrow and concrete and cyan blue. At the top, three Congolese women, also in navy coveralls, gazed up from where they were sitting, right there in the hallway, on overturned buckets. The youngest and prettiest was fiddling with a dustpan, knocking it against her plastic bucket, as if to test the noise. They said hello, first to Mamadou, and then to me. They seemed happy to see me, and said, "Good evening, Madame." It couldn't have been later than 1 PM.

"Left," said Mamadou.

We carried on down a narrow hallway painted the same cyan blue as the staircase and half the building.

"That's the MONUC cafeteria," said Mamadou, pointing to the right at a door held open by a latch. Interestingly enough, it led outside.

"Political Affairs..." That door was open, too. Nobody was there.

"Ulli?" I said, gazing back at the door in search of a name. *Ulli Mwambulukutu, Senior Political Affairs Officer.* I'd heard of him—all good things.

Just two steps on, still on our left, elephant-grey egg carton padded the walls. "The studio," I said excitedly, peering in. No one there either.

The newsroom followed, at the end of the line, in a place of its own, attached on only one side like a peninsula.

Where was everybody?

As if reading my mind, Mamadou said the journalists were out getting their stories.

"What time do they usually get back?" I said, hoping it was soon.

"Oh, I don't know… around two." I stopped at the doorway and took a quick look around. Blue-upholstered swivel chairs loitered in the vicinity of six dusty PCs spread along a large rectangular table upon which sat two telephones with twisted cords, a fax machine, a laser printer, months-old scripts, coffee-smudged spoons and Radio Okapi–branded pens and pamphlets. Light was flooding in from a wall of windows on the far side of the room. A photocopier tucked into the back corner reached the height of a small child. I noticed a mini refrigerator. Just a baby fridge — so small I felt the need to comment. Mamadou bent down to pull open its door: two shelves, heaving with MONUC-labelled water bottles. He said the journalists didn't have refrigerators at home. "There's no electricity, as you know."

The linoleum floor was peeling off at the corners, and on every grubby grey wall was a map of Kindu, of Maniema or of the Congo. Across from the biggest map, someone had neatly written out Radio Okapi's editorial values in black marker on a scrap piece of paper and taped it next to a dry-erase board:

We are **professional** and work with rigour.

We are **independent** from political and economic powers, which is crucial for our impartiality and credibility.

We have the **integrity** to report **facts** as accurately as possible, taking into account our biases, prejudices, life experiences and personal perspectives.

We **respect** pluralism, the dignity of each individual, and that human rights are **universal**.

I was following Mamadou into his office, soon to be mine, through a door at the back of the newsroom, next to the photocopier. Suddenly, an ee-*dum*, ee-*dum*, ee-*dum* sound slapped the linoleum floor. Mamadou and I stopped even before any name was called. I turned and saw a young woman — Congolese, pretty — gallivanting towards us in a pair of pumps the colour of cherries.

"Eh! Eh! Eh! Jenni?"

"Yes!" I said, spinning around and nodding wildly as if to say, *I know! I know!* When, what did I know? "Mamy!"

With a squeal, Mamy nearly bowled me over. I was still only slightly used to being instantly liked by strangers — and to such a degree. In this place, where you might have thought people had a reason to be distrustful, they seemed to be... refreshingly *normal*.

Mamy asked me some questions. We hugged again. Minutes passed. Finally, we were about to separate — she had interview tape to cut — when she started like a gazelle: "Wait! I forgot. We — all of us — wanted to invite both of you to dinner, here at the cafeteria, to say goodbye to you, Mamadou, and to welcome you, Jenni."

Mamadou nodded several times, before pressing his lips into a retiring smile. "Thank you, Mamy. That is very kind. Jennifer?"

I released my thumbnail from my mouth. *Out to dinner? And* they *meant to pay for* us? In Kinshasa, other expatriates had put me on guard. *We earn more and the Congolese know it. They all just assume we'll foot the bill. Just you wait, you'll see.* And so, thinking this, my eyes travelled Mamy's full face: it was comely, of even proportions and tone — more hardy than delicate but with a button nose and soft chin suggesting decency. Perhaps this was why part of me wanted to be honest and say, "Oh! That's a nice surprise!" (until a denser part rebuked, *My God, Jennifer, you can't say that!*).

"Well... yes, thank you, Mamy. That's really nice."

Having somehow been made to feel at ease, I suddenly became aware of the thespian emphasis of Mamy's one-word reply: "Okay," she chimed, coiling an extra syllable into a loud laugh that was at once sweet and gritty, like brown sugar.

THE JOURNALISTS IN KINDU had been together since the UN and the Swiss NGO Fondation Hirondelle first rolled out their ambitious plan to use the airwaves to unite a vast country wrecked by killing, kidnapping, rape and disease. The people I was to meet and work with had gone through tough times. Their families had, too. So when the UN-backed Radio Okapi network went live on February 25, 2002, Kindu 103.0 FM was welcomed as a miracle son. At first, the station played a lot of music – the Congolese love music – but then, gradually, it introduced local, national and even some international news. Although no one knew just how far a radio station could go in helping to achieve national peace, in one way, the journalists were already successful, simply because they were alive and providing for their communities. But just as Radio Okapi was young, barely two years old, there was a sense that the journalists were still in the exploratory phase of infancy – as if they had more to do, to discover and to see.

After Mamy, a total of seven others trundled into the newsroom singly or in pairs, their eyes narrowed with artless expectancy, as if gazing upon a present fallen out of the sky. Each time, I smiled widely as one of the others – someone else in the room, someone who'd been through the process before – would shove me forward and say, "She's here. This is her. Jennifer: our new *responsable*." Sometimes, in nervousness, I would titter or bite down hard on my back teeth. I'd even be liable to throw up my hands and clap.

With all this excitement, it was a pity I couldn't remember anyone's names. In my defence, they each had triple-, quadruple- or even quintuple-barrelled names. Their full names—their real names—if I have this right, were: Mamy Halili Tshibangu, Rigobert Yuma Ndwani wa Lona, Matthieu Ilunga Shambuy wa Monatschiebe, Tumba Dieudonné Mobile, Kasmu Mwinyi Ramzani, Gabriel Wamenya and Sadala Shabani. I think Gabriel and Sadala's names were, in fact, longer, only I never knew, or else they told me and I forgot.

There was a lot I'd have to remember, work-wise. One of the most important things was not to mess up the schedule. Like the network's other regional stations in Bukavu, Bunia, Goma, Mbandaka, Kalemie, Kisangani and Kananga, Kindu cut away from national programming once a day to air a half-hour local program. This was called the *décrochage,* and ran Monday to Friday, beginning at 5 PM and was repeated the next day at dawn. My job, a desk job, was to produce it, from story assignment to story vetting. I was also expected to feed the goat—and not the black, brown or oatmeal-coloured ones roaming about town, bleating at passersby. Our goat was Kinshasa. It was to be fed twice daily, morning and night. National editors and newsreaders were waiting on the stories we'd send to them in French and translated, if we could, into the other four national languages recognized by the network. These were Lingala, Swahili, Kikongo and Tshiluba. I understood none of them.

"Who gives us the information?" I asked.

"What information?" Mamadou was walking me through the chores of being a new UN staff member—all the mundane administrative stuff… Like I had to sign for the Toyota, which would now be an asset in my name, and get a Motorola two-way radio, and there was a security briefing that stressed the importance of actually using the Motorola instead of stuffing it into some drawer. MONUC ranked the security threat in each of its geographic sectors on a scale from one to five, with five being the highest. We were level three. Jim, the security officer who gave the briefing, spent a couple minutes talking about home security and not being afraid to fire any household worker who showed himself to be untrustworthy, and a lot of time going over insect repellent (minimum 30 percent DEET, he said). Plus, I must always wear long sleeves at night.

After the briefing, Mamadou smiled and said, "Okay?" and then moved me onwards to the next stop. The UN called this my "check-in." All substantive sections of MONUC Kindu were staffed by one or two civilian officers, with the exception of Human Rights, which had more, and I required the signatures of each "Officer in Charge" on a stiff form that had just given me a paper cut. Likewise, I required signatures for the office's administrative components, including Transport, Personnel and Finance, and a great many others, such as Security, IT, Movement Control and an enigmatic entity called General Services.

"What information? You know," I tucked my hair behind my ears; the humidity was rendering it heavy, "for the radio." We'd gathered most of the signatures and were walking back to the newsroom down the long and narrow concrete hallway whose thick coats of blue paint curled under our feet. "Do these people—I mean, like Child Protection or Human Rights—do they send us information on, I don't know, rape cases, or… displacement of the population? Like what that woman from Human Rights mentioned just now—that story on those two young girls who'd been kidnapped in… in…"

"Kailo."

"Yeah, Kailo. Suppose she'd just written that in a sitrep... or some other report, and I read it. Could we just take it, for the radio, or... Is it... classified information? How does that work now?"

"I don't think I've ever seen anything marked *Classified*," said Mamadou. He was shaking his head but not dismissively. "Some things are UN restricted; some things are for public distribution. But don't worry about story ideas for the radio. The journalists come with their own ideas."

"Right," I came back quickly. "They have their own ideas, of course. I was just... I was just thinking that it would be good to communicate... if we could use the material in UN reports — you know, food distributions, militia sightings, cholera outbreaks, this, that and the other — like, as leads. In our newscasts. To the population."

We were back at the newsroom door, where Mamadou looked at me a minute and then gestured me through. "Yeah," he said simply. "Sure."

AT SOME POINT during the two weeks I'd spent in Kinshasa prior to my deployment, I'd met a gregarious UNV from France who, as it turned out, lived in Kindu. That was Bérénice. When she'd raised the possibility of me moving in with her — apparently, some guys had just moved out — I jumped on the offer.

Bérénice was home when Mamadou dropped me off mid-afternoon.

"*Ay-lo!*" she said indulgently. From the beginning, *indulgent* felt like the right word — for Bérénice, not for our house certainly — because although the house looked big from the outside, inside it was barren and obdurate.

Bérénice gave me the tour as per her way of seeing things, which meant scooting through the living room so fast its furnishings were a blur. There was a dark wooden table in the place where a dining room would be, plus a number of wooden chairs. "Bedroom back there…. Another just here…" With a quick glance, I could see both rooms were empty. Empty—as in, no paint, no flooring, no nothing but low-grade, rock-dust concrete.

"And this is your room."

I cast my eyes about and said nothing.

The room was a large grey cube. By now, I was familiar with its particular shade. An attempt had been made to warm up the space in the form of a raffia rug at the foot of the frame supporting a king-sized bed: it was low to the ground and had four flimsy posts without which the nails tacking up the bed's wilting mosquito net would have had nothing to drive themselves into. An armoire made of thick sanded wood was pushed up against the wall.

Bérénice said the place was airy. I took another look and noticed two screened windows, plus a row of small square holes where the bedroom's far wall abutted the ceiling.

Not that it mattered, I supposed, but I liked it. That is, I liked being shocked by it. The idea that this was my house, that I would be living in a place so far removed from reality as I knew it, brought about a rush I hadn't felt since first arriving in Paris as an au pair in a swirl of smoke and small cars with loud horns.

A whizzing noise echoed off the floor. Something dragging?

"Oh, sorry," I said, suddenly realizing that Mamadou had been wheeling my black nubby Samsonite since he lifted it out of the trunk. "Thanks."

We moved on to the bathroom, the house's only one (we'd have to share), which again stunned me with a sparseness not to be described in words. There were three fixtures, to use the word loosely. A white ceramic washbasin with one tap hole had partially come off the wall and looked about to fall off. There was no shower to speak of, just a small showerhead attached to a rusty pencil-sized pipe running up the corner where a shower would have been.

"There's no hot water, I take it?" I said, half-hoping to be corrected.

MONUC delivered the water: I could see two large tanks propped one atop the other on a tower out the bathroom's jailhouse window. And although the toilet itself was porcelain, it was missing something—namely, a seat and a lid over its tank. Bérénice said the owner had promised to fix it, but we'd have to keep an eye on him because he was crooked.

Overall, there was an unvarying, unrelenting echo in the house from the lack of furniture, and an odour of burnt coal and wood fuel that wafted in from a fire pit in the backyard. Our charcoal came from clear-cut trees. Our kitchen didn't have a sink; in fact, that room's only feature was an unvarnished wooden shelving unit that gave me a splinter when I touched it. Plastic dishware, cutlery, a kerosene lamp, a bottle of palm oil, a few doll-sized tomato paste cans and a galactic-sized bag of rice sat on the shelves, none of which showed any signs of dust, thanks to either diligent cleaning or, perhaps, timely consumption. We had a cook, Roger.

"Fifty dollars a month," said Bérénice plainly, not clarifying whether fifty dollars was his salary or just my share.

"Look," she said, pulling me back to the shelves from which I'd just recoiled. "Right here." She picked up a Hilroy-style scribbler and opened it to the page that was making it bulge. Inside there was a cheap ballpoint pen and a thick envelope. Bérénice lifted the envelope's lip to reveal a generous purse of Congolese francs worth no more than ten dollars. She said it was for Roger to get what we needed from the market. She reached for the scribbler again and dragged her finger across a line of a random page. I read a date, an itemized list of provisions and a running tally. "You need to check it, make sure it's right," she said high-handedly. "And if you buy anything, or add money, don't forget to log it."

Besides Roger, we employed two unarmed security guards (Benjamin and Lumumba), one per twelve-hour shift. Bérénice said they were using the money to pay for their studies, which I believed and never checked.

4

FOR ME TO COPE IN KINDU, there were three separate aspects I'd need to get a handle on: one, Kindu itself as a Congolese city; two, the UN, a world of its own; and of course three, the radio, which in some ways straddled the other two.

As for Kindu, just coming to terms with the layout of the city was hard. It was scarcely built on a grid. Two main roads were dominant; they made up that inverse and distorted *T* on the drive in from the airport. Neither road had a sign. The top of the *T* followed the river more or less, with one tip leading to a dead end at the Uruguayan Riverine compound, where MONUC Kindu's Uruguayan contingent was based, and an offshoot took you out to the Basoko neighbourhood in the nearby municipality of Kasuku. The other tip, in the other direction, travelled over potholes and puddles past the city's largest shops, then another fifty metres or so straight through the MONUC intersection to a Catholic cathedral, where a smaller dirt track ran behind MONUC, past a large red-brick community centre.

From here, navigation became even more impossible, as the land wasn't level and the roads either looped around onto themselves or led in *U*s or *V*s to a scattering of shanty houses that no car could pass around or through.

So the city's major landmarks were: First, that Catholic cathedral, called Cathédrale Saint-Esprit, or the Cathedral of the Holy Spirit; it was a grubby shade of yellow with burgundy trim and two sets of side-by-side arched doors painted peacock blue. It had a green steeple the colour of the palm beside it and a small belfry covered with louvres to prevent the rain from getting in. A thin cross reached into the sky.

Then there was the Salle Champagnat, the community centre (also a theatre, I was told), which had been named after an early nineteenth-century monk from France who dreamed of a worldwide community of brothers devoted to making Jesus Christ known and loved among children and youth. It was set off from the road, behind a basketball court with one standing hoop.

Farther down that same road, away from MONUC, a small-based bright-blue stela climbed to a point in the centre of a roundabout. Someone had said it was a peace monument that long predated the war.

And of course there were the port and the rail station, both built in a style reminscent of Brabantine Gothic and neither one kept up. The train no longer ran, and only MONUC possessed motorized vehicles to cross the river over to the right-bank municipality of Alunguli. For everyone else, there were canoes dug out of a single log, to which enterprising makers added at least three rows of wooden slots for people to sit on. I would watch these pirogues push past one of the small islands in the centre of the river, which appeared superbly soporific and lush. I knew at once, as if by instinct, that to be so wild these little islands must have been deemed little more than weeds amid the great current around them, far too inconsequential to be worth the trouble of exploiting.

AT THIS TIME, NOTHING remotely resembling a restaurant existed in Kindu—only the MONUC cafeteria, which was just a part of our roof with some plastic chairs and tables set out. It covered a sizable area; it would've taken about forty steps to walk diagonally from one end to the stairs. We used a small portion in the middle, well in from the barbed wire around all sides.

On the night the journalists treated Mamadou and me to dinner, we went outside near 7 PM, after our *décrochage* had ended and our national stories had been put on the server for Kinshasa's nightly newscast. We found two empty tables and put them together to make one bigger table. Sadala sat down first. He'd just returned from the city of Bunia, meaning all of us were present, save for our technician, Kasmu, who oddly enough, was rarely around.

Some hours earlier, Mamadou had placed our order of cassava fries and fried chicken ("bicycle chicken," he called it), and by the cafeteria's shameful standards we were served promptly. For the one meal I'd had that day, my stomach was growling its hunger, though I was even more thirsty, waiting on our drinks to come.

When at last a listless waitress footled over, carrying a brown plastic tray of three large bottles of Skol beer, a Fanta orange soda and some glasses, she moved with a languid reach to group them in the centre of the table. Afterwards, she slipped into the muggy darkness.

"Bijou!" Mamy ordered after her—and it was doubtlessly an order. The tone struck me, for they were both women, children of the same tumultuous era, and both still here. "A bottle opener—and another glass."

Bijou uttered a lazy "ah," which Mamy acknowledged with a neutral mien. "We were surprised to see you were white," she then said.

"Really?" There was no question the remark was directed at me, as Mamadou's skin was too brown to classify as white. Of course, I didn't care they'd thought I was… black? But I wondered why they'd even thought about it. Had I… Were they … *disappointed*?

Someone laughed lightly and said, "No, no, no — it's just your name. It's African."

"Congolese even!" said Sadala passionately. "Right here in Maniema, in Shabunda. Near the border with South Kivu."

Mamy threw down her arms, whacking the table loudly, and scrunched up her button nose. "*Mais non, Papa!* That's Shakody!"

I had never before seen arms, hands and wrists wielded so extravagantly, as if casting a spell. It was easy to see why someone in the Congo might believe in black magic and child sorcerers; there was something otherworldly in mannerisms so large and hypnotic.

Bijou returned with the bottle opener and began a long drawn-out process of opening each bottle.

I sat up and said, "Bakody's Hungarian" — only to backtrack when heads began to nod. "I mean, the *name*, I should say. Not me." I told them my mother and her mother had been born in Wales; my grandfather was Italian American and Canadian; and my grandmother on my father's side was Native American. "Like what you'd call an Indian. So I'm a mutt really."

I waited expectantly for a polite chuckle. It never came. "Who knows…? Maybe I *am* somehow African — and just don't know it!"

This remark sparked the laughter of everyone present — including Bijou, who had remembered the bottle opener but forgotten the glass.

"*Maman, s'il te plaît?*" Matthieu prevailed on her, raising his soda like a lantern's dimmed flame. Matthieu was a teetotaller

— on religious grounds, someone had said — which I didn't quite know what to make of. The world's pious abstainers had always left me suspicious, if only of their intellect.

We went on talking and eating and drank liberally for the heat. The slumbering sun had cooled the air but not enough. "Guess it's always this hot," I said. Mamadou nodded with a knowing sniff and smile, but Rigobert said, "No, not always."

"It can get colder," said Gabriel. (I thought it was Gabriel.) "Not Canada cold."

"Yes, exactly." I laughed — "Would you believe minus fifteen or twenty?" — to which Matthieu quickly sat up and said that in Lubumbashi in the south, eight degrees was not unheard of.

"Really? Eight degrees. That low? I'm surprised." I paused. "Anyway, I love the heat. This is great. Being out here in a tank top like this."

All this talk about the weather ran its course. I was in the midst of prying off a spoke of bicycle chicken when Rigobert asked if I was married. Étienne had told me Rigobert was a *mwami. Mwamis,* said Étienne, were traditional chiefs of small kingdoms throughout Maniema and the Kivus — they even had them in Rwanda. Apparently, villagers would go to the Rigoberts of the world to resolve conflicts and find justice in the wisdom of their counsel. "Over what?" I'd asked with great curiosity. "Over anything," said Étienne. Land disputes. Disputes over "right" behaviour (for instance, is it right for a woman to drink beer? When, if ever, could a person eat a monkey?). The stuff of family quarrels.

I stopped to clap at a mosquito. Missed. "Nope. Not married."

No one spoke up — and why would they have? Still, I felt they weren't seeing me the right way.

"I… I do have a boyfriend, though. Well… I *had* one. It's sort of… on and off, really."

"And no children?" said Sadala, in a manner you might have guessed was delicate for him.

Someone in the shadow of the far side of the table – one of the men, judging by the voice – followed up by asking whether I even wanted children. I tipped my glass to pour more beer into it; no sooner had I finished than Mamy reached across the table to lay the cap back over the bottle. "Bugs," she said perceptively, in a tone so subtly empathetic I wondered if I'd imagined it.

"Umm… Well, it's more like… I mean, how could I have a child and be here with you in Africa?"

When Matthieu suggested I could leave the child with my parents, Mamadou shook his index finger vigorously and said things didn't work like that in Europe or America.

I laughed and said, "Honestly, I could never imagine leaving my child to be raised by anyone – not even my parents. And besides, I already gave my mom my cat when I moved away after university… and I think that's enough!"

This last point struck Mamy as particularly funny. "Ah, Je-nee!" she whooped.

Something in her rejoinder (a reproof?) prompted me to speak up, causing Gabriel to twitter: "Yeah, when *are* you going to get married, Mamy?"

The look she gave him could have pickled a potato. "Yes, I live with my parents. But I cook. I clean. *Oui, Maman.*"

Time passed and we spoke of other things. Then something occurred to me: "Wait – you were saying you cook?" I'd been under the impression that in a Congolese city the size of Kindu, moneyed families like Mamy's typically had help. "You mean your family doesn't have a cook?"

Oddly enough, Mamy began to tap her wig. Her grandmother, she said, had been poisoned by the woman who cooked for her. "People do that here," she said. "It happens."

Across from her, Gabriel clapped at another mosquito and shook its dead body off his hand.

IN A PARALLEL UNIVERSE, this might have been the point in time when I realized that six valuable resources were sitting right in front of me. Matthieu didn't help any; he kept saying how excited he was to learn from me—"a real journalist," he said. He had a doting way of looking at me, I'd noticed. As if he expected me to perform a miracle.

In any case, except for Matthieu, who said he lived just around the corner, and Gabriel, who said he was okay to walk, we all piled into the Toyota that night without me having asked much at all about the foreignness around me. It was possible generosity sidetracked me, with the journalists paying for the meal and asking so many questions of me. Whatever the reasons, later I would have to go to great lengths to find answers. In some cases, it would be too late.

5

THE DAY MAMADOU LEFT on the morning flight to Kinshasa, the journalists and I sat around the newsroom. The excitement was palpable. The source of mine was hardly a mystery, but I wondered what was causing theirs. They were eager for us to start making real radio, I decided.

"But Gabriel," Sadala was saying insistently. "You're forgetting that Kabambe wa Kabambe said he would *never* join the FARDC. I think the question we need to ask him is what's changed? Why's he making this announcement *now?*"

To hear Sadala sound off aroused my senses, as if I were a deer in his headlight. This man, Sadala Shabani, wasn't especially handsome and was the shortest of the group—even Mamy minus her heels was taller. He wore an uncommon hairstyle—bald, save for a fuzz of black hair on the dome of his head. His neck was too thick. Yet I knew my mother, for one, would have said there was something sexy about him. It was his disposition; it was edgy. Somehow, Sadala managed to give the impression of a man whose temper could flare at any moment: over politics, the treatment of a news story or just one of life's vicissitudes. From the beginning, Sadala struck me as the passionate one. Which said something in this group.

"Kabambe wa Kabambe…" I repeated aloud, like a child learning her first language. It was a kooky name to my ears… like Willy Wonka in *Charlie and the Chocolate Factory*. "He's a Mai-Mai leader, no? I mean, an *ex*-Mai-Mai leader…"

"Yes, exactly. He's from Kailo—twenty kilometres north of here. That's my story!" Sadala's head flapped like a fish in a pirogue. "Now that the war is over, Kabambe's going to take a position in the FARDC—the government army. They're offering him general. He's going to make the announcement today, that he's taking the position and leaving here for Kisangani."

It was a good year past the heyday of Maniema's Mai-Mais, who I knew were just people from Kindu and its environs who had taken up arms, killing and raping and recruiting children, same as any other belligerent, same as the national army. Nevertheless, the series of rituals and myths in which the Mai-Mais ensconced themselves seduced me. I was desperate to hear more about this emollient of palm oil and holy water I'd heard about—the one the Mai-Mais would supposedly grease onto their skin to make bullets bounce off their bodies and spatter into water.

"Right. But wait—"

Rigobert. King Rigobert.

"I know we need to ask the question," said Rigobert, his gold-framed glasses slipping down his nose. "But I think the subject has more to do with what this means for the integration of the Mai-Mais in the FARDC… DDR. And pressure from the international community… questions of justice—and amnes—"

With Rigobert waffling, others launched into simultaneous comment—until Sadala's voice triumphed: "Exactly!" he strained, pushing a sigh of vindication. "That's exactly what I'm telling you!"

"DDR?" I said meekly. (*What* was *that again?* Something to do with disarmament. *Reinsertion?* No, that wasn't right.)

Within minutes, the phone would ring, and I had no idea what I would say. The *how* part, at least, had made itself clear:

Do it however you want with your décrochage, *but don't let the journalists propose national stories. It takes them too long to get to the point, and we don't have the time to sift through their bullshit to find the angle.*

These were the general guidelines that dictated a process overseen by Radio Okapi's chief news editor in Kinshasa. Yves Renard was his name. His three deputies formed the triumvirate (as I called them in my head). Yves was French, whereas Martin, Leonard and Noella were Congolese. But nationality aside, the four shared a professional trait of high relevance to me – small talk was a waste of their radio-controlled time.

Every weekday morning, Yves and the triumvirate would call each regional station from Radio Okapi's production hub in Kinshasa (expecting at least one focussed story, though two would be better), and in a tone best described as surgical would utter this cue:

"What have you got?"

For if Yves Renard didn't say it, if the triumvirate didn't say it, if Mamadou didn't say it – anyone could have stated the reality of the times. The governments backing Radio Okapi – including the Americans, Belgians, British, Canadians, Dutch, Germans, French, Swiss, and Swedes – were using the rich world's tax dollars to buy high editorial standards in a country flooded with mediocre private and community-based radio stations, all trying to pick up the slack for the dud that had become the state broadcaster, the Radio-Télévision nationale congolaise (RTNC). Not surprisingly, foreigners (as in, anyone other than black Africans – called *"mundeles"* in Lingala, *"mzungus"* in Swahili) had warmed to the idea of Radio Okapi from the get-go. Often they would ask, *What's an okapi?* because the Okapi Wildlife Reserve — the only place in the world where you could be sure to see the brown, donkey-sized mammal with its black- and white-striped hind legs — was far-flung in Epulu, in the Congo's northeastern rainforest, and not all zoos had one. Even people who knew what an okapi was found the idea quaint. They'd say, *A national radio in the locals' indigenous languages? How clever indeed!*

But all exoticism aside, donors needed rationalizations. Measureable outputs, for one. Put simply, the station had to justify its annual $10 million operating costs, and we were but two years past 9/11.

THE DAY'S REMAINING story ideas broached relevant, newsy issues. There was the discovery of a cache of AK-47s ("but not an arms cache," Gabriel had fervently argued, for they only totalled six); the robbery of electric cable at MONUC's South African base in Basoko; the rape of a nine-year-old girl by a sixty-seven-year-old man in Kabambare; the reunification of twenty children from Kisangani with their families in Maniema; an illegal taxation checkpoint on the road to Kalima; and a decision by Kindu's mayor to tear down any bamboo fencing not in conformity with a new city bylaw.

"Oh dear, I have a bamboo fence," I said dramatically.

"Oh, that doesn't matter," said Tumba mildly. Although he, too, had ways to make himself heard as well as any Congolese, Tumba was lumbering in speech, too tubby to truly impose and, in contrast to Sadala, rarely worked himself up, if ever. "You're MONUC. They won't bother you."

For once, the loudness of my thoughts kept me silent. Amid their juddering conversation and the threads of other stories,

I shifted my weight on my squeaky chair, unsure of whether to be impressed or intimidated by the journalists' ken. They didn't have a staff vehicle, there were neither postal services nor a functioning landline system in the Congo, and at this point, we shared two cellphones among the eight of us. Where on earth were they getting these ideas from?

The phone rang and my heart leapt.

"It's Kinshasa!" someone exclaimed.

"Okay, okay!" I pushed back a band of air with my palm, and when I said hello, my voice echoed down the line.

"Hello, it's Kinshasa. Yves, Leonard, Martin and Noella."

"Hello, Kinshasa," I said breathlessly. After my two weeks there, I could easily conjure up an image of Yves and the triumvirate, clustered at one end of their long rectangular wooden table around a triangular speakerphone. Noella would be flipping through *Le Potentiel, Le Forum des As* or any one of the unabashedly biased dailies purporting to be national in scope despite circulating in the capital exclusively.

"All is well in your new stronghold?" asked Yves.

"Actually," I realized aloud, "I like it here."

There was a pause—which perhaps was the phone line's delay. "That's good, that's good." Yves's second pause in as many seconds sounded an awful lot like him smirking. "So…"

So: *What have I got?*

I drew a deep inhale. "Well… Okay. Well, the Mai-Mai leader. I mean, the *ex*-Mai-Mai leader, Kabambe wa—"

"Yes. That's today. What time is he supposed to speak?"

"What time? This morning, I—"

"Call us once he has," said Martin. "Who's going? Sadala?"

"Yes, Sadala." Out of the corner of my eye, I saw Sadala perk up at the mention of his name. Down the line, Yves pronounced the word "fine" in that unmistakable rising inflection that passes for "And?" He wanted to know what else I had, but stupidly, I hadn't stopped to think that far ahead.

"Oh! Well… Okay, there's also a story… Sadala has another story, about an arms cache… Well, it's not an arms cache… it's six AK-47s—assault weapons—that were found yesterday near Kal… Kal…"

"Kalima!" whispered Sadala excitedly.

I spoke Sadala's word before turning my back to him to hear the call more clearly. Moments later, while anxiously repeating, *"What else have we got?"* I shot a desperate look over my shoulder.

Mamy took a step forward. "The fences," she mouthed.

That's right! I said to myself, rapidly vivifying. *Hooray for the bamboo fences!* "So the mayor, he's ordering Kindu's police to tear down all bamboo fences… because a bylaw was passed two months ago, but it hasn't changed anything. Fines will be handed out at first. Then if someone doesn't pay, their fence will be torn down. They have a week to make the changes."

The journalists' eyes fixed on me as I hung up the phone. My shoulders rose with a breath that, once exhaled, left me lighter. "They're taking the bamboo story for this evening."

"Ah!" said Mamy. Her brown eyes were wide. "There you go! Congratulations."

"Vraiment," said Gabriel, encouraging me as if we were friends.

I ought to have been past being pleased about having a simple story accepted. To cover up, I started saying something about how, as a general rule, it was good to have plenty of stuff to fill the holes. Seeing Tumba's lazy eye brightening—for a man with such a big face and head, his ears and chin were remarkably small—I carried on inculcating my principles of best practices. Matthieu thanked me over and over again, and said hungrily, "Tell me more."

Once upon a time, there was a tailor. People called him *Frère*. He spent his days in a tiny square shop with bobbins and scissors and colourful scraps of numbered wax-printed fabric strewn like kapok leaves at his feet. He took measurements. He pinned. He referred clients to the styles of cutout pictures taped to the wall. (It could not be claimed that any of these pictures modelled new looks; that went without saying. But by looking at the wall, a person could certainly get an overall picture of the major trends to have taken a foothold in the town.) He was proud to say he had loyal clients. Whenever anybody would poke in their head or pass by the shop's open window, nine times out of ten he would know the person's name—and this from a man from Kasai, a province hundreds of kilometres away. It was his fine workmanship people appreciated. And he was fair in his dealings: the price was the price because word spread, and when it came down to it, everyone was his brother or sister. Now, individual personal circumstances—that was something different. Some people just couldn't pay—not up front or all in one go. Of course these days, more and more people were indebted to him.

This man's name was Matthieu. He was married to a woman inside the faith who was as young as she looked. Her name was Mwanvua. He'd met her in the Kingdom Hall. She was born in Maniema, raised in Maniema; she studied in Maniema, got married in Maniema. She'd had her children here. Mwanvua was a good clean wife who shared his modesty. Every day, she would squat down low to sweep the porch and stretch up high to protect the corners from cobwebs. She cooked what she could find. She always took heed of her physical appearance, good care of their three children and even better care of him. For Matthieu, Mwanvua's unwavering moral support was what really counted.

Not that she didn't spoil him. For example, whenever there was one last piece, one last spoonful on the serving plate, she'd always have the reflex to say no thank you, she couldn't; she was full, no matter how good it smelled. And never, even in the toughest times, would he ever have to go more than a few days without a bottle of soda to hand. Feelings fade, but as ever, he cared about her happiness. And despite their sixteen-year age gap, he confided in her as a friend.

No, the problem existed elsewhere, outside their home, with the vagaries of statesmen waging war. You didn't have to go far to see it (and good luck to anyone trying to get too far from here). Matthieu rose from his chair, said goodbye to Mwanvua, goodbye to his three-year-old, who was old enough to reciprocate, and left the house on foot. Another dusty day it was, quiet like a Sunday. There were no cars, no bicycles. Some people, like him, were moving about. The pale sand of the cemetery lay exposed in its desperation for a shadow, and every landmark looked as though it were pretending to be asleep. The cathedral... Collège de l'Enano. The commercial radio station, KFM. He squinted as he walked past a row of buildings — vendors, grocers, currency exchange houses. A hotel. All stripped bare, looted and abandoned. His wouldn't be too far behind, surely.

To one side of the hotel, or rather what *used to be* the hotel, right here off the main street, three men in loose jeans and sweaty chests were pounding long wooden sticks with rocks, driving them into the dry earth, which was splitting with each strike. A woman with a baby on her back and another on her breast was shouting something to one of the men as a clump of dirt flew into her face. Beside her, four children were playing, using the force of their feeble arms and legs to shake a blue-and maroon-striped tarpaulin like a tablecloth with crumbs, trying to catch the wind to get it airborne like a parachute and get themselves down underneath it.

How many families had come to Kindu over the past six months? Hundreds? People spoke of thousands. Every day, the remnants of another family emerged from the forest barefoot and in tatters, many with lacerations or malaria, some with skin diseases. In the worst cases, they had nothing left that was human except for the shape of their bodies. It was an awful sight. And the smell! Urine. Feces. Sweat mixed up with a sickly pungent smell of ammonia. Most of the new arrivals came from the south, from places like Kibombo and Salamabila, diamond and gold towns raided by the Mai-Mais and other armed groups. Most times, people would hide out in the forest for as long as they could hold out on a diet of leaves. They didn't want to be found for fear of being attacked or kidnapped or murdered. At the same time, no man or woman wanted to stray too far from their land. It was their livelihood and, however humble, their place in the world. Matthieu could relate.

The inhabitants of empty villages had nothing. In Kindu, there was a great deal less than there once was, and prices had skyrocketed tenfold. Fronted by a band of ex-Mobutu generals, RCD rebels controlled the city (RCD being short for Rally for Congolese Democracy), taking anything they wanted because they could. Fighting against them, the loosely allied militia group, the Mai-Mais, meant to put an arrow through each and every last one of them: tough talk for people who weren't even born by the time Matthieu had had his first child. By and large the Mai-Mais stayed lurking in the forest. Occasionally, they surfaced; the bullet holes showed that. Mainly, the Mai-Mais had parochial interests, achieved through extortion and plundering and rape, the young being so terribly short-sighted. Their presence alone was enough to choke off the city: there were no planes in Maniema; the train from Lubumbashi had stopped service in 1998; and then, at the end of last year — 2001 — traffic upriver from Kisangani had been severed. As a result, the breadbasket of the Congo now exported nothing and received nothing in return — save for new arrivals from the forest, new mouths to feed. And they were Africans. They shared.

Matthieu was coming up on the offices of the state broadcaster, the RTNC. It was supposed to be President Kabila's radio, but the RCD had done away with that. Lately, the stations had all started announcing jobs for journalists as part of a new UN peacekeeping mission they said was coming to Kindu. Matthieu didn't know any journalists, and he himself knew nothing about a journalist's vocation (though nice work, it would seem, if you could get it).

The reality was life on the ground was difficult. And he couldn't hold out much longer. (Because, really, at a time like this, who was thinking of buying new clothes?) No one wanted to leave anything for him to alter or fix, on account of the very real possibility of his shop suddenly up and closing. Plus, at any time, the rebels could come and make off with his entire inventory. The whole lot of it.

His co-worker — his employee, to speak forthrightly — was sitting inside the shop folding scissor-edged fabric in squares like pressed laundry, one on top of the other. Of course, he didn't need her. By now, one person could handle the work tidily. He couldn't remember the last time he'd had a charley horse after a long day of pedalling one of the machines. It was bad business to keep her.

After a moment, he turned to her. "It's a nice day," he said. "It's cool. I'm gonna go out and distribute some of these." He glanced over at a pile of religious brochures stacked on the far table. She smiled and nodded.

It was a Thursday.

6

EVERY MORNING BEGAN WITH the first of two Radio Okapi meetings convened daily. The journalists arrived more or less promptly at 8:30 AM to pitch the day's stories before heading out to do their interviews and cover any developing news. Although the afternoon meeting was scheduled at 2:30, people would straggle in anywhere from two to three. I gathered that Mamadou had been lax with this meeting, and half the time hadn't even bothered to sit down. So the result was more like a check-in. I might ask whoever was there: *Did you get the mayor? Did you make it to the prison? Everything okay?*

Aside from the Radio Okapi meetings, there was another meeting I had to attend every morning. This was known as the UN morning meeting. It was held at the other end of the long and narrow blue hallway and was attended by section heads, agency representatives and the commanding officers of military contingents (what would soon be called the "UN country team" in UN speak). It often dragged on for an hour.

And after that meeting, more often than not, if anybody had been looking for me, they would've found me in my office, sitting behind the computer.

On this day, I spent several minutes scrolling through the Radio Okapi playlist, which Kinshasa sent internally every day but Sunday. A song I felt I should have known was on. They played it a lot – as in, two or three times a day. It sounded French. It wasn't Congolese, anyway. I looked at the time on the bottom of the screen. 09:47 AM. Arrow down, arrow down... Arrow up... "*Tu trouveras.*" By Natasha St-Pier. I opened Internet Explorer, pulled up Google and put in the name. Natasha St-Pier – she was from Bathurst, New Brunswick. Bathurst, New Brunswick? *She could be me!* My whole life, I'd sung and danced. Growing up in Dartmouth, the radio had always been on; in later years, Mom bought a small Sony to put on top of the fridge. Partly, she wanted to hear the weather. Otherwise, she and I would dance through the kitchen, across the hallway and out into the living room, where the sheers were too dusty, too full of cat hair to ever think of pulling across the window.

Four songs from now was Jennifer Lopez, "Love Don't Cost a Thing." In between, there was a South African one I liked, if it was the one I was thinking of. "Pata Pata." I looked up the singer... Miriam Makeba. Did I know her?

At this time, most of Radio Okapi's morning programming was taken up by songs. There was one show – *Okapi Action* – that ran over the course of two hours. I'd have been inclined to call it a current affairs show, because it talked about timely things, but in fact, after listening for a bit, you'd realize almost everything had to do with what some local NGO was doing. So the name *Okapi Action* was apt. The show also aired a lot of music – too much in my opinion. It seemed to give the pacing a loose feel.

The host of *Okapi Action* was Nicole Ngaka. She was un-hurried in her speech and possessed a mellifluous, atmos-pheric voice: present but unobtrusive, the elevator music of conversationalists. Tina Salama, who was on now – a different show – went about things differently. She presented herself with the type of confidence that put a picture in people's minds. It was as if her smooth velvet voice was able to create a hologram: she was there, with you, sitting in the chair facing you or on the curb beside you.

I associated Tina with *Okapi Messages*, though she wasn't the only one to read them on air. Kinshasa ran them constantly. In the absence of commercials, they often took the place of stings – musical punctuation – or show promos, before or after a song or other programming. As the name suggested, they were just messages: a series of salutations hailing from Okapi listeners across the country.

I listened as Tina read out the latest string: Dieudonné from Gbadolite wanted to say hi to his mom and three sisters in Kisangani, to his brother in Goma and to another sister in Butembo. Bénévole in Lubumbashi wanted to say hello to Richard, Modeste and Adolphine. They lived in a five-to-six syllable place that started with a *K*.

The first time I'd heard an Okapi Message, Tina had been reading it. I'd just arrived in Kinshasa. It had been my first day at Radio Okapi. The newsroom, there in Kinshasa, the *rédaction centrale,* had been bustling with hurried steps to the printer, phones ringing, people tabbing between show rundowns and open games of solitaire. I was sitting next to Bob, one of the technicians – the one with the chipmunk cheeks. His head was shiny and red, as was my hair, most likely, the On Air sign being above us both. A digital clock counted down each second of a minute. Bob had two fingers on two sliders of the soundboard.

On the other side of the glass, a stunning young woman in television makeup was talking over the microphone, to us but not only. That was Tina. That was my first *Okapi Messages*.

I said, "This is ingenious!"

Bob had laughed happily, I think because he knew I'd meant it. He said when Radio Okapi had first started broadcasting in

2002, most people had had no access to phones or the Internet or mail. "Families who had been separated by the war had no way of knowing whether their loved ones were dead or alive…"

"So you started announcing these greetings?"

"Exactly," said Bob, nodding. "We invited people to drop off handwritten messages to their friends and family – and we began to read them out on air. We still do it today, even though almost everyone has a cellphone now."

I was thinking about that day, all those messages, as I got up for more coffee. This involved me going out into the newsroom, to the cobwebs that had taken over a small plastic table, on which sat an electric kettle, a jar of Nescafé instant coffee and a jar that once contained Nescafé but was presently being used to store granulated sugar. Its ever-so-slight saccharine smell courted a colony of ants.

"I've been wondering," I said, somewhat reluctantly. Rigobert and Tumba were the only ones in the newsroom. The others were out gathering their stories. Most times this meant they were chasing down the head of some local association, civil society or advocacy group, and interviewing him – usually a him – right where they found him: often on a low wooden stool in the yard of a thatched-roof house, or behind one of the many cement-powder pyramids heaped off the side of the road. On the drive in, I'd passed a mangy dog lapping a grey puddle from one of these pyramids and had felt bad for its measly existence. "Where do you guys get your stories from?"

Rigobert and Tumba both went quiet, long enough to be qualified as uncomfortable. Finally, Rigobert asked, "What do you mean?"

It was hard to picture Rigobert as a king: this neat, compact man, with a small head, sitting here in a khaki safari jacket and slacks. At the same time, he did have something. There were clues. For one thing, he generally spoke at half the volume belted out by, say, Sadala or Mamy. (Or me.) Yet his presence would fill the room — *command it* — as if he'd somehow discarded the dusty mirror we hold up to ourselves in our desperation to know how people cut us down to size. For another, he seemed to take more time than normal before answering questions, as if the quality of his answer carried import.

"What do I mean? I mean... How do you know what's going on every day?"

"We live here," said Rigobert, his voice taking on a higher-pitched lilt of confusion.

"People in the community talk and we pay attention," said Tumba, whose blunt, low-toned remark carried special credibility: Tumba, more than anyone, knew what was going on in the city.

I hastened to speak as if my normal good sense had simply taken leave. "Right. Of course. That, that makes sense. It's just... well... you come in with such great ideas. It's impressive."

I didn't think to tell them about the struggle I'd had in my first journalism job. It was with *As it Happens*, a well-established CBC news and current affairs show where the producers dialled out to generate what sounded like a phone-in conversation between the guest and the show's host. I was working as a fill-in associate producer. Just out of school.

I loved that program — I loved the idea of working with such smart people — but struggled with feeling the least smart among them. Parenthetically, this was around the time I discovered that false modesty was far easier for me to display than a version nearer the truth. I blamed my mother, for whom stress was a four-letter word. For her, staying calm and clear-headed took precedence over just about anything; in other words, never, *never!* allow yourself to get worked up, no matter what the issue.

Why? Not because she was ever afraid of making a scene… or of having a heart attack, nothing like that (though, as she'd say, if you had your health, you had everything). No, her reasoning was that stress sabotaged your mental well-being and ability to make good decisions. This went some way to explaining why, growing up, she'd ask me if I wanted to go to a movie with her the night before exams. And why she often missed parent-teacher day at school. ("You're doing well. I'd go if there was a problem. Of course.")

"Jennifer?"

I lifted my head. It was Rigobert.

"Huh? Sorry, I was just thinking."

I set down the mug in my hand with a loud thump and drifted to the door. Tumba turned to look, twisting his heavy-set shoulders away from the computer screen. He'd been reading digitalcongo.net.

"You don't need to go interview anyone," I said, with an air of indictment, "for your Kalima *tracasseries* story?"

"*Tracasseries*" was the French word we used for a range of harassment and hassling; in this case, we were talking about unnecessary and suspect red tape.

"I'm meeting the administrator at lunchtime." If my question had left him feeling defensive, he didn't show it. "He said he'd be here. He has a meeting with MONUC."

Rigobert removed his hand from his computer mouse and looked up expectantly. "Where are you going?"

Some lucky Radio Okapi regional stations could call upon a car and a full-time driver to shuttle the staff to and from their interviews. Goma availed itself of one. If memory serves, Bukavu did, too. In Kindu, we did not, which as I quickly found out, risked turning me into a quasi–soccer mom: all of us gathering our stuff and heading downstairs to the parking lot and into my Toyota, so that I could drop them off one by one in at least the general direction of where they needed to go. For me to be able to pick them up afterwards, however, I would have needed an ear to be wreathed to my Motorola radio: *Romeo Oscar One, Romeo Oscar One. This is Romeo Oscar Three. Over.* Or: *Romeo Oscar One, Romeo Oscar One, for Romeo Oscar Five. Over.* Already, everyone knew better than to waste their breath calling. Instead, whenever anyone wanted to reach me, they would radio the other Radio Okapi journalists—we were all Romeo Oscars, using the international radiotelephony alphabet—until they found someone who was close enough to tap me on the shoulder and say, "Jenni, so-and-so's on the radio for you."

Today, Rigobert was set to be disappointed: "Nowhere," I said. "I'm just going to the cafeteria." Potatoes had been promised yesterday, and although I'd be going home for lunch, I wanted to check for later. I wasn't used to not having anything to snack on, and the afternoon would quickly become evening, when my stomach would start to rumble. Unfortunately, Roger, our cook, would have gone home by then.

THROUGHOUT THE DAY, people working at MONUC HQ or visiting from UN offices elsewhere would go out to the MONUC cafeteria for a soda, a soda and a cigarette or just a cigarette. There was never a lot to eat, and there certainly wasn't a menu. You'd just go up to the metre-by-half-metre bar and ask one of the three or so people who sat behind or leaned into it, "What is there today?" The local workers all spoke halfway decent French or English, well enough to tell you there was chicken or plantain or omelette. I learned very quickly to follow up whatever answer I received with a second, yes-or-no question: "What about french fries? Do you have any potatoes left?" And if I was lucky, the tall, lanky guy who supervised the place would vaguely raise an eyebrow, push a burst of air out his nose, and answer, "*Oui, il y en a.*"

Today nobody seemed to be around. I leaned over the bar until it pressed my ribcage. Scratching my neck, I noticed a paper calendar tacked to the side of the bar. The month of March was up, but the dates were off. The printing was low quality and the pictures were generic scenes to the order of meadows, blue sky and rainbows. A flowery caption was written on the page you couldn't tear away:

The Congo: God-given potential. The country of the future.

The line was hardly the work of a great intellectual. Yet, simple as it was, it said something about the time—the inexhaustible number of peace accords, strategies, transitional justice mechanisms and political nominations, all attempting to right history's path. My problem was I'd arrived as a stiff tree introduced to the land. I had squandered my time in Mamadou's shadow. I ought to have listened better, and now wished that I had, for if I'd been told the names and affiliations of Kindu's political and military players, I never retained them. The Kabambe wa Kabambe stuff had gone straight over my head; I hadn't the foggiest idea who would bury guns, or why. And I *knew* I knew what the initials DDR stood for but would be damned if I could come up with it.

I could see I needed a plan. And so right there and then, I devised one:

Operation Ulli.

Ulli Mwambulukutu was an ageless soul, who nevertheless possessed rounded shoulders that pulled him slightly forward, and when he walked, he did so slowly, with some heaviness; cloudy areas appeared to be yellowing the outer circle of his deep brown eyes. Ulli was the head of MONUC Kindu's Political

Affairs office, but back in Kinshasa, no one had ever stopped there in their descriptions of him. People said he ran the place. It was a compliment, with grown men proclaiming, "You're going to Kindu? Oh, with Ulli! You have to go see him. He's the one who actually runs the place. Please tell him I said hi."

From what I could gather, Ulli had been in Kindu since MONUC first opened the office back in 2001. Before that, he'd been in other UN missions—the one in Western Sahara at least, because he'd worked with the person I knew from home. Whatever his postings, there was no doubt that Ulli knew DDR inside out (disarmament was one of the Ds—that was for sure), like he knew its inter-country counterpart DD triple R inside out, and like how after a great many years of peacekeeping, he'd come to know the UN like the lines on the back of his caramel-coloured hands. Ulli could explain things. Ulli could introduce me to people.

"Ulli," I asked, in a tone that in all probability whined for lack of being cute, "I need help."

I'd given up on the cafeteria and had been on my way back from the water closet off the hallway when Ulli had spotted me through his open office door and invited me in for tea.

Water was boiling. Ulli insisted I sit while he laid out a floral-patterned bone china service. The kettle released a cone of steam as water ran into my cup. Mine matched the set, whereas Ulli's was a mug that said *I Love My Dad*.

"How many kids do you have?"

Ulli stood up straight, as if to stretch each vertebra. At the top of a high cabinet, he slid back his hand to reach for a forgotten dish. "Four. All boys." The dish held powdered milk, in the smallest of faintly yellowed clumps. "But they're old now. They certainly don't need me."

"Where are they?" I asked.

"New York. But when I retire, we'll move back to Tanzania."

New Yorkers up and moving to Tanzania? It didn't seem likely, and to say so aloud felt sincere.

"They'll go," murmured Ulli, reflectively.

Ulli passed the sugar bowl, which I accepted with thanks while musing on the dull yellow glop in his eyes. My spoon made a *ting-a-ling* sound as it circled the sides of my cup. We drank the tea slowly because it was hot.

Finally, I replaced my cup in its saucer and announced brusquely: "I don't get what's going on. I really don't."

"Oh, Jennifer." Ulli smiled, with soft lines — squeezable cheeks — and a playful swat to the air. "A bright girl like you... One day this week, after you're settled, when you're passing by my office, stop in and I'll make you more tea. And we can talk, no problem."

No problem. *Hakuna matata*. The response was as nonchalant as a *pagne* draped over Ulli's girth. Ulli was unlike anyone I'd ever met. He was quick-minded but slow-moving; and unlike Rigobert, the *mwami* who shared Ulli's composure, there didn't seem to be an erratic bone in Ulli's body. He was grandfatherly, sagacious — yet with a sense of play. There was something effortless about the way he interacted with people — especially with women; I had noted it during his interactions with Mamy, with whom he was quite close. Ulli was a mature and thinking man.

WHAT WOULD SOON SLIP into feeling like my chief challenge in Kindu surfaced in the hours creeping ahead of our first *décrochage,* as I paced the floor and kept looking at the clock, like a parent whose teenager was out past midnight with the family car: 1:45. 1:55. 2:00. *When would they be back?* The newscast wasn't going to write itself.

Matthieu, who'd been hired on the Fondation Hirondelle side as a translator—so not UN staff like the rest of us—was first through the door at a quarter after two. "Hi, Jenni." He set down his Mini Disc recorder ritualistically, awaiting some form of amiable chit-chat. But I just clapped my hands. This made him laugh.

The flat thumping of computer keys gradually picked up, until at last it buried the voice of Radio Okapi deejay J.R. and the songs he played. By the time everyone returned, it was coming on 3:40 PM. We had an hour and twenty minutes until air.

"Matthieu!" I hollered out my corner office door.

"Present!" he hollered back.

Seconds later, a sort of trained puppy sat.

"Read it," I told him, placing a printout in front of his nose.

"Out loud?"

"You sound surprised. You've never thought to read out your scripts before? This is *radio*. You're a radio journalist."

At first, Matthieu laughed nervously, until with only the slightest of pauses, the nature of his laughter morphed. It was as if—just like that—he had decided to turn my censure into a game. "Matthieu, Matthieu, Matthieu," I wanted to say, suddenly feeling as though we had been friends since God knows when, when in fact, if I'd closed my eyes I would've struggled to picture his face. Matthieu was far from fat but carried extra weight in the middle. Or else his stomach muscles had relaxed. Either way, his waist looked sloppy, as if his shirt hadn't been properly tucked in. Showing an affinity for routine, he seemed to gravitate towards the same sort of button-up dress shirts as the one he wore now—it would require at least one pocket, to keep whatever he needed close at hand. Today, this was his MONUC ID badge, which was strung around his neck on a lanyard.

"All right, all right, let's go," I said.

"Okay, okay, okay," babbled Matthieu. He cleared his throat—in vain, for the problem was his tongue, which lapped his words as if sucking brine off one of the shelled peanuts I'd seen Gabriel eating earlier. "The International Committee of the Red Cross today, Monday, March 18th, 2004, reunified twenty children with their families in Kisangani, the administrative centre of Oriental province." Here, Matthieu paused in the way people do when making space for validation. Not receiving any, his voice thinned: "Of the twenty, four were girls and sixteen were boys. Their ages range from eight to fourteen. Matthieu Ilunga wa Monatschiebe reports."

After a second longer pause, filled with many ums and clearings of the throat, he asked whether he should go on.

"Please," I said intently.

So Matthieu obliged me. But when his next lines reprised more of the same—and word for word, at that—I noticed a clump of my hair entwined in my fingers. "Matthieu," I interrupted. "What's the story here?"

I didn't see the irony in me knowing I didn't know everything while still being convinced of the things I thought I knew. If that made any sense.

"*I'll* tell you the story," I carried on, over Matthieu's baffled face. "These young children were separated from their families because there was a *war* going on here." I said the word "war," insinuating I knew something about it that he did not, as if whatever idea I had of it was worse than what he'd actually lived through. "People were killed, raped, attacked... and children lost contact with their parents. And now these children —young children from ages eight to fourteen, *as you've told us five times*—who haven't seen their families in... in how long?"

"Three or four years."

"*Three or four years! That's interesting!* You have to say that. Go back and redo it, and then send it to me again."

Matthieu nodded compliantly. On his way out the door, he brushed past the next man waiting in the archway, who was Rigobert.

"Reee-go-bearrr!" I sang out, without thinking. Rigobert's shoulders shot back as his eyes and mouth opened like a sunflower.

"It's a commercial: Ri-co-la! In Canada. It's like, for cough drops or something."

There was a moment of silence before everyone laughed side-splittingly, as if whatever strange thing had just transpired had been the funniest thing in the world.

I pointed and said accusingly, "Wait—that's your story? You've written it on paper?"

A finger-picked soukous guitar on the radio masked Rigobert's reply. Or perhaps Rigobert had simply adjusted his own volume to make it appear that way. Either way, it seemed unlikely anyone could've missed me bellowing like a Mai-Mai made government army corporal: *"Waaaay* too long! Cut it down!"

LESS THAN TWO MINUTES LATER, Rigobert reached for the glasses he'd taken off during the read. "Okay, five lines, understood. Plus, I have another story—it's very short! I came across it while I was out doing this one."

"All right… But be quick."

I watched him smooth the folds of his trousers as he stood, moving to retract his loose-leaf paper in a quiet, furtive slide.

Mamy came next with her story. Then Gabriel, then Sadala, and then Rigobert again, with his second brief, the length of which made an oxymoron of the word. One by one, each of them came into my office with reports consisting of blah blah blah. The stories they had sold as war-torn families reuniting, secret arms caches, traditional warriors with *Jungle Book* names… It was the stuff that Pulitzer Prize–winning newscasts were made of. Now, somewhere along the way, all the peaks and twists had flat-lined and died. I would've mourned had there been time.

"Jennifer!" For a man so self-possessed, Rigobert had a strong voice and knew how and when to impose it, no question. "I need you to send back my two stories so I can start the Swahili translation."

This was how it worked: because I didn't know a word of Swahili, I would read over the journalists' scripts in French — make the corrections — and then they would go back and translate their text, allowing us to air a version in both languages.

"And I'm still waiting for mine!" yelled Matthieu.

Gabriel peered into my office and saw me in the zone: eyes two inches from the screen, fingers attacking the cursor, delete and backspace keys. "Jenni," he started hesitantly. "Could you print out the headlines? I've just sent them to you because our printer is broken."

"What do you mean the printer is broken?"

"I don't know. It's not responding when we all go to print someth—"

"Well, why aren't you calling the UN IT guys?"

"We did." Gabriel, more than anyone, had the Congolese way of talking, not with his hands but by leveraging the whole of his gangly arms, placing the tips of his fingers to his chest before snapping back his wrists to turn over his palms. And his manner of standing mirrored the way he always sat: seemingly comfortable enough to take up space around him but still drawing together his shoulders in a slight pliant stoop. For a man of any height, let alone one of five foot eleven—six feet perhaps—it was striking. "We called—twice—but no one's come yet. Maybe if you called…"

"Okay, okay. I'll call. In a second. Just send me the headlines."

There it was, on the bottom right-hand corner of my computer screen: 4:58 PM. The scale of the disaster would be ruinous.

I picked up the phone on my desk and the studio phone rang and rang. Where the hell was he? Atypically in the final minutes before the start of live programming—*No! 4:59 already?*—our technician wasn't at the boards.

"Where's Kasmu?" I hollered out the door, jumping to my feet.

"Jennifer, the headlines," reminded Gabriel patiently.

Over the next fifty-five seconds, I corrected the most glaring errors of two news items, printed out two copies each of the headlines, plus the presenter's introduction of Matthieu's *Okapi Actions* feature (which had aired in Kinshasa the day before: Matthieu had pared it down to recycle it for our *décrochage*). I tracked down Kasmu (who said he'd been in the bathroom) and read over a last-second addition, which Tumba had scribbled on the back of an old Okapi Message. The way he'd set it up billed it as the result of this year's Kindu football—soccer—league finals between B.C. Bisilabo and F.C. Nyoka, when in fact, the game had been rained out and postponed.

5:00 PM: Kinshasa has the airwaves to broadcast its hourly three-minute news flash. Inside the Radio Okapi Kindu newsroom, Gabriel, the day's Swahili news presenter, remains seated at his computer terminal, hurriedly translating the headlines from French into Swahili.

5:03 PM: Okapi Kindu takes over the airwaves of 103.0 FM. The *décrochage*'s opening theme is launched—in a loop.

5:05 PM: The musical bed continues.

5:06 PM: Rough transition from the musical bed to Bob Marley's "Iron Lion Zion."

5:08 PM: Gabriel rushes into the studio noisily.

5:09 PM: Marley is singing, "I had to run like a fugitive," when Kasmu cuts the song abruptly and opens Gabriel's microphone. Gabriel—short of breath—launches his opening greeting, *"Habari kamili."* At the same time Kasmu brings up the opening theme once again, burying Gabriel's voice underneath.

5:10 PM: The Swahili news begins. Names and keywords spoken in French help me orient the lineup.

5:11 PM: Kasmu launches the wrong sound clip in Sadala's AK-47 recovery story.

5:12 PM: Gabriel's apology for the so-called technical error in the previous item is followed by seconds of unexplained silence.

5:14 PM: Kasmu successfully inserts a sting.

5:15 PM: Rigobert signs off the Swahili news bulletin. Kasmu plays a Latin-influenced song, during which the singer trills "Maniema" several times in succession.

5:19 PM: The Maniema song ends. Mamy, the day's French-language presenter, sits up straighter behind the microphone in anticipation of a news theme that never comes.

5:20 PM: Having sussed out the program is running grossly behind schedule, Mamy goes ahead and says robotically in French, "Dear listeners, good evening," before booting through the first two items.

5:22 PM: Matthieu joins Mamy in the studio to deliver his reunion story live to air. He trips on several words, but Kasmu manages to insert the right clip in the right spot, more or less.

5:25 PM: The French newscast ends. Rigobert reads the introduction to Matthieu's bone-dry magazine feature on some twenty books that have arrived in Kindu. In it, Matthieu names each one, its author *and* its publishing house.

5:30 PM: Matthieu ends his piece and should be ending the program, but the press review—our summary of the national newspapers—has been squeezed out. Sadala returns to the studio to squeeze it back in.

5:34 PM: Sadala ends the press review and, by extension, the program. Kasmu reconnects with Kinshasa's signal in the middle of a song.

AT 5:54 PM, we placed the Swahili version of Sadala's report on the FTP site for Kinshasa. Confirmation of its arrival came five minutes later (a minute before it was due to air)—at which time, Sadala stood, showing just how short he was, and then moved to the door, weighed down by the computer bag over his shoulder, a MONUC water bottle in one hand and his palm-sized radio in the other. Its antenna could have taken an eye out. "Okay, well, good night," he said.

I took the water bottle in my hand and slammed it on the table. "Are you joking?" I said caustically. And with a stern look, added, "Sit down."

BY 7 PM, a mixture of man-made light and radio waves had turned my office into a cocoon. Neon-green insects pressed their wings upon the window to my right; its seal was far from hermetic, allowing bug after bug to squeeze through. I flicked their weary near-dead bodies off my keyboard and hoped that, at the very least, they preyed on mosquitoes. There weren't as many mosquitoes as I'd feared before coming, not in terms of their numbers at any given time. There was, however, no let-up, and I soon began to sense them circling my head or levitating off the floor, even when I couldn't see or hear them. If I wasn't clapping, I was itching.

Mamy, Rigobert and the others had all vamoosed after my harangue:

"'Jennifer, our *responsable!*' Well, you wanna know what? You're responsible for what's in your reports. Not me! God! You guys are like, fifty." (Which they weren't: only Rigobert, and perhaps Tumba, were close.) "I'm thirty. What is that?"

That was a disaster! Humiliating! There was no pleasure whatsoever in that!

Recalling the scene, I picked up the phone with a grunt and punched in a PIN. Hearing the familiar ringtone in the context of such foreignness struck me: here I was, in a cement room, under the hum of an air-conditioning wall unit in middle-of-nowhere Africa, bombarded by strange neon-green insects, using the Internet and placing a long-distance call to Canada. As the ringing trilled on, I looked out the window as if Canada was out there, somewhere in the darkness.

After four and a half rings, voicemail cut it. "I'm sorry," I said. "I've missed you." I started to recount the details of our disastrous newscast but bailed quickly, thinking, *What's the use?* Louis never listened through to the end of my messages, particularly when they had no immediate consequences for him.

And so I hung up and returned to my work, first sending our show's rundown (our *conducteur,* we called it) to the Radio Okapi network. I wrote a few emails. At last, at around 10:30 PM, I shut down the computer. In the hallway, a warm line of light seeped from the bottom of Ulli's door. I stepped forward and knocked gently.

Something in my squinting eyes or pallid complexion must have given me away. "Oh, Jennifer!" he said when he saw me. He walked to the back corner to throw his weight behind an upholstered chair, faded blue. "Sit," he said, with a light tap that set off the chair's dust.

"Did you listen to the newscast? Did you hear it?"

Ulli, I knew, always listened. Just as the Bolivians guarded MONUC installations, the Swedes ran MONUC AirOps and the Uruguayans tamed the river, it was Ulli's job to listen. More than this, he'd become one of Radio Okapi's biggest fans—and critics —often shaking his head in disparagement over how Kindu's *décrochage* butchered (his word) his beloved Swahili language.

"Did you hear what a total disaster it was? It was a fiasco! I can't believe it. Is that normal? Is it always like that? The writing, the presentation…"

Ulli's rusty-pink lips curled in a bemused smile. "Jennifer, these aren't BBC journalists. Don't beat yourself up thinking the radio needs to be something it isn't. Work with them on their level. It'll be fine." He leaned in to wrap his arms around my shoulders, squeezing them together like a pair of exercise bands. "Don't stress yourself over this."

Another of my sighs burst forth, this one summoned from low in my throat. "I know. I know. You're right. I... Agh!"

Ulli drew a deep breath. "Go home," he said with quiet influence, "get some sleep. Kindu Paradise," he whispered, "can be a tiring place."

8

HEAVY RAINS FELL OVERNIGHT, drowning the jungle's bleats; I never knew nature could be so loud. As always, it was too hot to wear clothes, too hot for a sheet. From the first night, I'd lie faceup, tossing and turning underneath my wilting mosquito net, with just my underwear on. *Buzz, buzz.* In times when I well and truly couldn't sleep, I'd scrutinize the net's rips and holes like enlarged pores, obsessing over which bugs were small enough — or smart enough — to find a way through. When the buzzing came too close, I'd know there'd been a breach and the ear whacking would start.

The rain did little to cool the air but by morning had brought a freshness of tropical fecundity: swampy foliage; the silvery-grey bark of umbrella trees; the distilled fruit of home-made hooch, wafting with sweet cane sugar. The rain gods had thrown them all into their giant blender in the sky and set aside the leftovers: Still. Obstinate. Undone. The smell reached my nose in bed, where I lay as late as I possibly could. Clothes on, contacts in. I suspect I brushed my teeth. Upending a glass of squeezed orange juice, I called out to Roger, "Thank you!" and "Goodbye!" and shot out the door, though not necessarily in that order. What Ulli had said the night before held no water in the morning; plain as the off-kilter nose on my face, there was work to be done—and it wasn't going to do itself. The challenge had been set. I had to get to work.

Outside, the dirt was dark-brown gunk. The muddy water soused the soles of my feet, causing them to slip and slide against my rubber flip-flops.

I scurried through the MONUC parking lot, past a group of women bent over at the waist, mopping up slicks with half-metre switches of reeds. Up the stairs, down the hallway—with a few casual, blithe hellos. When I bounded through the news-room door, far too hot and sweaty, Rigobert was nearest to it. He was setting down a cup of Nescafé to turn on the room's wall unit air conditioner but stopped to say good morning when he saw me.

"Holy Mackinaw, it's hot! Yes—*please*, turn that on."

Rigobert averted his gaze from me to the air conditioner, as if thrown for a moment, so that I had the feeling of having said something wrong. The word "holy" seemed the likeliest culprit, said if not in vain, then at least cavalierly—and on the very day that Matthieu was wearing an *I Heart Jesus* baseball cap.

Our technician stepped out from behind Rigobert's sil-houette, ending my dwelling on the matter. "Good morning, Jennifer," he said, coolly. "How did you sleep?"

I grimaced despite myself. More than I wanted the journal-ists to like me, I wanted—if not needed—to like each of them—so much so that I'd actually considered the matter prior to leaving Canada. ("Really? That worries you?" Louis had scoffed. "I'd say that's the least of your worries, Jen-Jen.")

I knew the others didn't like Kasmu. To begin with, no one ever made any effort to bring him into their conversations, and when they did—out of need or by accident—they used polite voices and spoke only of professional matters. Last night's dis-aster newscast had made their lack of communication painfully obvious. Kasmu seemed to be sitting back, just waiting for the next false move—though in fairness, the journalists' hand signals had been all over the place. Sometimes a finger point had been meant to call for a jingle; other times, a sound clip. When Kasmu messed up, as he inevitably did, they'd brandished the whole of their arms to scold him.

Okay, Jennifer, I now said to myself. *You just have to work harder.* I pushed forth a smile that hurt my jaw, but already he was skirting away.

Matthieu was at the room's far end, next to the photocopier in front of the windows, where the backlight gave him a halo effect. Every last smile wrinkle was in place, lines stretched deeply, to the point of naïveté. He was percolating over a simple hello. He'd held back purposefully to be the last person I'd greet.

"Hi, Matthieu." I looked from him to around him. "Where's Mamy?"

It was almost farcical the extent to which a couple of thoughtless comments had rubbed them the wrong way—and how little I realized it.

"Mamy?" questioned Matthieu. There was a pause. "She's not here yet."

I nodded and walked into my office to turn on my computer. Twenty-six new emails, the vast majority of which were scripts and announcer cues sent to Radio Okapi recipients network-wide. Some were personal. The night before, I'd sent an old wives' tale that Bob, the technician in Kinshasa, had told me, about how eating Congolese dirt could supposedly ease an upset stomach. One of the droller replies requested a healthy amount of dirt be sent to Halifax.

Disappointingly, Louis hadn't written. I wondered, *Did he get my message?* The one I'd left on his voicemail, how could he have missed it? Although technically we'd broken up (in Toronto, where I'd left him, though he was French from France), how many times had he said, "I still care for you, Jen-Jen"? And he did—care for me. I was certain of it. The problem was how to justify the fact he couldn't manage to send even two lines asking how I was, in a country he'd condemned on more than one occasion as godforsaken. I realized the dysfunction: to think him selfish and yet miss him all the same. For whatever reason, I excused it away: one: as a curse of romantic love, and two: as just the way he was.

IF I GRAVITATED TOWARDS Mamy it was because I perceived I could count on her. In the time that Mamadou had been with us, I'd watched how he'd gone to her first to satisfy any last-minute requests from Kinshasa's expectant producers. "Mmmmm, no problem" Mamy would hum with an air of unruffled facility. One time, when I'd picked up the phone—it was Jocelyne, from the youth show *Okapi Jeune*—Mamy stepped in and said, "Don't worry, *ma belle*. I have it covered. I'll be back in a half an hour." She'd picked up her purse, slid it to the crook of her elbow and pointed, triggering our eyes to follow an imaginary line appended to her manicured finger. Mamy's nails were never jagged or uneven. "Matthieu. I need your Mini Disc recorder, that one beside you. If you please." She sauntered out of the newsroom, her purse dangling from her arm. Two seconds later, we heard her purr hello to Ulli.

So Mamy was reliable but in a certain kind of way. I looked down at the right-hand corner of my screen: 8:32 AM: she was late, again. I was waiting because I was still unsure how to bring up the subject of my rant the day before, and it felt like whatever was going to be said or done needed to be said or done among all of us or not at all. I waited another three minutes. A fourth minute. And that was it; it was decided. I wouldn't apologize—an apology would give them the wrong idea—but I would acknowledge that the way I'd handled things wasn't professional. Or maybe I would just leave it. I would see how the meeting was playing out and take it from there.

In the newsroom, the others had been waiting. No sooner did I step out than a pair of arms flung into the air like projectiles:

"This morning at Camp Makuta—" Sadala fired fast and tensely. "At 10:15 AM, two hundred... maybe three hundred former soldiers during the troubles in Kindu... Mai-Mais, ex-ANC combatants—well mainly ex-ANC —"

"ANC are from RCD-Goma," said Gabriel. He was standing in front of our dry-erase board, holding a blue marker.

"Used to be based at the airport," said Rigobert.

Matthieu managed to squeeze in the acronym DDR a spit before Sadala's oncoming tirade.

I was trying to focus—*Ex-something soldiers. This morning. Goma. Airport. You can get this!*—when Sadala drew a deep breath and sat up straighter.

"No, no, no!" I said. "Just a second!" With presence of mind, I could have quipped J-A-S. "Go back, go back! I've missed something. So what you're saying is th —"

"I'm saying that even though the national DDR program hasn't started, the UNDP's arranged this—because the soldiers voluntarily demobilized."

"The UNDP is responsible for DDR," said Matthieu.

"No, the transitional government is responsible for DDR." Rigobert made the correction casually, scarcely taking his eyes off the pen he was fiddling with. "Under CONADER." CONADER was yet another Congolese acronym, only Rigobert had flattered it with real-word characteristics by pronouncing it *Conadair*. "But it isn't operating yet."

I thought a moment, longing to have answers but instead forming questions I was too frustrated to ask. Just then, Mamy traipsed in, strolling across the threshold as if it were a fashion runway and she, Naomi Campbell. "Good morning!" she pealed.

Rigobert winced as if in physical pain. "Oh, Mamy! Not black and red!"

And Mamy, she just laughed.

I strained to get a better look at what all the fuss was about, and yes, it was black and red. Mamy was black and red. A pair of red heels peeped provocatively from underneath the bell flare of a pair of black polyester 1970s-inspired trousers, which Mamy had matched to a red-and-black cotton blouse with a starched white collar that buttoned close to the neck. Wide strands of her jet-black wig had been coloured crimson and were crimped into place with small bobby pins. The clutch handbag she set down beside one of the computer terminals was the same shade of red as her shoes in faux patent leather. Plastic animal print bangles stacked themselves high up her forearm.

"What's wrong with black and red?" I asked shrinkingly.

"Ah!" said Rigobert reproachfully. "I *hate* black and red."

Still laughing, Mamy outstretched her bangled arm. "Rigobert," she cooed, her arm rattling like a snake.

I slinked back into my chair, ambushed and amiss to say anything about Mamy's lateness three days running. "Nice outfit," I said, of all things.

"Thanks!" said Mamy, prompting Rigobert to wince again.

I watched as Mamy brushed the dirt off her trousers' flouncy cuffs and then pushed back her handbag to win more space around the table. The tension in the room made her look around.

I honestly had no idea what to say.

Slouched at his desk, Sadala shifted his weight from left elbow to right. "So I just proposed a story about the Congolese army disarming ex-combatants today."

And Mamy nodded. "Oh yeah, the disarmament ceremony at Camp Makuta."

She had said it like that—so insouciantly—that it took a moment for the pieces to make sense. "That! That's the story? That a group of soldiers is laying down weapons in a ceremony today? That's easy enough to get! Why didn't you just say that?"

"I did," said Sadala, visibly upset.

"No… no, you didn't—not in that way. ANC, RDC, CDR, DDR, FAR—whatever… Good Lord!"

Gabriel fidgeted in front of the board. "Should I write it down?"

I reflected upon his blank regard with half a mind to snap something mean. Instead, I retook my seat clumsily.

"Okay, okay, *okay*," I said finally, in a single exasperated breath. "We can't go on like this. *I* can't go on like this. You need to understand that I… I don't have a clue what you're talking about." I hadn't meant to admit the last part, but—too late for me to take it back—I could only hope to distance myself, to bring it back to some sort of lesson or point. And so I racked my brain to find one.

"And… and… if I can't make out what you're on about, you'd better believe half our listeners won't either. You only have a minute ten—*one minute and ten seconds*—to make yourself understood. Do you get that? They'll change the station—they'll listen to something else!"

"Hmm," said Mamy, with due consideration that I now think was generous of her. Because the first thing was: our listeners, Ulli… *everybody* knew exactly what our acronyms meant, largely because of the second thing: that there was precious little else to listen to in Kindu.

In other words, everyone—but me—knew full well that FARDC stood for Forces armées de la République démocratique du Congo, the new reunified Congolese army; that Camp Makuta was its base up on the hill; that the ANC had been the armed wing of the Rwandan-backed RCD (-Goma) political faction against which Kindu's Mai-Mai civil militia had battled, and that CONADER (pronounced Conadair) was the nascent government commission responsible for DDR—a disarmament, demobilization and reintegration process that was supposed to somehow, magically, turn hordes of untrained combatants into FARDC soldiers, officers and gentlemen.

With so many things for me to learn, these first few weeks left me wanting to rip out my hair (which was funny, in light of what would come later; but later was another story). Slowly, the journalists and I were beginning to muddle our way through, as I trusted that in time I would learn enough to impart my lore. "You didn't go to university," I said on more than one occasion. I was wrong—in fact, some of them had attended university. But they never corrected me.

RIGOBERT, APRIL 2002

Rigobert Yuma Ndwani wa Lona was staring down a half century and didn't feel old yet. He still felt wanted. Someone from the UN—a big, strapping, important-looking man with dark, even skin, a Chadian—had arrived in Kindu, poking around for names. That was about four months ago. Two months went by and two *mzungus* came back. One was from the UN and the other was from a Swiss NGO. They said their organizations were partners in a new radio project. This, from their own mouths and to his face—at work—where they'd solicited him, albeit under pretext. They said they wanted to know about the current state of radio in Maniema, and could he, Rigobert, help?

So Rigobert sat down and told them all he knew, which was not nothing: His father was born in Maniema, his mother was born in Maniema and, as of 1998, after a series of rites and initiation, he himself had become like – well… royalty. In itself, the career path he took to journalism said something about the way the métier worked around here. He was a biochemistry expert. Became a professor. So he could talk – that was one thing. He also had a degree and, as a professor, had achieved just enough social status to have authority without having the stigma attached to those who'd served in public office.

In 1995, Rigobert made the leap to journalism, with a job heading production at KFM. But that's not where the two *mzungus* had found him. Back in 1997, after Laurent-Désiré Kabila – Kabila *père* – had overthrown Mobutu, the state broadcaster reverted to its original name, Radio-Télévision nationale congolaise, and appointed Rigobert director of news for Kindu. The position had allowed him the chance to work hard and assume responsibility, two aspects that were training him for life, still to this day.

Recently, the Chadian had come back, followed by a woman, another foreigner. She was recruiting. She'd installed herself in a big colonial house down by the Lualaba – the one with the big garden terrace not far from the KFM radio station – exactly the house you would've expected. Some people from work were heading down there now. In five minutes, after he finished tomorrow's lookahead, he'd be joining them.

ULLI POKED HIS HEAD into the newsroom just after our story meeting. Mamy's round face stretched. "Eh, *Papa!*"

Ulli walked over to where Mamy was sitting and bent down to hug her. "I know it says nine fifteen," he said to me, tilting back upward. A small rectangular cut-out invitation draped weightless in his hand. "But it's on African time. I'll leave here around ten or so. Sadala—you coming?"

"*Oui,*" said Sadala alertly, with an air of reverence that a man would usually reserve for someone as old as his father. Ulli and Sadala were perhaps eight, nine years apart.

"Good."

I asked, "So are you going to the MONUC meeting?" and Ulli replied neutrally, "Why not?" I admired the way Ulli courted effortlessness without disrespecting the mission or its work. How did he manage? If I'd said, "Why not?" I would've come across as sarcastic. Facetious, at least.

I looked at the clock. In a flit, my head whipped around, looking for something while waiting on my brain to tell it what. "Mamy!"

"Yes, *Maman?*"

"When Kinshasa calls, please propose your story about the youths of Kitoko and their neighbourhood watch. They can use it as a brief—even this morning. Just type it up quickly before you go. And Rigobert's *Grande Instance* story. Oh! And Sadala's story! *This* one—of course. That could be their lead, actually."

"D'accord, ma belle."

Rigobert winced again, though differently from the way he'd winced earlier over Mamy's dreaded black-and-red outfit. I thought, *Had he wanted me to ask him? Should I have?*

"And today—" *Notebook?* Check. *Pen?* "I want to see your stories by three thir…" I could see Ulli sauntering off and was trying to think. "No—make it… three."

I was already out the door, racing to catch up to Ulli, repeating, "I said, no later than 3 PM!" when Sadala caught up to me.

"Jenni," he said deliberately. An intimation of "please" popped into my head but popped out just as quickly. "I think it would be good to film the ceremony at Camp Makuta. I can do it, if you want."

MONUC Kindu Public Information possessed a small hand-held Sony camera to document notable events. The tape would be passed on to the next person going to Kinshasa, where the MONUC video team had editing facilities capable of producing real packages for broadcast on UN television and syndication beyond.

"Yeah, thanks," I told Sadala, smiling a rueful "but" before I said it, "but I think I should probably take a stab at doing it." It also occurred to me that I ought to write an article and load it with pictures for MONUC's magazines. Although my job title, public information officer/Radio Okapi station manager, implied an even split between the two functions, I sensed the UN hierarchy in Kinshasa and New York—people like my boss, Patricia—would have preferred a split closer to eighty-twenty, the way Mamadou had run things. He and people like him were forever talking about "the message" and how to get it out. I couldn't get over it: in the places I was used to, nobody would have dared tell you how to behave, so blatantly and without apology. But here in the Congo, people did so constantly. They called it "civic education" or, a new term that was swirling around, "communications for development."

Because, if anything, *I* would have wanted the split to go the other way; I wouldn't have thought that Sadala of all people would have been the least bit interested in doing not only quasi-MONUC PR but extra, unpaid work, too. Now I saw I'd perhaps assumed wrong. For after I'd declined his offer, Sadala replied, *"Ah, bon,"* followed by too many words, none of which made any sense. When at last he fell back, his posture was defeated.

BACK IN MY OFFICE, having turned the place upside down, I was desperately searching through mothballed, spider-ridden cabinet shelves for the stock of Mini Disc cassettes that I knew were *in here somewhere, damn it,* when Rigobert gently rapped on my open door. "Could I speak with you?"

I shut the flimsy sheet-metal cabinet to loud vibrations that left me with a strange impulse to apologize. "Sure, of course. Come in." I wiped my hands on the front of my jeans. "Dusty," I said, smiling. "Anyway—please."

Rigobert's silence was palpable as he moved towards the chair in front of my desk. He stood next to it, ramrod straight, with that regal posture of his, until eventually I clued in and invited him to sit. I waited for him to speak, but he remained silent; there was something else I was supposed to do. He helped me figure it out with a sidelong look at the door.

"Let me just shut this."

In the wake of such a prelude, I sat and waited for him to say… I didn't know what.

He paused. Several seconds went by. "I thought about what you said yesterday—about how we're responsible for our own stories. I even talked about it with my wife last night."

My eyes veered off in thought. "Oh…" My outburst.

"My wife gives me sound counsel on these things. We've been married twenty years. We have ten kids." He swallowed with an air of conclusiveness, so it was a miracle I didn't interrupt. "And… I think you're right." At this point, he bowed his head with ceremonial composure, as if accepting a gift. He sat exceptionally still. "It's true, we *are* responsible for our reports—for what's in them, and for getting them done on time. Like you said, no matter whether we have a *responsable* or not. It was thought-provoking, what you said."

I blinked once, then again, trying to get my head around the conversation. "Well… I… you're welcome. I… I…"

Rigobert pushed up his glasses before resting his hands on his lap. The space he left between my words and his hung in the air, humid and acrid, like "I'm sorry" waits for "That's okay."

His tactic—if I could call it that—had its effect on me, for I could suddenly feel my diaphragm sink. "I… I… Of course I shouldn't have yelled at you guys like that. It wasn't professional. I'm sorry." Saying this aloud, I coughed as if disgorging a wedged object. I realized in many ways I was a new person living a new life detached from her mechanisms of support. When I'd vented to Mom on the phone two days earlier, she'd simply said, "Well, that's good dear." I wanted to jump through the phone and shake her! And Louis—Lord-love-a-duck Louis!— who hadn't even deemed it worth his time to call me back…

Rigobert could see I'd drifted off. "Jennifer?"

I lifted my eyes to his, rousing myself. "I… I'm sorry. I just… want us to do better." I stopped, hearing my words; I'd formed them too lazily. They sounded defensive. "I know we can do better. I'm convinced we can do really good things with this radio. We already are, of course—but we can do so much more!"

With a glint in his eyes, Rigobert stood and moved to the door. "Well, I just wanted to thank you."

"No, no, no," I prattled. "Thank *you,* for coming. To see me, and for saying that."

Rigobert had a hand on the door to open it, and almost did—on top of someone.

It was Gabriel.

I ushered him in, this time closing the door. His countenance was as sober as Rigobert's. And on top of that, he was fidgeting. Gabriel fidgeted a lot, like a teenager who was overly aware of his own presence and a bit bothered by appendages and emotions he hadn't yet mastered. He was the opposite of Rigobert that way. "Actually… I… I just… wanted to… apologize, for yesterday. You were right. We should be taking more responsibility, and working with rigour."

The first time I opened my mouth, nothing came out—but *Gabriel…* My second try wasn't much better. *The Congolese may not be a sophisticated bunch,* I thought, *but they always seem to make up for it by being so damn… generous.*

Or maybe that was just the Okapis.

"Sadala!" I screamed out the door, throwing the video camera into my bag and fumbling for my keys. "You ready? Chop-chop! It's ten."

SADALA, APRIL 2002

There were two kinds of people in this world: those who were happy to sit back and do things halfway and those who ventured out into the frontier. By the same token, there were two kinds of journalists. There were those who went through the motions, the ones who came up with lesser-than, imitation knock-offs by assembling bits and pieces that others had created. And then there were people like him. True men of the field.

It had taken a lot for him to come back to Maniema. Nothing less than war. He'd seen it coming and had returned to Kindu two years before the fall of Mobutu. And because of where he'd been, working upriver in Kisangani as a reporter for the state-run OZRT (Office zaïrois de radiodiffusion et de télévision), his security had been compromised.

Really, things hadn't turned out so bad. Back home since 1995, he'd successfully reinvented himself in the world of the written press with the creation of his monthly newspaper, *La Petite Opinion*. Everyone in Kindu read it. It was a true paper of reference. Men would cite entire passages from the paper word for word—particularly when talking politics and the intricacies of the alliances, deputations and double-crossings that went hand in hand with the kind of war they'd seen in Kindu. And you couldn't say the same thing about all of Maniema's radio stations. They didn't cover news in the same way. The community radio stations were all too soft, too localized, too wishy-washy; the privates, too commercial. Of course, everyone knew that Kabila's replacement for Mobutu's OZRT—the RTNC—was still nothing but a government mouthpiece.

So he was happy. He'd done well. And at age forty-five, as somebody who'd been in journalism for almost twenty years, since starting at Radio Candip in Bunia back in 1983, he certainly didn't feel as though he had anything to prove to anyone—not anymore.

Still, there was something. Restlessness... He couldn't set it down. At times, he felt envious seeing the guys with their cameras and recorders, while he went around with his little notebook and pen. Being away from broadcasting, he missed... *broadcasting*. He missed the showmanship: give him a microphone and he could create art. "*Sauti nyororo…* You were talking to the 'beautiful smooth voice' of Sadala Shabani." That's how he'd always ended his taped interviews. People knew it as his signature. And they liked it; it made them feel good.

So he'd decided he was going to go for one of the new UN radio jobs. It was by far the best thing going in Kindu at the moment, and would be for the foreseeable future. And frankly, no one else here was going to be able to do the job any better. There were the new RTNC guys, but they all had far less experience than he did. And the money was going to be good. He was only old enough to remember snippets of the ONUC years, but in retrospect, the old UN mission had done a good job keeping the foreign mercenaries from completely taking over from the Belgians, and keeping the breakaway province of Katanga in Zaire, which, of course, was still called Congo then.

Sometimes—more than sometimes—his thoughts would wander to the OZRT and the early days… Remembering guys like Inga Mubukay and Modeste Shabani, and the trouble they used to get up to—guys he still ran into all the time but thought about as if they were dead. Back then, there was order, but also Mobutu, who, despite having once been one of them himself, made sure to control the flow of information (and, with no free press, journalists weren't exactly sitting around singing pan-African freedom anthems like "Indépendance Cha Cha").

All of a sudden he looked up, jarred from his thoughts by a smiley man who was approaching his small news kiosk with purpose. The man looked innocent enough—certainly nothing to be alarmed over. Sadala clearly saw him reach across his body to pull… *something*… out of an old canvas messenger bag. What was it? A paper? Was he actually going to try to sell him something?

LIKE THE NDWANIS (Rigobert, his wife and their ten children), the Shabanis were my neighbours. The Shabanis lived on my side of the street, about 100, 150 metres down. With their three small children, Sadala and his young wife (who was older than Mamy but younger than me) occupied the second, and top, floor of a low-rise. Although I never once stepped foot inside the place, every time I drove by, I would take a gander out the passenger window and consider how cool it was that Sadala had chosen to take up residence in one of the city's novelty multi-floor buildings. Theirs was constructed of brick-on-brick cement painted a pale shade of yellow that showed the dirt. A staircase ran up its right side. Out front, an old 1970s-style punch buggy in a deeper shade of yellow was rooted to the spot. To look at it, you would have thought its engine had never once been turned over.

At some point, I thought to ask Mamy: "Whose old car is that, outside Sadala's building? You know, the yellow one. The Volkswagen."

Mamy drew in her cheeks and raised the charcoaled lines of her perfectly drawn eyebrows. "Sadala's."

"Sadala's?"

"It was his taxi."

"*His taxi?*"

"He used to drive it."

"What? When?" I said. "Where? *Here?*"

Mamy erupted into peals of laughter. I waited for her to get it out of her system, and then asked, "Are you kidding me?"

"Ah! No, *ma belle*. Not kidding. Completely serious."

So there was my answer. It had been clear enough, yet for some inexplicable reason, it was as if the conversation that she and I had had that day had been instantly sucked up into the humid air, away from me like a shadow. From then on, whenever I drove past Sadala's and saw the car planted like a bulbous palm in its patch of green grass and refuse, I had myself convinced, *Jeez, Jennifer, you must have just dreamt that.* And oddly enough, even though it crossed my mind to do so on many occasions, in the end, I never did ask Sadala about his taxi. I kept meaning to—particularly, why wasn't he driving it? Or if it was broken, why wasn't he getting it fixed? For one reason or another, I would always get sidetracked, only to later chastise myself, *Oh, man, I forgot again!*

For all his passion and impulsion to put words to ideas, Sadala wasn't like me in one important way—he internalized what he perceived to be the errant behaviour of people he didn't know from Adam.

"Did you hear what Mutebutsi said?" he said in a sniff one morning as we were about to start our story meeting. Near as I could tell, it was a general comment made to no one in particular. "Something is going on in Bukavu. Mutebutsi is… too big for his boots." His voice was growing louder as if competing to be heard. "Kinshasa won't make him a general. The tenth military region won't give him the power he wants. He'll be disappointed."

"It was a good report," said Rigobert, temperately.

"En tout cas," agreed Gabriel.

When I asked, "What report?" Matthieu was quick to answer, "Serge Maheshe's from Bukavu."

"Okay…" I didn't know the name. By this point, after more than two years on air, Radio Okapi employed a great number of people — more than 150 Congolese reporters, translators, technicians, drivers and administrators nationwide. "And Muta… Muta…"

"Mutebutsi," they spit.

"He's a senior officer — an ex-combatant — in Bukavu," said Sadala. "He was backed by the Rwandans. *Dans la guerre.*" *La guerre* — the war — often came up in conversation, and when it did, the word came out contorted, like a temporary paralysis of the mouth. Sometimes people referred to it in the present tense, in the way one might speak of a close relative or friend recently passed. "He was part of the *brassage* — integrated into the new national army. But in the tenth military region, being a Banyamulenge —"

Gabriel sat up. "They have problems there."

Today, I would've asked the logical questions: What kind of problems? What's a Banyamulenge? Instead, I just nodded and cut off the thread with, "I see," realizing once again we were back there — where I didn't know Adam from Eve. Besides, close as it was, the tenth military region was outside our coverage area. We had the seventh.

So I just changed the subject. Sadala, however, kept fuming.

In short, six degrees of separation were wasted on a man like Sadala. (And for all I know, maybe he did know this Mutebutsi guy in Bukavu.) The upside of this trait of knowing everyone made Sadala especially empathetic — an eminence no journalism school can teach you. The downside had him taking to heart the wicked, imperfect ways of his country's oft-corrupt leaders, a quality that you could sometimes see in his veins. In his rage as old as the rubber trees, they would protrude like a drinking straw running the length of his short neck. Although once in a blue moon I would see him quietly brooding over thoughts I suspected he was guarding behind the polite line of anger, only once did I ever see him sad. Even then, I wasn't sure whether it was sadness or fear, whether it was his or my own.

But that point came later. On the day of the disarmament and demobilization ceremony atop Camp Makuta's plateau, Sadala was in his element. I watched him rove under the searing sun with the diligence of a sheep dog. They, the ex-soldiers, the sheep, sat cross-legged in the long crisped weeds that passed for grass. They were a sorry lot; if they weren't wearing dishevelled military fatigues, they were in jeans and hand-me-down T-shirts shipped en masse by international charities advertising brands from another world. Even those in uniform were shod in some neon-coloured variant of the rubber flip-flops sold at the local market. I myself owned a pair in royal blue, having asked Roger to buy me a pair. He had obliged, his only question being a raised eyebrow the first time he saw me leave the house in them.

Some thirty dignitaries and invitees were on hand to witness the day's event, including the seventh military region's new leader, General Widi Divioka. He'd been reassigned to Kindu around the time that Mai-Mai leader Kabambe wa Kabambe had announced his departure. Divioka was seated three rows ahead of me at a sharp angle, smack dab under the wooden lean-to that sheltered us. It reminded me of an old-time bandstand. I leaned forward with a creak of my plywood chair and looked over in the general's direction, trying not to stare. A man of Divioka's standing warranted an armed wing chair: his was made of wood and was cushioned with a square block of Styrofoam that had been slipcovered in a dizzyingly busy fabric—wax print, I thought it was called. *I wouldn't mind having something like that,* I thought.

With the general so comfortably seated, an officer a rank or two his junior presided over the proceedings outside the lean-to. His slender bowl-shaped chest jutted out to claim space—and still, he was crammed too close to the microphone, such that successive blasts of feedback had people recoiling. I glanced over to where the guys from MONUC Kindu's Generator Unit were attending to the workings of a large generator and cables. They squatted and poked about, until they looked up, saw me and smiled.

The ceremony had its order, I supposed, but how it dragged on! The Congolese anthem played at the outset, both grass and bandstand crowds stood and only after more pomp and circumstance did the officer even begin his speech. It was intolerably long, laden with such immoderate phrases as, "the time has come," "the next phase of your lives" and even, "your place in history." In between biting my nails and picking at scabs, I wondered who could've possibly written it.

All along, Sadala stood by and recorded. I gazed upon his extended arm and mine felt heavier with pain.

Finally, after what felt like an eternity, a military trumpeter warbled, as one by one, each former militant rose to his flip-flopped feet and pledged to abandon his illegal battle. (Or *her* illegal battle, for the group of about two hundred counted a handful of women.) Each demobilized person received a demobilization certificate, which was neither laminated nor framed, and chockablock with misspelled bravado, but was nevertheless something signed by city officials *and* with his or her own name on it.

With so many shorn heads and berets blocking my view, I strained to read the faces of those arriving at the podium but only saw sweat stains. During the course of people shifting, my line of sight fixed on a young soldier in his late teens or early twenties (*From which former warring component? I wondered. Mai-Mai? ANC? What did it matter? All reduced to their buttocks now…*). As with the others, my young soldier—I thought of him as a *my*—saluted Divioka wearily before returning to his place in the bristles and dirt. I studied him twirling his certificate and blinked twice when I saw that his toenails were painted fuchsia.

Next, a déjà vu of sorts abruptly transported me more than two thousand kilometres to Matadi, across the Atlantic and up the coast to Nova Scotia, to a high school upon a knoll off Dartmouth's Woodlawn Road. It is 1992, and I am graduating. My name has just been called. I rise from my bucket seat and smooth the front of my gown. My posture is as straight as I can hold it to balance my cap. I walk four or five steps onto the auditorium's stage. Do I feel hot—or is the room's central air conditioning up too high? Indubitably, I'm proud when a string of merits are awarded to me. Back in the buckets seats, my parents and older sister lead rousing applause.

"Jenni?"

"Hmm?"

I turned my head down and away in the direction of the voice, and there, crouched down near my lap was Sadala, whose roving reporter ways in all probability had brought on a trifling of conspicuousness. Or maybe that was just me—how I used to feel.

"Should we be taking some pictures?" he whispered eagerly. "I can film."

I nodded my head in spurts, mouthed, "Yeah, yeah, yeah," and handed him the video camera from my bag. Then off he went, putting distance between himself and those of us under the shelter as his hands took their slippery grip: one holding the camera, the other steadying his arm.

Like someone with a metal detector panning for lost gems or scrap metal will cordon and clear an area of sand or stone, Sadala and his machines trawled the expanse of the field, drifting like the breeze I worked to conjure up by fanning myself with the day's flimsy program. I first saw Sadala off in the distance filming a mound of rickety long-barrelled guns – in all, 111 AK-47s, M16s and SAR 80s, he and Ulli later told me – piled up like kindling for a campfire. And perhaps they should have been burned, but they weren't, for as soon as the ceremony was over, all armaments and ammunition were marshalled off to a MONUC-loaned container to be stored under lock and key.

Later, with the names and certificates still unfurling, Sadala lingered in front of a burlap sack branded *United Nations Development Programme* that was bursting open with pots and pans and jerry cans and galactic-sized bags of refined rice. *All this and fifty bucks,* I thought to myself grimly: the basics to survive – and they'd have to suffice, until each new national army soldier received his first paltry paycheque from the FARDC hierarchy in Kinshasa. Or – if he was too young, too old, too sickly or just too tuckered out to fight – until he acquired some new skill in a city where the unemployment rate was so high as to make the entire concept meaningless.

The ceremony lasted another hour. At its end, I stood on stiffened legs as men reached into their pockets for their scraps of cloth and people started shuffling about. I yawned and reached back to touch the folds of my sarong, expecting to feel dampness as I did.

People fanned out quickly, only to linger in clusters like the families and friends of those just conferred degrees. Ulli touched me on the shoulder and then turned to speak with a man in civilian dress who I assumed was some sort of authority. I looked around for my pink-toed graduate but to no avail. He had melted into the crowd of others and was gone.

OVER THE COURSE OF THE WEEK, Sadala pored over the audio he'd gathered from the ceremony. He would turn it into at least three separate scripts: one for our *décrochage,* a second for Kinshasa's evening newscast and a third for a special *Dialogue entre Congolais* program on national disarmament. Produced out of Kinshasa, DEC—pronounced like the chair—was Radio Okapi's flagship political call-in program. Congolese people adored it. I remember seeing Sadala on the phone with Jérôme Ngongo, DEC's host, listening intently and saying yes to the hilt. The others fell silent watching him. When he got off the phone and said Jérôme had asked him to put together DEC's lead story, Mamy's eyes narrowed to pinpoints.

"The sound you got of the trumpets," I said, trailing Sadala so closely I accidentally stepped on his heel. "Sorry. You know, the one at the beginning of the ceremony? That was good. Load that in—plus, the part where that kid told you… What did he say? That he was handing over his weapons to return to his family? You know, because his father died. And he has to provide for them."

"But that was in Swahili!" said Sadala, sounding personally affronted. DEC aired in French.

"Vraiment," said Gabriel, walking over. "You'll need to do a voice-over. I'll help translate."

Three nights later, when Sadala's story aired, Mamy laughed from her belly and called it a masterpiece. In it, Sadala reported on the ceremony itself before going on to explain how less than twenty-four hours later, hundreds of bags had been hastily packed as the wives and children of the former 85th Battalion had waited for their husbands and fathers by the banks of the Lualaba. That same afternoon, the families had reunited, at which point MONUC Kindu's Task Force One had granted them passage across the river to Alunguli. From there, they'd headed into the dense bushes of the jungle, all the way to Kailo territory by foot, en route to their new deployments.

During their interview, General Divioka had told Sadala—and our listeners, by extension—that two new brigades in Maniema were to be created. "I've named them Alpha and Bravo," he'd said, with great seriousness and pride. "I'm basing them in Punia and Kalima respectfully."

We'd understood he meant *respectively*.

"Sadala," I questioned later. We were working on an article that he, Ulli and I were co-authoring for several MONUC-branded publications. "How can they do that? I thought there was no formal DDR yet. So how can Divioka just... *demobilize* people and redeploy them?"

Imprecision could be my middle name, and in my own imprecise way, I was trying to get at the question of authority, and coordination. Was the UN aware of the plan? Who had cleared it?

Sadala answered in a whiff of breath, softly for him. He seemed very focussed. Consequently, I didn't quite catch what he said. I gathered it was something along the lines of, "He's the general."

Whatever his answer, clearly, something was going on; I slowly pieced things together and finally realized that, in the end, in our backwater jungle, something momentous was taking place. Kindu was blazing new trails in national disarmament, demobilization and reintegration. The Mai-Mais and other fighters who'd been told the war was over were laying down their weapons in droves and waiting to see what would happen next. When and where possible, the seventh military region was absorbing and redeploying the state's nascent army. In other words, that *thing* that the experts hadn't got around to fully planning was happening anyway, spontaneously, in Kindu. We were the transition's DDR guinea pig.

"Well, what do you know," I said, sounding vindicated, as if I could take some credit for the turn of events.

Sadala left me talking to myself to return to his computer. Save for me as *responsable*, Sadala was the only one to have claimed a particular workstation. His was the one at the end of the table, closest to the door that opened onto the hallway. Although he had never come out and actually said, "This is my computer," he always sat there. But more than that, he'd left his digital footprint. Years before the advent of the selfie, Sadala had turned a picture of himself into the computer's screen-saver — standing in the blueness of the background, looking out with a serious expression, as if to say, *See me? I exist.*

<hr>

IN JOURNALISM SCHOOL, we used to put together these things called "carts." Cartridges. To look at one, it was like a spool of audio tape, a quarter or half inch wide, inside a thin, rectangu- lar... well, *cartridge* – like an old Beta or VHS videocassette but smaller. The ones we used ran seventy seconds before they automatically stopped in the cart machine that played them. So you had a minute ten to tell your story and not a second more. First you'd gather your sound elements – interviews, ambient sound, music, what have you – and then you'd edit it all together according to your script. Using two different spools of audio tape – a feeder and a collector, side by side on a turntable – you'd take a razor blade to splice the tape on an angle at precisely the start of the word or note or breath, where if you were to join it back together it would sound as if all the pieces of tape coiled up on the floor never existed. Getting just the right place to physically cut and paste involved careful listening through your headphones, with one hand flat on the feeder spool and the other on the collector, while scratching each one back and forth like a deejay.

The final step was to record your finished edit onto the cart for broadcast.

These days—everywhere—carts were obsolete: they were a rotary telephone in a hands-free world. No use in talking about them.

The journalists in Kindu had edited audio online from day one because Radio Okapi was no mom-and-pop shop. It wanted more. Back then, in the beginning, six regional studios, including Kindu, gathered news onto digital recorders and loaded the sounds into multi-track Cool Edit software. New technologies allowed audio—even video and photos—to be transmitted online. All reports were sent to Kinshasa, to the national headquarters of the new UN peacekeeping mission, where the network broadcast the same news, the same music to everyone via three shortwave transmitters using a Marconi exciter, an amplifier and a three-element Yagi antenna pointed eighty degrees east, which was enough to cover the entire country.

In relatively short order, Kindu and other Congolese cities had had their own FM signals and had begun airing local news. The *décrochage* model took off; partnerships with community radio stations and their correspondents were now well underway. Expansion was on everyone's lips, and it wasn't too soon to start thinking of legacy.

"Vous savez," said Rigobert. He was behind a computer, his fingers curled around a Radio Okapi–branded pen. I wished I had one. "The Congo has an oral tradition. We're storytellers. We talk. We don't write it down—Swahili, Lingala, these are spoken languages. We don't have a lot of books. Radio Okapi is like our first national archives."

"Yes," I said, wistfully. "Yes. Of course."

Not just in Maniema—the whole Radio Okapi network was helping to professionalize the continent's most dominant mass medium. Did people actually prefer radio over TV or newspapers or the Internet? That would have been hard to measure, but in terms of flexibility, literacy rates and costs all in, radio had the better reach. Your basic analogue mixing console with headphones; some cable with connectors; a couple hundred batteries, or even a twelve-volt car battery; a microphone connected to a vertical omnidirectional antenna; a low-level transmitter – and you could broadcast within a two-and-a-half-kilometre radius, where a hill didn't get in the way.

I didn't know much about sound engineering – the actual broadcasting, the scientific side of things. Like Congolese politics, all the technical stuff confused me.

Still, I knew some things.

"A training session?" said Matthieu enthusiastically, sitting up in his chair. "We love training."

What I heard was *Thank you! We're excited to learn from you.* I suggested Saturday.

"Saturday when?" said Tumba. The raised freckles under his eyes bunched like stars. "This Saturday? There's a match Saturday."

Football was Tumba's beat. He was across the schedule, knew all the coaches, all the players. *And why not?* I supposed. But he was podgy, and dawdling. He was the same age as the others, Mamy excepted, but somehow old for someone under fifty.

After the usual hither and thither ("Not me, right?" said Kasmu; he wouldn't have to come?), it was decided the morning made the most sense.

Come the day, Tumba showed up with a loaf of bread he'd found heaven knows where, and I brought in a bunch of bruised-but-good bananas plus some mangoes that Roger had cubed and put into a plastic Chinese soup bowl covered with a lid. Rigobert made us Nescafé. He and I were the only ones to ever drink the stuff. "You sure you don't want any?" I asked the others.

We hung out chatting until Mamy arrived and had one of my handouts under her nose. Two words in bold print popped out at the top:

"Focus sentence," read Gabriel, in the slow, exaggerated way he read English.

"Yes, focus sentence. And read on below, for an example," I said.

"Jennifer is going on strike because she wants more money for all the work she's doing at Radio Okapi Kindu."

Even Sadala laughed, as I'd hoped he would, Matthieu being the most animated of course.

"Every story needs to be *active* — somebody… or something — a group of people — *doing* something, or *wanting* something. Ideally, for such and such reason."

Sadala reached to the middle of the table; seconds later, his fingers were yellow and gooey. The mangoes had gone days past tart to overripe. Sadala wiped his mouth with the back of his hand. Then Rigobert said something in Swahili, after which Sadala passed him the bowl. "Wait," said Rigobert and went to wash his hands.

The session was a mix of raillery, their respectful attention and my exacting standards. We covered a lot of what I'd wanted to get done, only I'd planned to do more performance exercises — script reading, improvisation, that kind of thing — and ran out of time at diaphragmatic breathing.

Near twelve o'clock, Tumba raised his hand and said my name shakily in the voice a man might use when fighting the urge to say Mr. or Mrs. "The match…"

"Right. Of course. Go. We're good. We can all stop here. What were we, two hours? More than two hours. Wow, went fast. There was some studio stuff I thought we could do. But anyway… We'd need Kasmu for that."

"*Vraiment,*" said Gabriel receptively.

Tumba moved to the door as Sadala and Rigobert thanked me. Rigobert stood up, but Sadala stayed seated. He was working on a script for *Okapi Action* for Monday. Monday was Kindu's day to file.

I started tidying up. Mamy reached for a Mini Disc recorder (we were two short of having enough for everyone to have their own) and put it into her handbag. Sadala said to her: "You going to interview that mechanic?" and Mamy nodded.

I knew her story. She'd come across a local garage worker who was looking to start her own business. Generators, cars, motorcycles: if it was broken, this woman could fix it. When Mamy had first brought it up I'd said, "A woman mechanic? Great story!" And then: "She can't be that busy," because other than our UN cars, trucks and boats—and the one Congolese army Jeep I always saw barrelling around—you could've counted the number of motorized vehicles in Kindu on one hand.

I'd said this and Mamy had replied, "Busy enough," because it was all relative. The peace that had come to Maniema was colouring the local economy, such that if one could ascribe the phrase "survival of the fittest" to times of war, famine or civil strife, you might've said Congo's transition marked an age of "prosperity for the pluckiest." In Kindu, the plucky tended to be great pilferers. In the city centre, around the markets and shops, men were busy carting around whatever building materials they'd managed to scrape up. Cans of paint were flying off the shelves (though there was only one colour to choose from: UN cyan blue—just as the only electrical cables had scratched-out labelling and the only gas and kerosene were in jerry cans or cut-up MONUC water bottles for sale off the side of the road).

The recent gains in security had also greatly influenced the city's foreign presence. As MONUC was scaling down its hubs and teams of military observers, redeploying its boots on the ground to politically sensitive areas elsewhere, local business (which had been on a steady decline since Kindu's days as a Belgian industrial centre) was scaling up from the drudges. Young Pakistanis and Indians were moving inland from the east coast to set up shop—nothing fancy, but business was business and welcomed.

Mamy had been just about out the door but stopped to glance at the green Cool Edit sound waves unfurling like a ticker tape across Rigobert's screen. Suddenly, her head turned, so mine did, too. A fine-featured man with lean muscles and smooth, plump skin stood devotedly in the archway. Judging by the smile that took over Mamy's face, I immediately thought, *Boyfriend.*

"Who's this now?" I asked brashly.

"*C'est mon petit frère,*" said Mamy, all smiles.

Her little brother! He and I moved towards one another, and before I knew it, his hand was warming mine. Holding his grip, I moved my thumb above, then below and then back above his, just to show I knew how to shake hands the Congolese way.

Mamy made it known that he was a student of the state-run University of Lubumbashi. He was attending classes at its extension here in Kindu, Uni-Kin, which had recently reopened but still lacked electricity, books or proper desks. From the outside—an odd-shaped side-split structure about a block long—you'd have thought the building was an abandoned garment factory and not a campus populated by the city's most ebullient aspirations.

"Ah, a university student. Well, you do have that look."

Mamy laughed, while her brother looked from his laced-up shoes and beige trousers up to the crisp button-down shirt that had been tucked neatly in. The pants, which were high-waisted, fit loosely at the waist; he must have bought them somewhere along the bumpy, potholed street that ran away from the river, where sellers splayed out rows of second-hand mass-market clothes. Those kinds of goods didn't come in all sizes. Belts, as you could imagine, were hugely popular.

Rigobert sprang up and said, "It's true, it's true," seemingly oblivious to the scourge of mosquitoes running circles above his head.

"Mmm," I said, taking an exaggerated whiff, and there had been no need to lean in. "You smell *good*." *Good* was the assault engulfing my nostrils, the scent of musk cologne that all but dripped off Mamy's brother's skin.

Within seconds, I realized how I must have sounded. Nevertheless, only now did I discover Mamy's brother's dimples. As he fought off a blush, we all laughed anew.

HERE WE WERE, a Saturday with no *décrochage,* and everyone but Tumba and Kasmu was in the newsroom (and Tumba was out doing a story). Yet only one person — Matthieu — needed to be here. In other words, he was the weekend's *permanence.*

"Jenni," said Matthieu, in a slightly supplicating way, though he would've known he was at present my only child, so to speak. "I sent you my story. Kinshasa's waiting. They're going to use it today."

"Come!" I said. I'd printed it out. I had plans for it.

From the beginning, Matthieu invited my babying, not only because of the pains he took to right his mistakes, but also because he dealt with his emotions demonstrably, like a child. His face would go slack when contented. His forehead would pinch when confused. And even the lightest questioning of any of his stories would cause his cheeks to cave in like deflated balloons.

"Okay. So, turn over the paper… That's right. Flip it over… right here, on the desk."

Regarding me with wonder, Matthieu shuffled his chair closer to my desk before finally turning over the paper as asked. With elbows on the table and fingers interlaced, his thumbs circled one another nervously while he waited, disoriented and dreaming up what I might be after.

"Now, tell me the story—the one you *meant* to write on the other side of that paper."

Matthieu leaned back and guffawed. When I didn't laugh too, his forehead creased along several distinct lines. "Umm, well… well…"

"Well, okay," he said, suddenly game to play along. "So, a training the trainers seminar…" (In Kindu, the NGOs were forever "training the trainers"—which was just an unadulterated seminar, pure and simple, except for the notion of passing it on: I train you; you train him.) "In Kindu… that started on… on Wednesday and runs until today, Friday… about, um… the preservation of self-injected blood products, is… destined to the attention of medical practitioners —"

"You mean doctors?"

"Yes! Doctors." Matthieu nodded encouragingly, as if I were getting his meaning. "All the doctors of the seventh military region… will, um—after the seminar—explore ways of storing the blood for future medicinal usage."

No one liked a good seminar better than Matthieu. WHO-sponsored seminars, human rights seminars, gender-based violence seminars, you name it. They were easy stories to get, and easy to get right.

"Did you just hear yourself? Future medicinal usage? Who says that?"

Matthieu's head dropped slightly. He reached for the paper to turn it back around, but my hand shot out to stop him. "That won't help you. You know, Matthieu —"

"Present!"

"Agh, why do say that like that? Present? I'm not your teacher! You can just say yes, you know." How many times a day did I sigh, and at him? "Matthieu, your little seminar is actually quite interesting. *Minus* the rigmarole. A group of doctors is looking into ways that people can store their own blood, right here in Kindu—in case they need it later. We're talking heavy-duty technology for a place that doesn't even have regular electricity supply. Is that even feasible? Nevermind Kindu—how are they gonna do it in some rinky-dink place like Tunda?"

"Be a reporter," I told him. "Stop regurgitating everything you hear!"

"Okay, okay, okay," said Matthieu, rising hastily and snapping up his script as if I were capable of swallowing his hand.

Seconds later, I flicked up my eyes to see him standing at the door. I thought he'd left.

"You know, my church doesn't believe in blood transfusions. For us, blood is sacred. 'For the life of the flesh is in the blood... No soul of you shall eat blood.' It's written in the Bible: Leviticus, Chapter 17. Verses 11 and 12."

I hesitated. A Bible quote. In the midst of casual conversation. "Oh! You're a... Jehovah's Witness, right?"

"Yes, yes, that's right," said Matthieu, beaming. In fact, he often said, "That's right," with a smile. I suddenly realized I'd met people like this before: people who were pleased to see any indication that others had noticed the things that made them *them*.

"I didn't know there were Jehovah's Witnesses in the Congo," I said.

Matthieu said they were a small church.

"Are you a believer?"

"Am I a believer?" I twirled a strand of hair, which came out in my hand. "Well, I believe what I believe. Yes."

Matthieu nodded and smiled at me yet again. By now, I was starting to wonder whether his smiles were more a bellwether of his eagerness to please than a sign of his contentment.

"How's your daughter doing? She's still in … Kasai province, is it?"

"Yes, that's right. In Kananga. With her uncle."

When I asked how that was going, Matthieu said it was going well and thanked me several times for asking. He said his daughter didn't have as many problems down there. Her uncle—his brother—was great to her, he said. She could even act independently. *"Vous savez,* she's a teenager now."

Don't ask me why, but schizophrenia came to mind. "She's lucky to have you for a dad." I'd intended to say more. But then there'd be the question of how to phrase it.

Matthieu went quiet. Then he looked at me, as if he'd spotted something new. When he smiled again, I thought, maybe he's just a happy person?

He left, ruffling his script. "Keep correcting me! I can do better! You'll see," he said.

DAYS AFTER THAT FIRST training session, Radio Okapi Kindu had not seen the last of the focus sentence.

"I want to see it at the top of every script you write!"

They might have thought I was joking—at first. Gabriel kept saying the words in English—"focus sentence, focus sentence," over and over again. Every time he did, he laughed.

IN RETROSPECT, it took about three weeks — fifteen *décrochages,* more or less — for us to pass the first hurdle, to arrive at the place where everyone had at least a vague notion of what I wanted, and where I stopped being the annoying person who'd walked into the movie theatre late — *that* person, the one who keeps asking everyone around her to provide running commentary on an emerging plot. ("Why is she saying that? Who is he again? Are those two in cahoots? Do they not like each other?")

By now, it was clear the tropics agreed with me. The morning light injected a rush of vitamin D, the sunshine vitamin, which helped to ward off the day's rising temperatures. The yellowness of the sky ran the risk of ouching your eyes, but if you had the presence of mind to forgo a nap, clouds would float in by mid-afternoon, soon fluffing like the feathers of an African grey parrot looking to ease its tension. The pale-blue sky would thicken and turn grey, dark clouds would swell, and then, *kaboom!* People going about their business would vacate the streets, vendors sweeping off the cookery, clothes, used sneakers and whatnot they'd had on display. Nobody used umbrellas. They'd just move out of the way — somewhere, *anywhere* under shelter, like how a cat knows where to go to get out of the rain. Usually, just afterwards, the grey sky would turn into a canvas of colours, like one of the paintings we *mzungus* used to pick up and gush over.

Maybe Kindu *was* just the jungle, but then again, who was I, if not just one lowly person on its land? I was slowly starting to see the difference between fact and impression. Like the first time Roger served me coconut: I'd always thought that coconut was sugary — too sugary for my liking — but when fresh off the tree and cut into wedges, it tasted rich, not sweet. There was no milk inside but coconut *water*. Roger used it to flavour our rice. "W-w…Well done," he said affectionately, with his slight stutter, when I managed to crack my first coconut with the blunt side of a cleaver. I set down the heavy blade with the pride and satisfaction of a grown woman able to solve her own problems.

There was another thing I liked about the coconut drink: how refreshing it was. Because Kindu was as hot as blazes — so hot that blotches of wetness woke me in the night. I would toss and turn to try to find a dry spot, until I could no longer withstand my own restlessness. I'd throw back my mosquito net, unlock my bedroom door and grope my way along the dank stone walls. Slap after slap on the concrete. Sometimes I would take my cellphone and press random keys to light my way. However I managed, I'd wind up underneath the shower with icy water pummelling my skin into numbness. Ten minutes later, I'd be back in bed, counting the gaps between cricket chirps. Someone had once told me you could gauge temperature that way.

My best sleep came in the cooler air an hour before dawn, as families on all sides of me were rousing. And because I slept so poorly, I was shocked when Benjamin, our guard, came into the house one morning — something he never did — to say that we (or rather I) had been robbed.

"What? Robbed? When?"

Benjamin led me into the small concrete room where Roger hung the washing. The twine he'd strung up was threadbare, stripped of all articles of raiment.

"Somebody was in here? Last night?"

Benjamin nodded. And sniffed.

"You're saying we were robbed? Did you see them?" I could hear my voice waxing louder and nasal. "Did you hear anything?"

"No," said Benjamin; probably when the robber had turned up, he'd been around the back of the house, near my room. "That had to be it," he said. And it was true that Benjamin often walked around the house, doing his checks.

At some point, Roger must have come to situate himself beside Benjamin, because suddenly they were both before me, slouching, telegraphing a look of contrition and empathy, tinged with curiosity. Wondering, perhaps, how Madame Jennifer would react.

As it happened, my head turned towards the window. Its wire screen was torn.

"Oh, God."

Nothing else had been taken, said Benjamin; he was trying to console me—I got it, I got it, but cripes! Didn't they know I didn't care about the clothes? They could have the damn clothes, the bulk of which had come from the deep jumbled bins of the Nova Scotian second-hand store we all called Frenchy's. I'd brought nothing of value, in case it all went to hell in a handbasket.

"I'm alone here," I said, my voice echoing in emptiness. "Bérénice is away. It's just me." This was pointlessly said, for they knew, of course they knew—the whole city knew; they talked and talked, leaking information like a sieve. My question about how the journalists came up with their leads had been naïve in the extreme.

"I can't have somebody coming in here. I can't have that. You understand me? *Tu comprends?*" My regard singled out Benjamin. *He* was the guard.

THE FRONT, BACK AND SIDE YARDS of our house were all part of the same dirt gradient, with patches of grass and trees. Each day I went out to the car, I would marvel at the beauty of the hulking rubber tree and how it had taken over the land with its roots that spread above ground like arteries and its tendrils that hung like party streamers. On dry mornings, Roger groomed the dirt flat until it lay like powder. The grass stuck up in whimsical, haphazard fashion in dabs of yellow and green.

Morning was a loud and busy time, with bands of biddable children coming together in all their noisy glory, despite their best efforts to behave. A large elementary school was just next door, and depending on the time I left for work, the last of the morning-session pupils were either wending their way to the schoolhouse or already somewhere on the property, running in all directions in the moments before class resumed. The children were truly sweet, I thought, in their uniforms. The boys wore pressed white shirts and navy trousers; the girls wore skirts, and many sported thick blue ribbons to hold back their hair. They all carried square book bags on their backs — even the little ones — perhaps so that none of their papers would dog-ear or wrinkle. Most days, like today, I was too late to see the children going in. Which was always a bit disappointing.

As I turned onto the main street heading to Radio Okapi, I glanced back at the school in the rear-view mirror. The schoolhouse itself was about the sturdiest-looking building a person could've expected to find in Kindu. It was a long rectangle, made of durable material that had been painted white and blue. It was hard to gauge just how big the place was inside, but it was safe to say it held eight, maybe ten classrooms. Tumba had done a story about Maniema being dead last in terms of national schooling. Authorities had bemoaned a lack of schools, but parents said the issue went well beyond that; you could always build the most rudimentary shelter and call it a school, they said.

Although no one had put it in quite these terms, the real problem was people were poor. For starters, very few people were qualified to teach and parents had to pay the teachers directly, money very few people had. NGOs were in the business of building schools, not paying school fees. Supplies were often pillaged. And once a child was old enough to have several brothers and sisters behind him, the choice was stark: spend the last of the family's money or secure more. So many parents would take one or several of their children out of school and put them to work. It was basic household math, which in many cases, saved lives.

Listening to Tumba's report and all the others, you couldn't help but notice a pattern. Often you'd hear someone say something to the effect of, "Eh! Eh! Eh! The poverty that's ravaging Kindu!" Or "We Congolese are poor." But a person would never call themselves poor. Never. I wasn't sure if it was a question of pride. Just the other day, as we'd been out doing something, someone had caught up to Rigobert and me to ask if he could have one of the MONUC-branded T-shirts we'd just received from Kinshasa. And as I was looking at this man and thinking, *We just got those shirts yesterday. How could you have possibly known we even had them?* Rigobert jumped in. He said, actually, there were only a few T-shirts left, and the last ones had been earmarked for the orphanage and the kind of down-on-their-luck people the Congolese liked to call *les sinistrés*.

I was thinking, *Is that true?* when, to my surprise, the man started nodding. After that, he said something nice, then turned and walked away. So there clearly was a sense that no matter how little someone had, there were others who had even less.

BY THE TIME I REACHED the newsroom, my story of an overnight robbery had become like a dropped oar in the Lualaba, entering a new realm and ready to be swept away. Given my anticipation to divulge every last detail, you would've thought I was almost happy to have been robbed. And I suppose I very nearly was. My first dreaded incident in the Congo had passed, no harm done, and now the sun's natural energy was girdling me like a second skin. Plus, journalists can be like that: inveigled into a story by events.

I was barely through the door, however, when an acerbic, accusatory expression kissed my spry mood goodbye.

"Hi," I said bunglingly, arranging a smile. "Good morning."

It was Kasmu, of course. Only he could do this to me.

"I'm hungry," he said brusquely.

"So go eat something."

"I can't afford to."

Not liking the insinuation, I slid along the wall to brush past him. "What do you mean you can't afford to? I know what you make"—which as a Radio Okapi technician was in the neighbourhood of US$800 per month—"and I know what it costs to live in Kindu. You can certainly afford to eat something."

"But we are twenty," said Kasmu sharply, as if pleased to contradict me. "My wife and I, and our children, and their children. I feed and educate them all. So we only have one meal a day."

I eyed Kasmu skeptically. Eight hundred dollars, at approximately two dollars a meal... That was about four hundred meals. Twenty people. Three meals a day. For thirty days...

Not being sure, and not wanting to be conned (if that was his intention), I let his point go and defended my argument, as if it were the argument that mattered most. "Well, one of you—one of your children, I'd think"—I was referring to the older ones of course—"should be able to work. But, as I say—your call."

Kasmu walked away in a huff, perhaps suspecting but not sure that I wanted to take my words back.

"Good morning, Jennifer," said Sadala, breaking into my thoughts.

"Hi," I replied, relieved to be engaged in a new conversation. Then, "How'd you sleep?"

"Well. Thank you." Sadala sounded pleased by the question, though the truth was I'd only thought to ask because they always asked me. "We were just discussing the report Serge Maheshe filed on Colonel Mutebutsi—the deputy regional commander of the tenth military region who was dismissed and summoned to Kinshasa."

Even when just talking casually among themselves, the journalists spoke of news precisely. They bestowed respect upon it, as if afraid to cheapen the facts.

"Oh, that's funny. You're talking about that report. Serge Maheshe, in Bukavu—that's right. I was planning to print it out. It was really well written." I'd heard it on Radio Okapi during the drive in and had especially loved the drama of its first sentence: "The news, fallen like a thunderbolt." It was the kind of narrative storytelling I was hoping we could adopt.

"You know he is ex-RCD," said Rigobert. He was tucked in the room's front corner, beside the kettle, which was just beginning to boil, its steam reddening the ruddiness of his face.

I nodded glibly and was drawing breath to segue into my story when Kasmu's voice cut the air: *C'est un Banyamulenge.*

"Huh? Who? Banya... *mulenge?*"

Sadala gave Kasmu a look I couldn't interpret. "Colonel Mutebutsi," he said. "In Bukavu. Remember? I mentioned the Banyamulenge in my DEC piece. After the DDR ceremony?"

Just as I was starting to grasp hold of the Congolese military, its acronyms and restructuring, along came this new strand. Were they talking about some sort of tribe? I wavered a bit and then leaned in to Sadala's monitor to see this word, "Banyamulenge," in an article on digitalcongo.net. To my surprise, there was even a picture of Kindu: it had been taken right here, at the intersection just outside the MONUC gate. You could actually see the police officer.

"Right. The Banyamulenge. They are… ethnic Congolese?" As soon as it came out of my mouth, I realized that "ethnic Congolese" was strange phrasing. I think I'd meant "indigenous."

"No, *Maman*." Mamy's tone was definite and laced with reproach. "You can't be ethnic Congolese."

"You can be ethnic Congolese," retorted Kasmu. "Of course you can."

"Of course you can't!" Mamy shot back. "You know as well as I do that the Europeans drew up Congo's borders *years* ago, without any notion of who was ethnically," she paused to make air quotes, "Congolese —"

"Yes, exactly, the Banya —"

"May I finish?"

Yikes, I thought. I knew that look, though it was the first time I'd seen it on Mamy's face. *If this gets out of hand,* I thought, *I'll say something. I'll interrupt.*

"*So,* as I was saying… Today, the Democratic Republic of the Congo is a country with about 250 different ethnic groups…" —here, she turned to me— *"including the Banyamulenge,"* and then she turned back to Kasmu, "and no one group is any more Congolese than the other."

Matthieu cleared his throat. "The word 'Banyamulenge,'" he said for my benefit, "is Swahili for the people of Mulenge. And Mulenge is in the Congolese province of South Kivu. It was on my test—when I was recruited for Okapi."

"Oh! You all had to write tes—"

"Exactly," said Mamy, looking visibly satisfied.

Rigobert approached me with a mug of Nescafé. "Careful. It's hot."

I thanked him for the warning and then rashly burnt my tongue.

Kasmu sighed churlishly. Mamy rolled her eyes. And just like that, the conversation petered out.

When at last I got around to telling my robbery story, Mamy's face pinched. "Eh, *Maman!*" she exclaimed.

She and the others followed up with a few pointed questions: they were commiserating with me but, more than that, trying to figure out the extent of the damage.

Finally, Rigobert normalized the situation by uttering "Eh! Eh! Eh!—a throwaway phrase, a commonplace filler, a cross between "Appalling! (but to be expected)" and "That sucks!"

Gabriel said, *"Le Congo,"* and sighed fatalistically. *"N'importe quoi."*

13

ESPECIALLY AFTER THE ROBBERY, though even before, one
of my biggest pet peeves was to hear someone ask, "What is
la Monique doing?" As if it were the UN's job to solve people's
problems.

"It's your country," I said to the police officer, the one outside our MONUC gate. It was always him, this same small guy,
standing in the dust of the cratered crossroads, quick to draw
the whistle he held in his white-gloved hand.

From the perspective of an air-conditioned car with rolled-up
windows and the radio on, the officer putting the whistle to his
mouth seemed to be enacting a futile, laughable exercise. But
now that I was on foot and fearing his whistle's loud shrill, his
range of motion seemed wide and imposing. His navy-blue shirt
and trousers were as ragged as ever—that hadn't changed. But
up close, his gloves looked bleached and crisp, and it was amaz-
ing how far the simple passing of an iron could go in instilling
respect and authority.

For all this illusion, I hadn't anticipated hearing the "What
is MONUC doing?" question now, and from him. Luckily, I had
my answer ready. It hadn't been hard to work out. From the
first time I'd surveyed the roving chickens, their feathers flitting every which way but down; seen the FARDC Jeep barrelling

down the road, gun-toting *boys* in the back in shades as dark as their regard; watched parents sending their toddlers off to fetch water from the dirty river… it seemed painfully obvious that people needed to start putting onus where onus was due.

The police officer nodded and gave me a tight-lipped smile. I wasn't surprised. Whenever I shared my thoughts on such matters, people typically fell silent for the insight.

Still, taking in the man's slump and dejected expression, I suddenly had a doubt. After all, wasn't I prone to self-righteousness?

A week or two later, Mamy interviewed this same police officer for the biography program *Okapi Portrait*. He sounded tired. He said he was. Then he said something that stunned me. He said every day but Sunday he got up, got dressed and went to the intersection—his regular beat for years and years—despite the fact he hadn't received a paycheque in nine months.

Mamy said the money hadn't come from Kinshasa. "Well, it's come," she said. "Probably." It just hadn't reached him.

"Is that normal?"

Mamy pinched her eyebrows and laughed through her words. "Yes, *Maman!*"

I MET MAMY'S FATHER quite unexpectedly. A clear resemblance was there, but I didn't see it at first.

The first thing anyone would have observed that day was a carefree, contented man who was happy to be out running errands with his daughter. I came across them outside the Salle Champagnat one sunny day with birds singing. I was bounding up the wide, low steps that went up to the community centre's front door—in a great mood, for such a beautiful day—when I looked up and saw Mamy coming out.

"Mamy! What are you doing here?"

"Eh! *Ma belle!*"

"Is this your dad?" I used the kind of dramatic tone, the inflection that captures a sense of *I don't believe it!* And, *Tell me more!*

"Ah, Jenni," she said, with a laughing sigh. "Yes. This… is Papa Tshibangu!"

Mamy's father put his arm around her shoulder and squeezed it hard, as the entire lower half of his face stretched into one giant circle; it was as if his body had suddenly been seized by energy that had to have some place to go. Because Papa Tshibangu had turned to face the smiling, tall, thin foreign woman in front of him, I witnessed all of this head-on and was reminded once again of the look of instantaneous fondness.

Papa Tshibangu was a teacher, and he and Mamy had been inside for something to do with that. Over their shoulders, I could see a wooden stage with theatre seating, all of it empty, not a soul. With the bright sun at my back, it appeared very dark inside, though, of course, my eyes still needed time to adjust.

"So you have the pleasure of working with this one," said Papa Tshibangu puckishly. He gave Mamy another squeeze and then thanked me for all that I was doing for his daughter and the radio and Kindu. And I did feel like I was doing something but certainly nowhere near as much as he seemed to be giving me credit for. I told him his daughter was very smart and I'd come to count on her for just about everything.

"You have to come for dinner. When are you coming?"

I laughed.

"Mamy will cook."

I laughed more. "Mamy? She will?"

"*Oui, Maman!* I can cook!"

They asked if I liked *fufu*—cassava root, pounded into a dough-like consistency—which I didn't unfortunately, because it might have helped to fatten me up. Roger always made us rice—Muslims in Kindu tended to choose rice as their starch as opposed to cassava or plantain—though I'd noticed Roger had recently started making plantain, too.

As for the dinner, it turned out to be a capable rendering of tilapia and goat meat in palm oil and tomato paste—served with both plantain *and fufu,* and I ate five full spoons of *fufu.* Honestly, I thought it was tasty. Mamy was the perfect hostess. She served the meal directly at the dining room table. Each dish was presented in a floral-patterned plastic pot, set upon a doily. Which made for a lot of doilies. In fact, the house was full of these round white-lace paper snowflakes, whether they were spread out on the coffee table in front of the family's jacquard chenille-upholstered sofa or on one of the end tables on either side of it. From where we ate, I could see the living room and, across from where I sat, unframed posters and family photos that had been printed on A4 paper and taped halfway up the wall. Green, gold and red garlands hung down in decorative *U*s. There was a clock on another wall, plus more posters, some of which were Christian. Artificial flowers filled pots and vases.

At times, we were as many as six at the table, but for the most part, it was just Mamy and me. Early on, Mamy's father—and her mother, briefly—had sat down to talk. But then they went away without eating—I didn't know where. I thought it was strange, because there was more than enough food for all of us. Mamy's brother—the one I'd met at the station—joined us later, and actually ate, though soon he, too, excused himself from the table. He had to study, he said.

The light was leaving us. Mamy got up and pushed through the African wax-printed fabric that draped across the door frame into another room I could sense but not see. When Mamy returned, the running drone of one diesel generator, then another and soon another heralded a growing radius of electric lamps and bulbs, announcing the night.

"Mango!" she exclaimed, with her eyes cast down at the bowl in her hands, as if she knew I could smell it.

We were both still laughing when a little girl came out of nowhere to crawl onto her lap. Mamy smiled and in a single gesture both caressed and prodded the girl into the chair next to her. Mamy introduced her as her niece.

"Your brother's?"

"No, another one's," she said. She'd understood what I'd meant. "An older brother. He's in Kinshasa."

"How many brothers do you *have?*"

"Three."

"And no sisters?"

"Nope! Just me! And Esther." She let her hand drop to the side of the little girl's leg and gave a quick smile, as the girl leaned forward for a mango slice.

I went home that night as tired as ever. But it was a different kind of tired. And for once, it led to proper sleep.

MAMY, APRIL 2002

The idea of it was crazy. And the more she sat here, buckled to the back of the sofa, watching his lips move feverishly, the more disconnected she became.

"Mamy, you can do this. Are you listening? You're smart. You can do this. You catch onto things quickly!"

"But she's an accountant!" her father cried. He was up, pacing their living room. "What's an accountant got to do with journalism? Nothing, that's what!"

Silence fell over the room. Mamy looked down at the concrete floor and began to tap the coarse rows of braids woven tightly to her head. This tapping was her only nervous habit.

"She should just take her resumé. They're looking for women. She has a chance at this. I know it."

Papa Tshibangu's large charcoal lips disappeared into his face.

Mamy lifted her gaze to the opposite wall but did not see — not the red, gold and green garlands strung in loops halfway down, or the wooden cuckoo clock that was stuck at nine o'clock, her brother's graduation photo tucked into one of the bottom corners.

Frankly, her father was right. "What? Who me? Journalism?" she'd said when Mr. Bagalwa had come bursting through their curtains with his fly-ball idea. He knew she was an account-ant. All those years she'd come down to do work for him at his NGO … Yes, it was rule of law stuff. But that wasn't journalism. For three years, he'd watched her scribbling out calculations, working through cash flow statements … Assets = Liabilities + Owner's Equity. She had a degree now. From the ISC. From *business* school. It was almost insulting that he couldn't see that.

Her parents remained keyed up for hours after he'd gone. She would think the issue was behind them — like later, when they were all eating at the dinner table, and her younger brother, Laurent, stabbed his plantain with his fork and made some off-colour joke about them learning how to eat with a Mai-Mai arrow. Mamy expected their father to scold him. Instead, he sank back into his chair and muttered, "Journalism!" under his breath.

That her boss at the NGO came back the next day was… awkward. Her mother opened the bamboo fence that enclosed their parcel of land, and there he stood, with a lopsided smile, as if to say, "What can you do?" The message was the same. He was still begging her to go. Only this time, a stillness in his voice had replaced the excitement of the day before. Just go, he said. Go take your resumé. And she could take it from there.

After all this hoopla, Mamy was actually considering it. Her parents, however, remained dead set against the idea. They said, "Mamy, think! Journalism is practically the same thing as politics. And look at our politics! RCD!"

"Honey, you don't want to get yourself messed up with any of that," said her mother.

The next day, Mamy walked down to where the recruitment was being held. Everybody knew the place; it was a huge colonial house with an equally huge, lush backyard that people said was the size of a Rwandan tea estate.

Mamy walked up the front steps, across the porch, peeped in cautiously – and gasped. There must have been two, three hundred people. For a moment, she stood paralyzed on the doorstep. She hadn't expected to see people corralled together as if trying out for some grand contest that promised to lift them from rags to riches. To change the course of their lives.

More applicants were coming in behind her. Having no place else to go, she hugged her resumé to her body, then twisted and stretched out her torso, stepping over the open toes of dangling feet to find a place to stand and wait. Here, with her back against the wall, which was vibrating from all the noise, the glare of the crowd began to fade. Soon, she could make out faces. All the *grand reporters* were there: the heads of KFM and RTNC. Inga Mubakay. Sadala Shabani, the guy who ran that paper. Rigobert Yuma Ndwani (him she knew, vaguely; he'd come to the house once to see her father). He and all the other newspaper, television and radio guys sat together on the room's plush upholstery set, slapping their suit trousers above the knee.

Just then, the person standing next to her let out an ear-splitting squeal. And all of a sudden, just like that, without even having to look over, she could see it. Why someone who knew her, who'd worked with her, who knew Kindu and how people raised their daughters to become the wives of other peoples' sons, had been so insistent on her applying. She'd sold herself short. No, she couldn't compete with the sofa gang. But none of the women — not even the RTNC girls — had her confidence. They didn't have degrees. They didn't have her strengths.

A Lebanese woman called Mamy into one of the bedrooms for an interview that went as well as Mamy had suddenly expected it to. "Come back tomorrow," instructed the woman, "with a story."

Mamy returned home as the sun was dropping in a spectrum of yellow and orange, a red lip on the horizon. She stopped shy of the gate at the sight of her father standing with his elbows pointed to either side of the door. She realized an impression — a lens — had been there all her life until now. Now, she saw a tall, broad-shouldered man gone past his prime standing at a loss for things his bigness and warm heart could no longer manage. She was twenty-two years old. Suddenly, twenty-two years seemed long enough to have lived your life as someone's pride and joy.

Her father was still staring her down as she approached him, smiling and swinging her handbag from the crook of her arm. "I think I'm going to get it."

Papa Tshibangu's mouth fell open. He went inside and called for his wife, who came out of the kitchen with her hands at the ties of her apron. Mamy set down her handbag, took off her shoes and slipped her feet into a pair of babouches at the door. She walked over to the sofa, primped her skirt and sat down.

Her father's right leg began to bounce involuntarily. "There's just one thing," he said agitatedly. He just wanted to know — and for her to tell him — had she lost her mind? "An accountant going around pretending to be a journalist!" His leg was jackhammering for dear life. "You're an accountant," he said, already with a lugubrious undertone in his voice. "An accountant."

THE CONGO RIVER, this impressive picture of mightiness when seen from the position of man's metallic conquering high above, was many things altogether different down on land. The upper part of it—the Lualaba—that barraged through Kindu, at once dividing the city's municipalities from each other and uniting them (in theory) via a national network of currents and tributaries—was raw, secretive, inhospitable. In Kinshasa, brave souls would jump in and ride the current, snatching from overhanging branch to overhanging branch until they arrived close enough to where they aimed to go. I never saw anyone attempt such a crazy thing in Kindu. For one thing, I supposed, where would they have gone? For another—crocodiles aside—there were rapids on either side of us, out of view but coming down the line: whitewater, wild and frenzied, bubbling atop the vast flow that had taken on the reddish-brown colour of the organic waste it swallowed like a whale does krill.

But here, we were far from the ocean. The cannonade of water before us, at times shooting waves several metres high, averaged more than twenty-eight degrees Celsius. That's what the Westerners said. Although the water was calmer at some times than others, this time of year, our part of the river had fallen into the habit of flooding. The fishermen complained.

Tumba spoke to a couple of them, who said that the undercut banks posed a real safety hazard and slack waters had become nearly impossible to find. I read Tumba's story and decided not to admit to him that I'd never actually seen anyone fishing the river, even though I had crossed the Lualaba on a number of occasions, both by MONUC's ferry and by pirogue. I said nothing because obviously the fishermen were there: we had fish to eat; it had to come from somewhere. They must have had their spots.

Technically, Kindu was a port—just like Matadi or Kisangani —only there were no container facilities in Kindu, and the only commercial goods that came in did so by plane, or after being pushed upriver in dugout canoes. The barge between Kindu and Ubundu (where the rail linked up north to Kisangani) took four days. Then it was another seven days back, upriver.

There was a pedestrian trail that followed the river. In fact, it wasn't a trail; it was the disused rail tracks overgrown with vegetation. I went down there one day on my own, to research a MONUC magazine story. There were a number of other people there, too. They used the route to transport things directly on their bodies, which struck me as an intelligent thing to do— because they could say for certain where the path led, and from a safety standpoint, they were out in the open where the chances of anyone sneaking up behind them were reduced.

It was quiet. Birds were chirping and the stream of the Lualaba drew my ear. Standing among unkempt grass, verdant shrubs and fragrant wildflowers, I took in a deep breath of the view. It felt unspoiled and undeveloped, bucolic as opposed to isolated. As if all that was missing were a blanket, a picnic basket and a book.

A dark-skinned sinewy woman with a large vat balanced on her head paced by; if she looked at me, I didn't see her do it. The nape of her neck was wet with sweat and the muscles around her shoulders were locked tight. However far she'd travelled to reach this spot, there were kilometres yet to go.

At this point in the Congo's transition, you got the feeling that anyone who could was beelining it out of Kindu: UN, expatriate, Congolese, you name it. The crocodiles swimming the Lualaba; the last of the forest monkeys, antelope and pigs—all fleeing, before they became bush meat. You could almost feel the grit in your teeth from the dust being kicked up on the roads.

"All change!" my Irish colleague Shane quipped as we smoked and shared a can of Coke in the MONUC cafeteria. A lively expression, I thought, if not an exaggerated one; for like the pesky mosquitoes I kept swatting at, which left large patches of red on my arms and legs, the new order—men like General Divioka—weren't likely to leave. Not before sucking out their fair share.

Nevertheless, every *décrochage* seemed to start the same: "*Habari kamili*—and now the news: X, Y or Z person left today for Kinshasa"—or Kisangani, or Bukavu. Still others were being sent northeast to Bunia, where despite the success of a recent French-driven military mission—Operation Artemis, it was called—Radio Okapi held fast to its roster system: journalists in, journalists out. Only the station's technician was permanent staff, and his name was never spoken on air.

"It's been awhile since any of us has been to Bunia," said Rigobert purposefully.

"I know." I'd been singing along to the radio, until the music had changed from Shania Twain to Congolese rumba and I could no longer keep up.

"Martin manages the rotation," said Rigobert, in a tone that implied instruction. "From Kinshasa."

I know! I wanted to cry out defensively: Martin—the triumvirate. The rotation… Bunia…

Bunia. Since Sadala's return, our rotations to Bunia had halted, simply because I'd allowed them to. I'd intended to keep them up—I honestly had—and it was still my intention to, *eventually*. The thing was, those in positions of responsibility make decisions, and frankly, sending them into harm's way seemed low priority, particularly when reporting in a safe place like Kindu struck me as being complicated enough.

Yet you could see they all itched to go. As if a whirlwind trip to Disney World was on offer.

"Well, okay… Whose turn is it to go next?"

"I don't know," said Rigobert bluntly. "But Sadala's been twice. And so has Mamy."

"Jenni! *Maman!* I've only been once," said Matthieu, appearing out of nowhere.

"I'm not your moth—"

"As have I," said Rigobert over top of me.

So they were keeping count.

"Has anyone *not* gone yet?"

Matthieu and Rigobert eyed each other. Matthieu's brow furrowed. "Perhaps not Tumba," said Rigobert.

"And Jean-Serge," said Matthieu.

I looked at Matthieu quizzically, not getting the reference. Then, as it dawned on me, Matthieu's face looked truly pained. "But… I don't know, I know, he's… maybe… that's different."

"Uh-huh." *The drunk guy.* It was one more thing to deal with.

Later, I called Martin, during a rare let-up in our pre-*décrochage* rush.

"Yeah, we can work Kindu back into the schedule," he said, above the noise. Like us, he was obviously busy doing a million different things. "Send me the names."

If only it were so easy! I thought to ask him to send me his records. I suspected I would need my facts in order.

"Tell me," I said, "Why does everyone want to go to Bunia so damn badly?"

"For one, they get a per diem. But it's not just that. Everyone wants to go on mission. And going to Bunia, it's, ah… fun."

"Fun to work where you could get shot at?" In the midst of fidgeting, I'd lost a flip-flop under my desk and had begun toe-ing about to find it. Martin chuckled at my comment. I'd always liked the way he laughed: short, sweet and nicely to the point. I could instantly picture his dark brows lifted above his wide-set eyes, spreading the bridge of his nose. Of the triumvirate (and I liked them all), I had a soft spot for Martin.

"No—not fun to get shot at. They don't always get shot at. And it's not just in Bunia. You know, Kindu was quite touch and go for a while—with the RCD and the Mai-Mai. Everybody had to sleep at HQ—for a whole week, I think. Rigobert almost got whipped to death by the RCD. We'd all thought he'd died. They threw Mamy in prison." He paused for a breath. "And Gabriel received death threats after a story he did about the RCD eating daw—"

I could hear activity mounting through the line. "What? *Dogs?*"

"Listen, Jenni, I have to go," said Martin abruptly. "I'll send you that list later."

Our line of business could be like that—abrupt.

After hanging up, I sat a moment. I wondered, why hadn't I ever asked the journalists questions about the past? I *had*—in a work context, relative to some script, or as background to a story. But never out of curiosity. Not personal questions, questions about their lives. Perhaps because it seemed… I didn't know… Voyeuristic? Intrusive? Like going to the funeral of someone you barely knew. And, also… beside the point. *We* were the storytellers.

So not surprisingly, with me still waiting for that proper sit-down with Ulli, the only background information I was getting was the kind I'd just heard from Martin, in dribs and drabs. That, plus the things made apparent by closeness. Recurrence. The funny thing was I didn't realize I was seeing as much as I was. That it was all there, waiting to be connected.

Gabriel was seated nearest my office door, hunched over the computer. He must have sensed my eyes on his back, for immediately he looked up. *"Ça va?"* Curiosity threaded the question, which he'd asked tentatively, as if guarded against my reproach. I'd noticed Gabriel wasn't the type to sit with his back to a door. He must not have had Matthieu's blind trust.

"Ça va," I said gently, not wanting to sound disingenuous. "So… how's your story coming?"

"Ah," said Gabriel. His shoulders relaxed. "Good. Yeah."

Gabriel was putting together an *Okapi Action* report for Kinshasa on the unsanitary conditions of Maniema's foremost slaughterhouse. One of its workers had taken him on a tour of a process run by custom rather than law. No government inspections, no rendering plants and little-to-no cleaning.

I read over his shoulder. "God, is that where our goat meat comes from?"

"Some of it, possibly. But I know Roger. He would take care. He'd make sure he was getting good quality."

"I wouldn't think you'd be able to tell, would you?"

"Sure you can," said Rigobert, beside us. "Sometimes."

All in all, that day's *décrochage* showed great promise. There was Gabriel's story on the dirty abattoir. Plus, Sadala had caught wind of another Mai-Mai group upriver wanting to disarm. The children would most certainly be handed over to child protection specialists, whereas the adults would be seeking the monetary and security entitlements they'd heard about on Radio Okapi.

Rigobert had looked into the appointment of the first two homegrown graduates to the Maniema bar. Tumba was back following football, plus a new school opening across the river in Alunguli. Matthieu had heard the 5th Celpac association was convening a seminar on gender and microcredit in its Pentecostal church down the road. They and the Baptists were Kindu's most prolific financiers and organizers of community events: Bible study, African cabaret, recipe exchanges.

Like Tumba, Mamy was behind a couple of stories. One had been practically in the can, and once that was done, she'd hit the road for Elila to cover an afternoon seed fair. Catholic Relief Services, a Christian aid agency, was serving dozens of families long displaced by the Mai-Mai and RCD rebel fighting in an area some fifteen kilometres north of Kindu. Each family was to receive ten kilos of vegetable, bean, maize and rice seeds to tide them over until they returned home—as early as the following week, if all went well—to where their goats, pigs and poultry once foraged. Then, with succour from the nebulous international community that the Congolese liked to go on about so much, they would start rebuilding their parcels.

"If you need a ride to CRS—for your story—let me know," I'd said as Mamy had been preparing to go. "Maybe I, or else Ulli, could drive you." Drive her as far as Catholic Relief Services' office, I'd meant; like most places in Maniema, the village of Elila wasn't accessible by car. A motorcycle, a bike or two feet were the only means of transport able to traverse the road, and in six months' time, when the rutting rains would come, even they would no longer find traction in the soil.

"No, *Maman.*" Mamy's short black wig didn't shunt an inch as she shook her head with a satisfied, if not smug, smile. For weeks on end, I'd been keeping at her to, *please,* put aside her vast collection of wigs, even for a day, so that I could see what her natural hair looked like. "One of the program officers said he'd pick me up downstairs. We're going on his motorbike. He's coming for me at eleven."

"Well, great," I'd replied, adding the words, *Of course he is,* silently in my head. For, sometimes, I had to laugh at Mamy. The oomph she put into her every word and move intimated a certain need for attention common among women in their twenties. You could see it was that—and not just her looks, or the fact she had her own tailor—that drove people to mollycoddle her. Men especially.

MAMY, APRIL 2002

The very next day after Mamy had gone to the UN recruitment event, she returned to the crowd at the Lebanese woman's— Eliane's—garden house. It seemed as though there should have been fewer people. Sadala, Rigobert and all the RTNC people were back talking among themselves on the sofas. But for some reason, Gabriel Wamenya—another RTNC star—was standing off to the side alone. So Mamy went up to him and introduced herself. "Eh! *Mon frère,* tell me something," she said. "What's a story?"

Wamenya didn't seem to mind the disturbance, and although Mamy was the kind of woman that men seemed to like, being of a robust womanly shape and having smooth chocolatey skin at its softest on her face, he showed no sign of any design to distort her question. "It's like RCD attacks X-X village. And then you look at it like a dissertation or an essay. Beginning. Middle. End. You flesh it out with information."

"So you do research?"

"No," said Gabriel. "You go out into the field."

Mamy said, "Where's the field?"

The next day, Mamy came back with her story, and Sadala Shabani took notice. He filched the paper out of her hands, scanned it and then handed it back. "Your writing is terrible," he said. But all the ideas were there. "Come see me tomorrow," he said, "at *La Petite Opinion*."

Even *she* knew what and where that was.

Over the next few days, Mamy hung around Sadala's kiosk like his little apprentice. She listened as he pontificated, his words barely passing her chest—; not because his eyes were affixed there—not necessarily—but because in his flourish of activity, he was always too busy to address her head-on. He gave her little exercises. One day, he picked up a pen. "Open your mouth," he said. "Put this in." He whirled behind him to grab one of his newspapers while saliva built under her tongue. "Now," he said, handing her a section. "Read this"—he pointed—"out loud. No—keep the pen in there!"

Mamy raised an eyebrow. After all, Sadala's girlfriend was an RTNC reporter who was also vying for a spot.

Still, Mamy went ahead and pushed the pen to her back teeth with her tongue. Already at the first apostrophe, she couldn't stifle a giggle. By the end of the first paragraph, she was gagging.

Sadala said she had to keep going. "It's going to train your pronunciation. And your diction."

That night, Mamy went home with her pen. She read the dictionary. She read the calendar—everything with the pen. Days went by and she kept on doing it, determined to master the exercises because something was working for her. Whether Sadala intended it or not. She was learning things.

15

AFTER ONE MONTH IN KINDU, I'd established a routine of scarcely interacting with anyone. Of course, as a public information officer, I organized community outreach events. And it was true I often accompanied MONUC colleagues to places like Kindu Central Prison (to take pictures of new mattresses being handed out) or to Kisuku elementary school in Alunguli (on the day UN-funded desks arrived – to replace the old ones that had been used as firewood for cooking during *la guerre*). But those were just QIPs. MONUC possessed a budget to allow NGOs to implement these small-scale projects – QIPs stood for Quick Impact Projects – that were meant to have an immediate and visible effect. They were gifts. Their primary purpose was to build goodwill towards us outsiders. As Sadala put it, with his odd mix of condemnation and self-importance that none of the other journalists possessed, we were winning hearts and minds.

And because I retained a certain distance – I was never going to integrate into the community, not a *mzungu* like me; that was clear – every time I found myself swept up into the city's experience, I was caught unaware. The robbery had been one. What the cleaning ladies said to me about it some days later was another:

"Madame Okapi! Your clothes are in the market. Do you want us to get them back for you?"

At first, I was unable to grasp it.

"We can go buy them for you, Madame."

There was no mention of money… no mention of how they knew whatever clothes they saw were mine. All I could think about was my underwear, for sale in the market.

"Madame?"

At least they were clean.

"Madame! Madame…"

With an "Umm" and a "Yeah," I sputtered in sudden pain, becoming ever-more conscious of the jabs that would work my stomach like a pestle in a mortar. By now, I was convinced the anti-malaria drugs I was on, called Lariam, were taking their toll. I'd had a dream the other night involving a bestial creature with multiple appendages. And it had been strangely sexual. Also, I was getting very thin.

"Ma-dame!"

I suppose I could have told them to yes, go fetch my clothes, thank you. But I didn't. For one thing, I had my focus—which presently had me rushing down the long and narrow blue hallway. I was conscious of being late for the MONUC morning meeting, dangerously approaching the cut-off when you could no longer slide into your seat as a supposed straggler; rather, you were just that smidgen late enough to be brought into disrepute. And once you were there, at the doorway of disrepute, there was no going back. You were expected to own up to the lack of respect you'd demonstrated and pause in the threshold—the time for others to take measure of your late entrance—before coming up with just the right gesture: the set of your jaw, the pursing of your lips or, better yet, the rounding of your neck and shoulders. You must act commensurately sheepish and, above all, ill at ease.

At the archway, I pulled out my steno notebook from under my arm and slid into the chair beside Ulli. He was talking:

"And so my friends… over a year and a half in Kindu Paradise, but we are here to serve. And I must go where the higher-ups chose to send me." Both his elbows were on the table, exposing his bare forearms. "Such is mission life."

"I'm sorry—what?"

"Ulli's being redeployed to Bunia," said the Uruguayan contingent commander with lavishness that gave the sneaking suspicion of his pleasure to be the giver of the news.

"What? Redeployed to Bunia? You're joking! What?" I shuffled to face Ulli directly. "I've just arrived! You can't leave now. I'm being cheated!"

"Oh!" Ulli swiped the air, as casually as one of the four cows on the patch of grass opposite the Catholic church on the corner would swipe a tail at flies. A gift to the parish, they were the only four cows in Kindu—none milked, slaughtered or bred.

"You don't need me," said Ulli sincerely.

I wondered what he was talking about and determined, then and there, that only an inherently needed person could ever say such a thing and get away with it.

THE JOURNALISTS AND I wanted to throw Ulli a party. He refused. On the eve of his departure, he circulated a three-line email inviting anyone who was still around—and available and interested in doing so—to join him in the cafeteria for a drink. I read his note with sadness and regret but in the end resigned myself with a shake of the head and said, "How very Ulli!"

AS ULLI'S OFFICE SAT EMPTY — when I would walk by and out of the corner of my eye see his desk cleared but for a dull knife lying beside two teaspoons — Maniema's transitional process was beginning to take shape.

One day, Mamy proposed to cover a parade in honour of the province's new administration, which was due to arrive soon. "Come with me, *Maman* Jenni. Do a MONUC article. Be a star!"

"Hey, that's *my* line!" I said, and laughed.

With Mamy having actually used the phrase "political parade," why, then, was I so surprised when we drove up and saw monolithic blocks of women and students parading down the road? Each group was wearing matching T-shirts with slogans I couldn't read and *pagnes* touting politicians whose names I didn't recognize. Some championed the face of Jesus.

Mamy and I parked the car on the dirt shoulder and jumped out with a Mini Disc recorder.

"Wait a second," I said, straining to read the incomprehensible red scribbles on two large cloth banners:

Karibu a Mesieurs Sumaili et Mendes de la par de GADEMA!

AFILMA *wellcomes* RCD-KML *to Maniema!*

In another context, I might have quipped something like, "Spelling isn't people's strong suit, is it?" But the banners were written in three languages — at least. Plus, it was so loud: Who would have heard me anyway?

"Mamy!" I had to shout to be heard over the ululations. There was even a marching band.

"Mamy!"

She stopped and turned her head. "I thought people here didn't like the RCD." That's what Rigobert and Tumba had said. The three of us had been in the newsroom one day, talking about the new transitional government appointments — these very same ones — and I'd asked, "Who's coming here to Kindu?"

And in his usual sluggish and lumbering speech, Tumba had said they didn't know. Nothing had been announced.

"Well, who do you think it's going to be? If you had to guess."

They'd both thought awhile before Rigobert said, "Not anyone from the RCD, not after what they did here." He said people wouldn't accept it.

It felt — to me — as though forces from the Rwandan-backed Rally for Congolese Democracy were long gone from here, though in truth, they'd controlled most of Maniema well into 2002. Gone not even two years. Their presence had led to widespread famine and abuses, particularly against young women and girls. At one point, they'd reportedly implemented a ban on anyone leaving the city without their authorization. Sadala mentioned something once about Kindu having been used as a base for launching military operations. There'd been a lot of mortars fired, he said. And he'd often bring up the name Tango Fort through gritted teeth, as if the two had once been friends but had had a violent falling out. I knew Tango Fort as General Gabriel Amisi Kumba, one of the country's many ex-combatants, who had, or was about to be, made major general in the new Congolese army. He was the one with the dead-looking face, the one who never seemed to be looking at you straight on. Sadala said he'd led the RCD's military operation in Kindu.

Now Mamy shook her head swiftly. *"Non, ma belle. C'est pas ça.* Here, hold this." She wriggled her handbag down her arm and passed it to me. Although I'd just had some of my belongings stolen, I'd left my purse in the car and hadn't even bothered to lock the door. (Plus, we'd just fetched our monthly allotment of potable water from the MONUC treatment plant in Basoko.) "It's RCD-KML. It's a different party. From Kisangani."

I slung Mamy's rock-heavy handbag over my shoulder. "So... not Rwandan?"

"Not Rwandan."

"So people like them, then?"

Mamy was giving such careful thought to my question that I'd actually forgotten what it was I'd asked. Finally, she let out a gust, almost a scoff. "I guess."

She turned to press record.

So it was true that Mamy and I weren't striking up a friendship, not in the traditional sense of the word, where one of us would have called up the other just to talk or to make some special plan to spend time together. Neither of us ever sought that kind of friendship from the other. I couldn't say why. You might've thought we would have, as we were the only two females in the newsroom and were relatively close in age.

Perhaps it was another shared trait—proclivity—that set the parameters of our relationship: that she and I were both "close family and good friends" people. For me, in Kindu, this meant spending most nights after work in my office on the telephone with my two best friends, my sister and my niece, my parents—both of them, on speakerphone—or Louis. These days, Louis and I spoke nearly every night, largely about his plans for a fishing-themed travel show. He'd just finished producing a pilot and was pushing it on sponsors. As for Mamy, I supposed she was home with her family, because with the exception of her brother, who from time to time came to fetch her at the station, I only ever saw her around us.

If I hadn't known better, I might've called Mamy's lack of friends conflicting because youth and good looks aside, her on-air personality had made her a celebrity about town. Étienne had told me so before I even got to Kindu: "You'll see. It's incredible. You're in this small, small place, and you walk down the street with Mamy, and they call out her name. She's like… a star." In fact, I'd discovered that people sometimes went so far as to point at her unabashedly, as if Mamy was still behind the studio glass and not standing right in front of them.

After Mamy finished her interviews and I'd taken several pictures, we returned to the car. A group of darker-skinned *mamans* in busy, brightly coloured *pagnes* were sitting on their knees with their legs folded, hooting and carrying on. Rows and columns of miniature tomatoes were splayed out on cut burlap in front of them — all soon to be squished and simmered alongside ground red chilies and, in the absence of lemons, several squirts of anything tart. I call them *mamans* — and they plainly were, even if some didn't have a year on Mamy.

Red-lined eyes stared as we went by, but Mamy didn't flinch. I opened the car door and moved my purse off the front seat.

"*Alors, ma belle,*" said Mamy, smiling very brightly. "Your first *défilé à la congolaise.*"

"Yes," I said, with a short chuckle. "That's right, my first Congolese parade. Yes, I guess it was."

Mamy asked me what I thought, and when I told her I liked it she nodded, visibly pleased, as if she'd had a hand in its planning. "By the way, I'm going to your aerobics class tonight. I brought my stuff."

"Oh, great!" I said jubilantly. We pulled out onto the road. "That's terrific. It's going to be fun." Today was Tuesday, one of the two days a week I taught aerobics down by the Lualaba at the Uruguayan Riverine gym. It reprised what had been the most popular staff activity at MONUC Kindu's Welfare Club until, wrenchingly (or so said Bérénice), the Swedish government had sent the previous instructor off packing with her air unit to Liberia. A sizable Indian contingent was in the process of taking over the job.

I'd been hoping to get all the journalists to attend the class — imagine Tumba with his belly! But Mamy would do for a start.

As it stood, the peanut gallery of bodybuilders who used the equipment at the back outnumbered us aerobics enthusiasts. A few more participants, and men like my friend Shane who'd taken to mocking our efforts would start to feel rather silly, on the outside looking in.

I FOUND OUT THERE was to be no replacement for Ulli per se. The higher-ups in Kinshasa had decided to nominate a head of office. Also at this time I learned there'd *used to* be a head of office for MONUC Kindu—before, and not long before, I'd arrived. It had been a South African, a certain Colonel Lawrence Smith, who'd headed the UN fighting force headquartered in Kindu, Task Force One—then more than three thousand strong. It still existed—still in Basoko—but with a dramatically reduced troop ceiling at about one-tenth the size.

This time, the head of office would hail from Political Affairs. The person to occupy the role would be my new boss.

"Jenni," said Gabriel, in the thin, deferential tone he often used to address me. "Do you know who the new head of office is going to be?"

"Agh," I said, slinking into the chair beside him. "Don't talk to me about it."

"Eh!" said Rigobert with a sudden alertness, recoiling as if stung by a bee.

"Oh—*sorry*." I was starting to figure out that Rigobert was sensitive—not to criticism necessarily, not like Gabriel. Rigobert was sensitive to stimuli: to noise, sharp tastes, colours. Red and black.

"I just… I…" I exhaled sharply. What was it about this new head of office that bothered me? Because I didn't have a problem with authority, though I'd come to like the autonomy of my situation: I reported to the head of Public Information in

Kinshasa—my boss, Patricia—who knew what we were doing and never said boo. Otherwise, on a day-to-day basis, we dealt with Yves and the triumvirate, and despite all our editorial haranguing, the arrangement was clean.

"I... I don't know who it is. But I just don't want somebody who doesn't get us. You know? I don't want some... *I don't know* ... coming in here and trying to tell us what we should and shouldn't put on air. They're going to think we're UN radio... that they can *direct* us."

It was crucial, I thought, that whoever was coming respected the radio's role—vis-à-vis the transitional process, yes, but also, on the most basic level, because people trusted us. They'd say: "If it's on Okapi, it must be true." There was no room for meddling.

Rigobert, for one, must have seen my point, for he took on a rapt look before nodding slowly.

Generally speaking, Radio Okapi Kindu was in MONUC's good books: with all the rapes, chronic shortages and harrassment, it often happened that something we were broadcasting was the subject of some UN dossier or investigation. The same local groups to approach us—Haki za Binadamu, for example (human rights organization in Swahili)—would know to alert la Monique (because our listeners possessed the kind of smarts of people who knew their options). So we'd all double up, which made the most sense for us at the radio: in one go, we'd get the story, *plus* the reaction from the one authority in town most capable of dealing with the matter. The UN wasn't perfect. But it had resources. It had reach.

AS WE AWAITED NEWS on the new MONUC Kindu head of office, Maniema's new authorities arrived, albeit several days late. They were flanked by soon-to-be-sworn-in Governor Koloso Sumaili and Vice-Governor Pierre Masudi Mendes. A third person, another vice-governor, was also appointed, a woman who was in charge of housing and social welfare and had no real power.

Not long after the trio was formally inaugurated – another day, another public rally, with more pageantry and speeches broadcast on Radio Okapi – Rigobert and I climbed into the car late in the afternoon, hours after everyone had started saying good evening. We drove about two kilometres to a dilapidated two-storey building. It was up the hill to Camp Makuta and around its right side, next to Kindu general hospital. The building had seen better days. Its concrete was split and its windows smashed out. Long-stemmed rubbery vines had climbed the ochre-washed walls, utterly encroaching on the interior, stealing every last morsel of sun, such that a person could've never known the building underneath was once a swanky hotel. Rigobert said he remembered it as a child.

The governor received Rigobert for forty-five minutes, during which they talked about government plans for Kindu's reconstruction and growth. Rigobert probed the governor's priorities, inquiring about roads that had never been gravelled, schools functioning without paid teachers, illegal checkpoints and Kindu's recurrent electrical outages – and learned that the governor was a proponent of hard work. Sumaili said the very first project would be the refurbishment of his and Mendes's offices – spaces most undeserving, he said, of a city of Kindu's stature.

Rigobert went back to the station that day and packaged a report reflecting the substance of what Sumaili had said. We aired it locally. Then we sent it to Kinshasa.

About two or three days later, Mamy reported that some of the remaining civil servants – those lowest on the food chain – were grumbling over their new working conditions. They were set up outside under a mango tree.

16

WE KNEW WE WERE on to something big when people right across the Congo took to saying, "If it's on Okapi, it must be true."

Rigobert said Radio Okapi was a new social institution.

"Yes," I said aloud. What a wonderful way of putting it.

It seemed to me that if Rigobert was right, the station was justified in billing itself as "the frequency of peace": peace, as in, stability. Structure amid chaos.

Gabriel read the Swahili newscast most nights, because he was good at it, number one; and number two, again—structure. By now, people felt comfortable hearing Gabriel's familiar voice start our *décrochage*, and in the language they knew best.

On the particular day I'm thinking of, I was at my desk cleaning up our rundown—the *conducteur*—and not listening live in the studio for once. Gabriel's voice saying, *"Tumu sikiliza"* was streaming through a small Sony radio plugged into a socket. *Tumu sikiliza.* Gabriel would always say it before throwing to a sound clip. Let's listen, it meant—as if asking for it.

So I ought to have known.

Knowing the stories and the lineup, and now having made out this phrase, I knew Gabriel had reached the start of his own report. Earlier in the day, he'd crossed the Lualaba and made his way to a squalid conglomeration of buildings for a story that, when I'd read it over, I'd thought wasn't half-bad. A group of women was squatting the space to sell stuff. Alunguli authorities had imposed taxes on their revenue, but the women were holding out. They said the buildings were abandoned, and, by all rights, nothing in the provincial nomenclature justified the tax.

I was only half-listening when my reverie was shattered by the last thing I expected: a human voice—misplaced, an octave too high, the low tones banished. But the syrupy, timorous tones couldn't lie. I froze when I heard it. Then I began to shriek.

In one leggy leap I was out of my chair, flying past Rigobert and Mamy, whose jaws had dropped to the floor because they had heard it, too. The studio door was open—it always was—so I rushed in to stand beside Kasmu. He looked tormented. In front of us, Gabriel was calmly seated behind the glass, as if nothing out of the ordinary had happened. He'd already moved on to the next story.

I couldn't get that voice out of my head.

"That sound!" I exclaimed, not necessarily to Kasmu, but he was there. "What the hell was that?"

Kasmu cast his eyes at Gabriel dramatically before turning to face me. "I tried to tell you. I tried to tell you it sounded funny."

What it had sounded like was a man putting on a falsetto voice, live on air.

Gabriel had impersonated a market woman. We'd all heard it. *God, live on air!* What had he done? And how? I knew at once that whatever it was, he'd done it for me, and the thought made me ten times angrier.

The program took twenty more minutes to end. When the door to the recording booth finally opened and Gabriel was out, I led him like a bailiff into the newsroom.

"Maybe you didn't hear me? I said, *What… in the name of God… was that?*"

Gabriel ran the fleshy part of his fingers across his lips. He scratched the back of his neck.

"That sound, Gabriel! What was it?"

His brown eyes turned ashen with thought. Then he shifted. "Yes"—a pause—"you know, sometimes in Alunguli... men dress up as women."

A poorly stifled cough (from Sadala?) reminded me there were other people in the room. I looked over and saw Matthieu cowering.

"It was you! Gabriel, it was you! This is a serious, serious error. *Faute grave! It is a* faute grave! People get fired for these kinds of serious errors, and I ought to fire you right now. Right now! On the spot! This is such a serious mistake... it's a question of our very credibility. All we have is that! Our listeners trust us, sometimes with nothing to trust but us. Everything that we've worked so hard to achieve goes right out the window—into the garbage!—with this... this..."

Mamy began to tap her wig. Sadala, Rigobert, Tumba—people who normally had so much to say about news—and yes, about the right way of reporting it—weren't uttering a word. They scarcely looked up.

After some moments of silence, Rigobert asked, "Jennifer?" like a child seeking permission to leave the table. I nodded and they all moved to stand. No one wasted any time leaving.

GABRIEL, APRIL 2002

The UN people just had to pick him. It was all coming together. He was back on track; he could feel it. That nice woman from MONUC—Eliane, the Lebanese woman—said they'd all be given a test. He needed to pass it.

A job like this was a dream come true, going all the way back to elementary school. His parents had their dreams; they wanted him to be a lawyer, which sounded okay enough – for someone else. Gabriel Wamenya Mugala N'samba was eleven years old, with a rich world of imagination spurring him into the corn-fields, because nothing made a better microphone than a fresh ear of corn off the stalk. Out there in the tall dense stubble, he would become Kabwe os Atocho, the voice of Zaire, calling sporting matches in Swahili before an audience of cornsilk, as loose husks tickled his long skinny legs.

In 1990, the boy, now a man, had his chance: the Zairian state news agency, OZRT, offered him his first recruitment test – and he passed! But then the bad break came, far too soon afterwards, the day the broadcaster's whole radio system broke down. Of course, with all the pressure on Mobutu, and the country indebted beyond bankruptcy, one lowly old radio making no money wasn't about to get fixed. He needed to find a new job.

Unfortunately, all this was happening as the country was being squeezed by hateful politicized acts next door. Come 1994, as many as a million Rwandans fleeing the genocide broke the back of the Zairian government's ability to cope. A crisis, a great depression, ensued. And for years, Gabriel went without work. All dreams aside, how could a man provide for his family without work? Had God intended for such soul-crushing things?

He had to adapt – there was no other choice – and was lucky at last to find gainful employment teaching French and history at several Maniema schools.

In life, things often have a way of working themselves out. As it happened, all the writing, reading and spelling that went with his new job left Gabriel perfectly positioned for the RCD's arrival in Kindu. In 2000, the Rwandan-backed rebels hired him to work for the new state broadcaster, the RTNC. What's more, they sent him across the border, to Butare, Rwanda, and gave him three months of journalism training.

So somehow he'd managed to overcome enough obstacles to now be in a position to give something back. He had a social debt to repay; he felt that. And was there any better way for him to do that, to help his fellow citizens, than to launch himself into the exact thing he'd always known deep down was his true passion and calling?

Radio Okapi appeared to be all the things that would enable a newsman to produce the kind of journalism worthy of the name.

He just had to pass that UN test.

THE MORNING AFTER OUR Alunguli debacle, noise woke me near 5:30, before the heat had its chance. *Fine use of a generator!* I cursed inwardly, rolling away from the light. Gospel music chirruped over the twang; plus the animals were chatting—loudly, as was their way. Oddly for someone living in the jungle, I'd only ever *heard* animals: civets, gorillas, forest elephants, or big cats or birds—that's what people said, anyway. I did see a monkey once; it was tied to the back of a bicycle, sitting on a metal rear rack. A young man with his hands on the bike's crossbar and handle was steering it through the street. I passed them on foot. Of course I couldn't help but look.

"*Tu veux?*" the guy said to me, stopping and holding my eye.

"No!" I said quickly, backing up to break the hold. *No!* Goodness gracious, no! I didn't want it. What was I supposed to do with a monkey?

Keep it as a pet, Rigobert said later. "People used to sell monkeys to foreigners all the time. Not so much anymore."

"Where do they get them from? These people who sell monkeys?"

He swallowed. He was drinking coffee. "The bush."

So: it was five-something in the morning and I was in and out of sleep, thinking about the bush, when suddenly, chanting—

deep, bottomless chanting—resounded in the room. It was coming from outside. *War chants.* It was unmistakable, even for someone who'd never heard them before. Instinctively my toes stopped rubbing the edge of the bed. Heavy footsteps grew louder.

They were soldiers; they would have guns. They would use them to rape, not to shoot—that much I knew from Radio Okapi and all our stories about ex-combatants. On air, we laundered a whole host of untrained, underfed, undisciplined warriors—often vermin of men, flat-out killers and rapists—in this sweeping term "ex-combatant." I closed my eyes and pictured the long barrel of a gun ripping my innards to bloody shreds. People tied to trees.

Not knowing what the hell else to do and desperate to be invisible, I lay very still and blenched. Then I could hear it: the sounds, fading away. Within seconds, there was silence but for the roosters that had been none the wiser and the electric guitar next door. It must have been a church.

The next thing I knew, I was falling back asleep.

When my eyelids opened two hours later, the footsteps, chanting and underlying dread swept over my body like the vague recollection of a dream. With a large o-shaped yawn, I rubbed the inner corners of my eyes, getting sleepy dust on my fingers.

The sunrays were burning. I laid a hand on my cellphone to check the time and—*damn it!*—I'd slept in. Like a coil come unwound, back went my mosquito net and on came a sarong and stretched-out T-shirt awash in lavender. Teeth brushed, contact lenses in. Car keys in hand. I had ten minutes to get to Okapi.

The coziness of cohabitation echoed through the clangour of forks and knives against plastic dishes, and of glasses and mugs plunked on our vinyl polka-dot tablecloth. I suppose the argument could have been made that, technically, Roger and I didn't live together; his wife, her mother and their three children would've surely claimed that he lived with them in the small flophouse they occupied inside the labyrinth off the road to Basoko. Nevertheless, whatever the hour he set off on his dark crickety path, Roger was part of my every morning's fog. At lunchtime, I'd come home and he'd be there, milling about the house with a sureness that left things unsaid.

At the table, Bérénice was nursing a hot drink. "Ah, hey, good morning," she said in a drawn-out yawn. Her back teeth had mercury fillings, like the kind we used to have in Canada. "We're both running late, I see"—and we had the Congolese army to thank. To her, the fact they'd chosen 5 AM to train made them "brilliant."

"So that's what it was!" I said, too quickly. "I heard the chants. I didn't know what was going on."

Bérénice cocked an eyebrow. "You were worried?"

"Well, not worried really, no," I lied. "I was just... kind of puzzled... curious."

On the table was a glass of fresh-squeezed orange juice still filled to the rim. Bérénice might have had something to say. Instead, she sat with her hands cupping her mug and made do with the silence of watching someone drink. Maybe the silence suited her. Incidentally, she and I had not become friends either.

I ARRIVED IN THE long and narrow blue hallway—a new day, a new agenda—and told myself that yesterday being yesterday, I wasn't angry anymore. At the door, the smell of musk beguiled like a handsome stranger at a party. And I almost forgot.

"Parfum!"

Mamy's brother, once again whiffing of cologne, stood over her as she typed. Rigobert, Tumba and Kasmu had also arrived and were seated. Gabriel was at the far side of the desk, typing.

"Bonjour, Madame," said Parfum, which was the last time he ever called me Madame. As we talked, I thought, *Such a lovely and handsome guy* and almost told him so, because it's usually clear when someone likes you and won't take things the wrong way. Our exchange drew in everyone at times, save for Gabriel. I felt bad but not bad enough. I wanted him to keep doing penance—to be the one to say something first to make it right.

Rigobert stood. I turned: "What time's Sadala due back?"

At dawn, as I'd lain in panic, UN transport had picked up Sadala from his second-floor walk-up to take him to the airport. Eibhlin from the UN's Office for the Coordination of Humanitarian Affairs had secured a helicopter flight to Punia, a mining community 175 kilometres to the north, where a cholera outbreak was feared.

Rigobert said Sadala would be back by four.

"And my MOP for next Wednesday?" said Gabriel. His voice sounded strange—though his own. "I… I put it on your desk."

"Yes," I said punctiliously. "I saw it. I'll sign it."

The Movement of Personnel form allowed people to fly on UN flights. It amounted to an airline ticket, free for all passengers but hard to get unless you were UN staff. It was a lifeline in Kindu, and for us at the radio, our only way to reach the hinterlands. Whatever the reason, whatever the destination, we didn't care. Provided MONUC AirOps granted us a seat, we would always cover the goings-on that justified the roughly $15,000 cost of the flight, which more often than not was some kind of joint civilian and military verification mission looking into a public health crisis. Sometimes it was an alleged crime; other times, a purported foreign army sighting. On average, there was one flight a week.

"Ask me if Radio Okapi has an agenda," I said to Shane later that same morning, as he was questioning me about my work. A flirtation, more like a coupling, was forming between us. "We do." I brought my cigarette to my mouth and rapidly inhaled. "Of course we do. We want people to be informed. We have to get the facts out."

"And *then* they can put in their bias," said Shane, with his barefaced simper.

"And then they can put in their bias. Exactly."

Day to day, our assignations—Shane's and mine—remained routine. First, from his long desk downstairs in the small low-ceilinged office of MONUC Kindu's Joint Logistics Operation Centre, Shane would send me a one-line email, as cute as it was concise. This morning's had been, "How's our little Benny Mulengie?" after which—as always—I'd come running out to join him in the MONUC cafeteria. All so he could simper at me.

"Who's Benny Mulengie, by the way?"

Shane just laughed, as I laughed, too—for let's face it, we were out here for the laughter. The coffee was fusty, the mosquitoes were a constant nuisance and the skin beneath my sarong kept sticking to my chair.

Other than the occasional rant (mine), Shane and I never traded opinions on Kindu's politics or predicaments, or went into any great length about who or what occupied us back home. I supposed I could've told him about the stories I edited: of village wells running dry... the crimes, the extortions, the *tracasseries*... or the way the Kindu police locked up people like barn animals. Several days ago, Mamy had reported that some prisoners down the street were verging on starvation—among them, a boy of eleven mixed into the general population; he'd been jailed without trial for stealing someone's cellphone. MONUC and the province's human rights groups, including the Haki za Binadamu people, were forever campaigning for the due course of justice, calling for the respect of *this* or *that* international treaty to which the Congo was party. MONUC Kindu's human rights section had met Governor Sumaili and his deputy, Mendes. I couldn't imagine what either of them would've said. Sumaili's comments to Mamy had been a bunch of baloney.

I RETURNED TO THE NEWSROOM TO FIND Matthieu—and Gabriel, who caught my eye and asked if he could speak to me privately. I'd expected as much and ushered him into my office.

"It was me yesterday... pretending to be the woman."

We had just sat down. And although Gabriel's confession had come swiftly, the words had barely escaped the diminutive space between his chest and fallen chin. He'd gone to Alunguli the day before, he said, and met a woman who'd said all the things he was hoping to get. "But when I got back to the newsroom I realized none of my interviews recorded—it was too late to go back over to Alunguli, and I remembered exactly what I wanted to use from her, word for word. So..." He drew a short breath. "So I quickly wrote it down from memory and recorded it."

He was... *It* was... The whole thing need never have happened. How easily he could have paraphrased and just... *attributed* it to her! I asked him why he hadn't.

His head shook with compunction. "I don't know. I don't know... It was just so good, what she said. The sound didn't record—I don't know why. I thought I could fix it."

"Oh, Gabriel," I said, collapsing the bridge of my nose into my hand. "Let me tell you something..."

It was an easy story to tell: me, having just started working for the CBC in Fredericton, New Brunswick—conscientious but inexperienced. The community meeting I was covering had finished late. I was tired. "So I get back to the station and prepare to file for the morning, only to realize that I left the Mini Disc recorder locked in the school gymnasium. And it was too late to go back to get it, I had no idea who to call."

I paused, noticing Gabriel's chin was higher.

"And, yes, I could have called my news editor. But I didn't want to come across as amateur, and I thought I could work around it."

The corners of Gabriel's mouth started to twitch. Even unconstrained, Gabriel often looked down when he smiled, as if his smiles embarrassed him.

"So what did you do?"

"Well, I started to prepare a report using tape from a previous interview I'd done the night before on the same subject. I left that night with the story in the system, ready for broadcast. But the next morning at 5 AM, I woke up in a panic and called the newsroom. I said, 'Don't use that story!'" I chuckled, remembering. "It's funny, because the news editor told me he'd listened to it and had already decided not to use it. He must have known. He never said anything, mind you—but he must have known."

I shook my head and breathed out my last memories on the subject. For a moment, Gabriel and I sat in silence, not looking at each other. Then suddenly, like a girl next to her sister on a church pew, I spurted.

"Gabriel, it's not funny. None of this is funny. It is serious."

Another spurt. What was wrong with me?

"I meant what I said yesterday. You know I really will fire you if you ever pull anything like that again."

Gabriel nodded abstemiously. The last word out of his mouth was "bye," even though he was set up at a computer not two metres away, where we could see each other through the open door.

SADALA RETURNED late in the day, hugging a flimsy charcoal-coloured bag of mangoes that was slipping.

"How was it?" said Rigobert.

Mamy rushed for the bottom of the bag, and she and Sadala heaved it back into his arms. "Good," said Sadala, wresting control. "It was very good. We saw lots of people—all sick."

"Cholera?" said Rigobert.

"No, not cholera." Cholera was often the first guess—*pray for the best, prepare for the worst*—for what later proved to be a case of bilharziasis: parasitic worms. Although neither was a picnic, public health authorities feared cholera's rice-water stools and shrivelled skin because the disease rapidly spread and killed. Bilharziasis could be readily treated.

Sadala let the bag fall on the table. "Bilharziasis. Maniema's chief medical officer and the World Health Organization doctor were with us on the flight, and they both confirmed it."

I looked over at the mangoes and swallowed hard, the sweet juice of their mottled green tips bringing spit to my mouth. Bérénice and I had eaten every last scrap of food Roger had prepared at lunch, and the MONUC cafeteria had cut its last potato days ago. I wondered if the staff had managed to get some plantain or anything that Bijou could quickly fry up in a splotch of palm oil. Not that Bijou ever did anything quickly.

"It went *really* well," Sadala went on, looking squarely at me. He said he had four stories to write—stories for Kinshasa. "I say we save them for tomorrow morning—except for a news brief about General Divioka making a quick tour of the region. We should use that for today."

"Divioka was on your flight?" My surprise was unjustified. MONUC was all about supporting the transition, and one of the foremost areas of support was to provide transport for the whole kit and caboodle of transitional leaders. "So you saw Divioka again? My, you two are getting pals-y!"

Sadala scoffed. I took the rumpled paper out of his hand.

"I wrote it in the helicopter on the way back."

Seeking my approval, perhaps? It wasn't that I thought Sadala didn't like me. It was that the others seemed to appreciate me, look up to me even; whereas Sadala, no, I didn't think that he did. "The general," I read aloud—his handwriting was faint, a pen running out—"was... aboard the UN flight to Punia... to assess the conditions of the local army base..."

I read on to learn that the general had gone to fire up the soldiers. Congolese military types called this a *causerie morale,* a phrase that always made me scoff, *Well that's the least they can do!* The Congolese army lacked training, equipment, food and even water to back up its front line. There were no wages to speak of either, for the FARDC was no better than the government at paying salaries. All week, Sadala had been following a story about an envelope gone missing. Soldiers of the seventh military region had been told the three months of pay they were owed had arrived from Kinshasa—only the officer purported to have transported it denied that it had ever been given to him. *Détournement de fonds* such stories were called; and if we'd got a dime for every embezzlement story we covered, we would've been able to pay each soldier his sixty dollars ourselves.

I handed Sadala's rumpled paper back to him. "Okay... but... didn't General Divioka say anything interesting? Anything worth taking a clip?"

"No. Nothing."

"Really? Well, I guess then —"

"Although I noticed about 150 soldiers and their families were moving, in line with Divioka's orders to redeploy. You know — the redeployment he announced at the demobilization ceremony, the one last month? They're going to Kasese. Divioka himself confirmed it to me."

A sudden rootsy, Latin-tinged guitar riff on the radio nearly knocked me down. "What do you mean nothing? Wouldn't you say that's a story?" *Why do I always have to be teaching grown adults a lesson?* "You've got to write that! That's new —"

"But I can't," said Sadala, heatedly.

"What do you mean you can't? This is *exactly* the kind of story that shows your army's doing what it said it was going to do. That it's starting to get its act together."

"We can't report military movement!" His veins popped out about as far as veins could go. "And not this kind... on foot. In the bush!"

"Oh, yes we can. You *saw* it. And I thought you said that Divioka confirmed it."

Some ten seconds earlier, at my last *What do you mean?* Rigobert and Tumba had crept nearer to where Mamy, Sadala and I were standing. Now all four pushed in simultaneously, the words of one banging like gunfire against the words of the other three.

"Sadala's right," said Rigobert. "If we report this, any militiamen still in the bush, like the RCD, could attack the soldiers. We'll be announcing to them that the soldiers are on the move — and they'll know which way they're going. They could be ambushed."

Tumba and Sadala nodded in sync. "We never announce this kind of thing on Radio Okapi," said Tumba, almost ruefully.

"It would be irresponsible," said Rigobert.

"*Vraiment*," said Gabriel.

Matthieu rose to his feet and pushed back his chair, only to stand and hover.

My tongue set to clucking. "That…" I started, "that certainly makes sense. *Perfect* sense, actually. I just… I don't know, I never thought about that."

Matthieu playfully patted my shoulder. "Ah, Jenni," he said, smiling. "It's not your fault! You just don't know war!"

I flushed.

"Just because it's common sense to us, doesn't mean it would be common sense to you," said Rigobert matter-of-factly.

18

I WAS IN MY OFFICE, scrolling through the Bunia rotations spreadsheet that Martin had sent, when I overheard Mamy raising a fuss about something in Swahili. When the conversation switched to French, I stopped typing to hear more clearly.

"I haven't seen him in hours," said Rigobert.

"Figures," Mamy sputtered.

Matthieu began to chuckle. "Mamy! Why don't you call him on the radio? He'll answer. IT just gave him a new one. I saw him get Jenni to sign the form yesterday. He said technicians need them the most."

"They do when they're never here," said Mamy crisply.

THEY DON'T SAY first impressions stick for nothing. As time went on, the notions that others had passed on to me found sufficient proof to solidify into absolute judgements: however devoted his labours, Matthieu couldn't file a compelling report to save his life, and — it had to be said — Kasmu belonged in a studio about as much as one of the feral kittens outside belonged in the MONUC cafeteria.

Kasmu was a real problem. Afraid that any approach I tried would give me away, I was content for us to work around him.

Matthieu, however, I liked. He, like none of the others, hung onto my every word of tutelage, and his listening ear and ready laughter had a way of making me feel I had value, even when I wasn't sure what for.

Matthieu said the others thought that he and Mamy were my favourites.

I was surprised to hear they would have had such a discussion and thought, *I'm not sure that's true*—that he and Mamy would have been my favourites if I'd had to choose.

"They say Eliane liked Sadala best. Étienne liked Rigobert, and you like me and Mamy."

We were sitting on the asphalted ledge outside Kindu's airport terminal, both of us intermittently saying, *Non, merci* to colourfully dressed women trotting out nuts and bananas. We were waiting for Rigobert to finish an interview with the head of the airport authority. The airport's weather-gauging equipment—humidity data loggers, wind speed instruments, vanes and the like—were showing material signs of wear, reportedly recording gusts of up to seventy-five kilometres an hour on hot, windless days like today when I dreamt of the slightest gust of air on my neck.

"What about Mamadou? Who do they think he likes?"

"We didn't talk about Mamadou." Matthieu fished an old cut-up undershirt from his pocket to blot his forehead. "Probably Mamy."

I went to nod my head, saying, "She is relia—" but instead jerked it oddly as my hand shot down to swat my leg.

"Jenni! You are strong!" Such declarative praise. Over a dead mosquito.

My hand poked about for a small package of cheese puffs inside my purse. The South Africans flew in provisions once a week from Pretoria. There was a store at Basoko Base where you could buy anything from toothpaste to entire flats of Simba brand potato chips.

"NikNak?" I offered, and Matthieu took just one.

"Take more—they're small." I paused for Matthieu's hand to dip. "See the little prize thingy?" The entire range of the Simba brand came packaged with round paper collectibles that I systematically gave to Matthieu. The Ilungas then had four children. Three were at home. *His* eldest (because Matthieu's wife was entirely too young to have birthed someone who was now a teenager) was still away for her problems. Mrs. Ilunga—Jeanne, Matthieu said—was into her third trimester with their next baby.

We sat and listened to the birds. By the time I returned to Matthieu's point about favourites, his fingernails were orange. "I don't have any favourites." I pulled up my left leg and inadvertently skinned my calf.

Matthieu fended off a *marchande*'s reach, and when he briskly nodded at me, I thought: *He doesn't believe me.*

"I don't see it like that… favourites. I really don't. It's about the work. And I honestly think that each of you has something— you know, your own little things. You…" There was a silence. "You're always trying… putting in effort, listening and wanting to do better. You're very thorough. You have a great work ethic."

Matthieu's lips curled under sharply so that his face was all pink gums.

"Mamy is quick. I can count on her. Tumba is prolific—and good at sports. Sadala knows all the military stuff. And Rigobert is consistent. He has real leadership skills—and his voice sounds great on air. And Gabriel can really write. He makes an effort to prove his talent. I love his scripts."

It was true, what I'd said. All those strands in my head had felt strangely… *good* to have articulated.

Out of the corner of my eye, Rigobert emerged from the wideness of the terminal's entrance as a collected, slight figure. At a distance, he looked undistinguished in a brightly patterned short-sleeved shirt, belted beige trousers and polished penny loafers, unencumbered but for the small square Mini Disc recorder he held in his hand.

"Get what you need?"

"*Oui, merci. Il était correct.*"

"Good," I said, hopping up, then down.

The plan was to drop off Matthieu at his next interview, and then go get some gas with Rigobert on our way back to HQ. We UN staff filled up our vehicles at the only gas station in town, the South Africans' in Basoko Base.

"I… also have to drop off the last of those damned magazines in the back." (Our MONUC magazines, I meant; it was part of my job to disseminate the ones Kinshasa sent in batches every so often.) What else? Ah…"

Down Airport Road, as I called it, I caught a glimpse of an SUV like ours when the road suddenly dipped. I squinted in the sun and realized Shane was in the passenger seat. *Where is he going?* There was one of two possibilities: to the airport or to the Indians, whose nearby Airfield Services Unit received guests in a large officers' mess with arm-to-arm sofas and a flat screen TV.

As we passed, I waved to Shane and the man he worked with, his boss. Shane was wearing sunglasses, but in the set of his jaw, I could see that simper. I think it made me blush.

"Jenni?" said Rigobert.

"Oh!" I stammered. "What was I saying?"

ALTHOUGH HE'D NEVER ACTED as a chair, or even as a formal moderator, the MONUC morning meeting had come to lack focus since Ulli's departure. For this reason if none other, I was looking forward to the arrival of my new boss. I found out it was to be a woman. Her name was Marie-France. She was French but had raised her family in Boston, which I knew because both times we'd spoken on the phone, I'd noticed her strong command of English, made more striking by the accent that rounded out her words. She wanted to know about housing and the availability of fresh produce and meats in the market. When I told her there was none, or next to it, she harrumphed and said, "Really? Oh my!"—after which she gave a long tumbling laugh before concluding, "No matter." So long as she could manage to find the right yard, she would plant a garden of carrots and tomatoes and chives and little hot peppers for homemade pili pili sauce. She'd brought seeds with her, she said.

Marie-France was to arrive any day now. She would become the fourth woman around our MONUC meeting table, joining me, Fernanda of Human Rights and Eibhlin, who, though not staff (she worked for OCHA, the UN's humanitarian agency), helmed the UN's humanitarian dossier in Maniema, an important job.

Eibhlin was Shane's roommate. Both were Irish, and both had distinctly reddened scalps along the lines where their hair naturally parted. Shane was five or ten years younger than Eibhlin and behaved so, but they used the same phrasing and laughed over things that to me felt incomplete. They shared a large furnished house in the old colonial style. Rigobert said Eliane used to live there. It was only five minutes away: after passing through the MONUC Security container (and after the old police officer blew his screeching whistle), you'd hang a right and make your way down the cratered residential street that sloped to the river. It was a nice, easy walk. And had I known to look for it, and been able to see around corners, I could've easily scoped the place out from my office window from day one.

On the last Sunday in April, Shane invited me over to see some chicks that had hatched in their backyard. Afterwards, we took some sun, lying in our bathing suits on towels arranged side by side atop tall bristly grass that pricked like straw. There, the tiny chicks thrived, their yellow heads poking out. Shane said the dense growth probably protected them against cats and other chick-eating creatures. And I could see their mother loping in confidence nearby.

When Eibhlin and I passed in the kitchen, her meaty, freckled shoulders bunched as she moved about from the cupboards to the table to the sink. There wasn't much for us to talk about; still, I felt judged by the words she didn't say. I suspected she didn't like me.

During one of our MONUC meetings — two or three days after Sadala's trip to Punia — Eibhlin chose her words assiduously. Her regard of me was devoid of emotion — nothing put on, no spite or otherwise. "It is a very serious matter to announce a cholera outbreak when there isn't one. Radio Okapi should check with me first on these kinds of stories. Cholera is extremely contagious, and the humanitarian community's response to it is measured accordingly. There are serious ramifications for the local population when the wrong information is broadcast. The radio needs to double-check its sources."

The radio needs to double-check its sources? I could feel my cheeks heating up. "We didn't report that. I'm pretty sure we didn't say cholera. And we *do* double-check our sources."

"My national officer said he heard it on Radio Okapi."

What? I wanted to say. *Had he listened? Did* you *listen?* It was on the tip of my tongue. Instead, I asked more neutrally, "Here? Or in Kinshasa?" It wasn't a moot point.

Eibhlin didn't answer, effectively dismissing both the argument and me.

"Hey," I announced later, barrelling into the newsroom. "Did we say the outbreak in Punia was cholera?"

Mamy looked up from the computer. "No, *Maman*."

"I said bilharziasis," Sadala pushed out, as if rebutting an affront. "I told you, remember? My script? We said bilharziasis."

"I know! That's what I thought. I didn't think so. I told her we said it was bilharziasis. I don't know what she was talking about. Nobody listens! They just... Did Kinshasa say cholera?"

"No!" said Sadala, denying for dear life, as you'd expect him to.

"Maybe in one of the translations? In the local languages? Maybe somebody in Kinshasa made an error and just..."

"The word for bilharziasis in Swahili or Lingala doesn't sound anything like cholera!"

"Not in Tshiluba either," said Mamy, who always told people she was from Kasai (the land of her father's ancestors, the Luba-Kasai). Yet she rarely spoke Tshiluba—at least not in my presence, though she was capable of translating for Kinshasa in a pinch. "This happens all the time. People say they heard things on Okapi when we never said it."

"Really? What else do people say that we didn't say?"

Mamy blew a gust out of her mouth.

"So they lie?"

"Not necessarily," said Sadala finally.

I gave him a look.

"Maybe... someone said it to him."

"So *they* lied."

"Or just got it wrong," said Mamy thoughtfully.

"Well... Somewhere along the line, someone said they heard something they didn't. Why would they do that?"

And so it was that I came to see that war wasn't the only thing I didn't know much about. It seemed I also possessed scant experience in the areas of rumour, misinformation and politically motivated attacks. It hadn't occurred to me that anyone would ever seek to discredit our radio. I'd been taught that sticks and stones could break my bones, but words would never hurt me. It was a kind of naïveté, I suppose, which I'd one day wish could be returned to me. Because ironically, with all I later learned on the subject, my mind could never work through the multitude of reasons why spoilers would instigate misery, let alone their own. I could only reach the sad conclusion that some things in life remained impossible to know or to ever fully understand.

MATTHIEU, APRIL–MAY 2002

On the Tuesday morning after Matthieu had distributed his Jehovah's Witness pamphlets, he was at his sewing machine, guiding a pair of pants along the seam, when his seamstress came running in.

"*Frère!*" she said. "*Frère!* They need translators! People like you! Throw on some good clothes!"

She led him down to the centre of the city and a small kiosk where a short corpulent man was selling newspapers.

"Hey, I know you," said Matthieu enthusiastically, though he wasn't yet done brushing the dust off his trousers. "I'm the person who came to your house last Thursday. With the brochures. Remember?"

And this was how Matthieu would come to meet Sadala. And although he wasn't given the full pen treatment, like Mamy, Sadala told him what he'd need to do and where he needed to be.

On the day the Lebanese woman administered the test, Matthieu, Rigobert and more than fifty others sat down with a breathless, fluttering feeling of possibility. Already, their candidacies had triumphed over two hundred applicants who'd failed to make the short list.

The test paper arrived face down on Matthieu's desk like a piece of buttered toast dropped to the floor begging to be picked up and flipped over. His body ached, his energy depleted like a lantern burned long into the night. He'd committed every last aspect of capital *N* news to memory, for it was certain that if he was to get this, if he was to stand out among the other candidates who could also speak several national languages, he had to prove more than the ability to translate French into Swahili, Tshiluba or Lingala. He had to make them see he had the makings of a journalist.

At last, the signal was given: "Okay. You may begin."

Matthieu turned over the test paper at its top staple. He read the first section. He turned the page. Many of the questions he'd prepared for were there – questions of a political nature, e.g., "Name the head of the RCD-Goma." And: "What is the Sun City Agreement?" But there were other questions. Another page. General knowledge questions. Some looked very easy, *too* easy – as in, you couldn't be Congolese and not know the answers. Matthieu picked up his pen and spun it about his thumb, turning things around in his mind. He thought a moment longer… and then… That's it! He'd figured out the trick: they wanted you to let down your guard, to write the first thing that came to mind. They wanted to see just who they were dealing with.

And so it was that before writing a single word – not even his own name – Matthieu petitioned the hearer of prayer for the inner calmness to detect his biases and weed them out.

When at last the list was out, Matthieu said to his wife, Mwanvua, "You look! I can't!"

Of all the people who'd applied, only two would be recruited as full-time UN staff. He never thought he'd get one of those jobs; he fully expected the *Petite Opinion* guy, Shabani, would be number one—or at least number two. And as it turned out, one it was. The *mwami* was the other. Below their names were the names of three other people who'd be retained on a freelance basis by the UN's international NGO partner, La Fondation Hirondelle. Two were RTNC guys, and the third was that girl, the young one whose soft even skin cried out to be touched, the one who always had her hair done up pretty. He wasn't surprised to see she'd gotten a spot. She seemed very smart.

Under a separate heading at the bottom, the word "Translators" was added like an appendix. Two names followed underneath: Jean-Serge Shindani and Matthieu Ilunga Lukengu Shambuy wa Monatschiebe. He'd done it!

19

MARIE-FRANCE ARRIVED as April turned to May. And because it was obligatory even for heads of offices, General Services put a form in her hand and told her to go collect signatures. I had to sign for Public Information. I was meant to brief her on Radio Okapi's mandate, structure and outputs, but an assistant showed up in her place. He entered the room tentatively, smiling widely. Only a young frame could carry such suppleness. I heard him say something to Tumba in French, as if for my benefit. Then he came up to me, grinning with the kind of excitement usually reserved for a child — as if there was a new teacher at school and he'd been chosen to carry out her first task.

"*Bonjour,* Madame Okapi," he said, still smiling. He placed the half-completed form in front of me and pointed a long thick nail bed to a line for me to sign jutting out from my name, below Samuel's of IT and above Jim's of Security.

Marie-France and I had barely exchanged more than a few sentences, but I liked the look of her. She was unfussy, clean and tidy. She had short brown hair, which she was allowing to grey. If convention had allowed her suspenders, she may well have worn them to keep her sensible trousers in line. Her cotton shirts always came together in a column of buttons. Her sleeves were either short or three-quarters rolled up to half length. She herself measured no more than five foot two, if that. She wore glasses with wire rims.

Her arrival came in the midst of the dry season, as birds rustled the low banana leaves being harvested to wrap fish for the last *liboke* of the year. Spidery fissures ran through the dirt. As if the land could withstand no more. The cafeteria had gone without potatoes for a week. Could our food supply, which already felt negligible, be further diminishing? On Saturday, Rigobert came out to the cafeteria to find me. I was sitting by myself, eating a plain omelette with onions. He was eating something too, out of a small clear plastic bag. And the bag was moving. *By itself.* I looked more closely. There were small, black, shrivelled... *things*... in there. They looked like raisins, though somehow I knew they weren't.

"What is that? What are you eating?"

Rigobert answered rather nonchalantly. I thought I was hearing things. "What?" *Termites? Did he say termites?*

Of course I didn't want to sound shocked, or repulsed. Like some prejudiced, closed-minded foreigner. I took a quiet breath and changed tone. "Termites."

Rigobert nodded, using a short range of motion, and passed me the bag.

"No!" I had to laugh. I drew another breath and composed myself. "Thank you."

For the record, Rigobert said he didn't want any of my omelette either.

That day, a Saturday, Rigobert was our *permanence*. Regardless, Mamy, Gabriel, Tumba... even Kasmu was in. I expected the others would make an appearance.

Rigobert had a script he wanted me to look over. It was about a reported rape in Pangi, the capital of a provincial territory of the same name, located some eighty kilometres away. Rigobert said he'd just spoken to the territory's administrator, and the young survivor was being sent to Bukavu, in South Kivu, for care.

"That's probably for the best," I said, knowing that South Kivu had far more resources than we did in Maniema. Kindu's hospital—l'hôpital général de référence de Kindu—was a small, almost romantic place, with a grassy interior courtyard where you could sit and barely ever hear a peep. It was like a convalescent home on the outside and a museum on the inside, where some old creaky beds, 1950s equipment and wooden cabinets filled with browned acetaminophen had been arranged. Civil society could only do so much.

We went back and I read Rigobert's rape story. It was good, if you could call a story about rape good. How many of these awful rape stories did we cover? Enough to desensitize me and, I hoped, the others, too. The facts as we reported them dispelled my last naïve notions on the subject: the grim reality of savage hands overpowering vulnerable women and girls—sometimes boys and babies, too. Men exhausted of spirit would insert piercing objects into other people's genital orifices. Branches, gun barrels, whatever they could find. Many survivors lived with the misplaced shame of leaking malodorous excrement through abnormal passageways. A new case of fistula came up every second or third day.

"Right," I said, driving my fingertips across my face, after I'd changed just a couple of words. I always changed "victim" to "survivor," for example—provided the person who'd been attacked hadn't died.

"JENNI?" said Gabriel some hours later, after I'd come back from lunch. He was eating shelled peanuts. He seemed to like them. "We're out of paper."

"Okay." I threw down my purse and leaned into his computer screen. "Is that your *Okapi Action* piece? You done? Can I listen?"

Although the temperature in Kindu never dipped more than a degree or two, lately the heat felt stuffy. On my way back in, I'd seen a group of men wearing T-shirts hiked up over their bellies, watching children race wire hoops with wooden sticks. We were all desperate for ventilation. At this point, it seemed the only nip in the air was coming from the stirring sawdust of backstreet ateliers where ex-combatants-turned-carpenters were making rudimentary furniture.

I placed a battered set of headphones into a computer jack and sat down to listen to the tape that Gabriel had gathered on the subject. "Oh yeah, this is good," I said of a two-toned sawing rhythm: back and forth, back and forth.

"Don't do it," Gabriel cautioned when my eyes lit up. "They're wobbly."

Kasmu chuckled sardonically and made a remark in Swahili. I thought I'd heard the word "Banyamulenge."

I said, "I don't care."

At this—at me—Mamy laughed. "Jenni! You can afford a proper table."

"I don't want a proper table. I want this! I want a… I think it's a good program. I want to support it."

Mamy laughed again, as if the thought of an ex-combatant job-training program was laughable. Her definition of progress was probably not the same as mine.

My computer chimed. It was Shane. I reached down hurriedly to pull out a desk drawer.

"If you need me, I'm in the cafeteria," I said, in my flurry.

Rigobert waved a hand goodbye. He and Mamy were squeezed together behind a computer, watching a film.

"Any good?" I called back.

"Not bad," said Rigobert.

"What about the paper?" asked Gabriel.

"I'll get it. On my way back. You can wait? Or you need it now. You need it now?"

Gabriel said he could wait.

The cafeteria had picked up considerably since the morning. Groups of people, some I knew, some I didn't, sat leaning over plates of bicycle chicken—and some kind of grilled fish by the smell of it: the sweetness of deep-fried plantain, mixed up in the fat of the palm oil it had been cooked in. By the look of it, you would've thought the bar was unstaffed. I was about to go up to call someone for a Coke—(*or a Fanta?* I never drank as many bottles of Coke and Fanta orange soda as I did in Kindu). Then I recognized the short-faced, wide-necked profile of a man seated at one of the white plastic tables. He sat alone with an unopened bottle of Primus beer in his mouth at a near ninety-degree angle.

"What are you *doing?*" I cried out.

I watched aghast as Sadala placed a cupped hand under his opened mouth. Silently, like a loose tooth, the bottle cap fell into his palm.

"It's okay," said Sadala, lacking conviction. "Rigobert still in there?"

"Rigobert? Yeah. Sure. He's in there watching a movie with Mamy."

You would've expected—*I* would have expected—Sadala to say something. Sometimes you had to prod Sadala a bit. It was funny, because he could be absolutely loquacious sometimes.

"Those Nollywood movies are a little violent for me," I remarked.

Sadala took a chug of beer, then set down the bottle before replacing the cap he'd just bitten off.

"Where's Bijou and everybody? Going to get a bottle opener perhaps?"

I'm not sure whether Sadala laughed, or even got my joke, because Shane then appeared and instantly distracted me.

"Hi, pet," said Shane.

"Hi," I said.

"Hi," said Sadala.

"Hello," said Shane.

It really went like that—so awkwardly! Of course, the polite thing to do would have been to introduce them properly.

"Bring the ciggies?" said Shane, after a moment.

I exhaled. "Yep."

Shane reached over and slid a cigarette from the package I held up to him before drifting off to a nearby table. I followed, throwing the words of disjointed sentences behind me as Sadala smiled tepidly.

In no way, in all my time in Kindu, did the journalists ever reference my personal life. How people who were generally so loud could be so discreet was beyond me. I knew they could see what was transpiring. They were journalists, after all. Observant. But it was more than that. They—all of them, for all their differences—possessed the uncanny ability to keep a steady eye on the actions of others without ever looking askance. In their line of work, as in life in general, I suspected it served them well.

MY AFFAIR WITH SHANE began not out of emptiness or boredom, not out of a lack of anything, but for the simple pleasure of affection. I honestly can't remember the circumstances under which we came together. Once we had, we maintained our schedule of mid-morning and afternoon smoke breaks and added to it a string of social engagements. I continued to teach aerobics on Tuesday and Thursday nights. I'd be jumping about up front, while somewhere along the gym's periphery, Shane would be flat on his back pressing an eighty-odd-kilo load. I'd try not to look over because as soon as our eyes would meet, he'd hand his barbell to a spotter and then fling about his arms to mock my girlie movements.

On Friday nights, we went to Basoko Base to sing karaoke and shoot pool. On Saturday, we worked. Then it was pizza at the Uruguayan Riverine Club. On Sundays, we had more time. Sometimes we'd stroll the orangey potholed streets next to MONUC, looking for treasures. The old artisans would see us coming and rush to their garbage bags, yanking out Teke, Kifwebe and Songye masks and Kuba ones with raffia beards. All were antiques, of course. When we asked, the sellers would insist they'd made most, if not all, themselves.

On Sunday nights, MONUC Kindu's Welfare Club would go out to the cafeteria and hook up a laptop to a projector. They'd angle it towards a white roll-down screen and then stretch a long cable to one of the plugs inside, and *poof!* we had an outdoor theatre. We called it staff movie night, though recently someone just back from leave had brought a DVD of the American TV series *24* and we couldn't get enough of it. To accommodate the demand, more plastic chairs were brought out, but there was never anything more to eat, unless some-one had worked it out well in advance. One Sunday before heading to the cafeteria, Shane and I caught the tail end of a one-day volleyball tournament among the Indians, South Africans, Uruguayans and Bolivians — every contingent in Kindu except the Chinese, who ran the city's hospital for UN staff and had either declined to participate or hadn't been invited. No patient ever had anything nice to say about their food.

I still called Louis in the nights after our *décrochage,* though less frequently. I mentioned Shane once or twice, anecdotally, in the context of some innocent thing I did or said.

One night while Louis and I were talking, I noticed the bugs had changed. Gone were the days of the green sci-fi insects; now colonies of flying termite swarmers were wedging their wings into the tape around my window. They wanted in, and I couldn't blame them.

THE SINGULAR FOCUS of a life without distractions a crackling phone call away prompted my sister to start one of her sentences by saying: "When you get back to the real world…"

I knew what she meant and with a turgid exclamation point, swiftly disputed, "You're wrong!" I was happy, yes—and a good deal happier than a person might dare ask of the dreaded real world. Still, no one could tell me for one iota of a second that our lives in Kindu were any less *real* than any other. Come 9 or 10 PM, the journalists and I would pick ourselves up and slump out the door, same as anyone else after a long day's work, and no less as though we'd been through the wringer. Mamy had managed to pick up typhoid fever. Matthieu fell sick with malaria. I knew Rigobert was midway through dusty cement piles of home renovations left in limbo until his next paycheque because he'd come into my office one day to ask for a loan. I said no. I didn't want money matters damaging our professional relationship. Just him asking felt like it already had.

So we had real-world problems. And not just real-world gripes, like never having enough paper for the printer, or always having to rely on UN dispatch to get anywhere. Because in the Congo, in Maniema, the real world was also full of cruel, unforeseen events that had a way of making our everyday problems seem at once luxurious and trite.

We were going about our normal routine one day when the phone rang—once. Once was called a "beep." Placing a call had its costs, but if no one picked it up, it was free.

Gabriel checked the number and dialled back. Mamy had just started saying something. Then out of nowhere there was panic:

"That was a friend on the phone. Just now," said Gabriel. "He says they've found two Rwandans. And a mob is stoning them. They're killing them."

"A public lynching!" cried Sadala.

A public lynching? Something lightly dusted my arm, causing me to jump. I spun my head to find a fallen strand of hair.

"Somebody!" I called out breathlessly, clawing the table for my keys. "Somebody come with me. Grab a Mini Disc. We'll pass by UN security downstairs on the way to the car. Let's go! *Now!*"

20

IT WAS STILL EARLY AND STILL WARMING UP, the time of day when everyone was installed where they needed to be but was having a coffee or taking a short break before gearing up to be productive. I was running through the blue hallway, down the stairs, around the corner, people with bewildered expressions on their faces stopping and asking with as much anxiety as officiousness, "What's going on?" Rigobert was keeping up. I could hear him saying things to people, things about crowds and people attacking people on the street. *Justice populaire.*

Jim, the head of Security—a Kenyan—was up on his strong, skinny marathoner legs and about to leave when we got to his office.

"Jennifer, Rigobert," he said, as if his next words were about to be, "Oh, okay, right, you're here."

Rigobert said good morning.

"So you're coming," said Jim, in a brisk but even tone. It appeared as if he was looking only at Rigobert. He—Jim—was wearing photochromic sunglasses, so I couldn't be sure.

"I'll take Rigobert with me in my car," said Jim, in such a way that now I understood.

The two of them returned an hour later, after we'd already heard that the crowd had finished what it started.

"They weren't Rwandan" was the first thing out of Rigobert's mouth.

We'd known that, too. Calls—beeps—had come in saying people had seen foreign faces in military fatigues and assumed the worst.

"They were Banyamulenge," said Rigobert. "FARDC soldiers from South Kivu, under *brassage*."

The dreaded army integration. I gave a strained, sorrowful sigh. "So they're dead." In my head *they* were faceless but young and cute, like an animal you could cradle in your arms. "What will happen to the people who did it? The people who killed them?"

"Nothing," said Sadala.

"Eh! Eh! Eh!" said Gabriel, with a heavy exhalation.

Popular justice.

Rigobert sat down at a computer and started to load his clips. Sadala called General Divioka, who agreed to come into the studio, for what would be only his second interview on our airwaves.

This time, the general spoke clearly and concisely; I suspected media training. Rigobert did the interview. I stood in the studio and listened as Divioka explained that under *brassage,* soldiers could hail from anywhere, all to serve the nation as army rank and file: soldiers from Bukavu in Kindu; soldiers from Kindu in Kisangani. Their interview carried forth on the process, procedures and modalities of securing the state: I found it tedious, dry as a riverbed, and praised Rigobert up and down for having delivered exactly what was needed.

There were other angles to cover, and between the two of them, Tumba and Sadala interviewed three people: Fernanda of MONUC Human Rights; an officer from Haki za Binadamu, the human rights organization; and a member of the Maniema bar, each speaking to the ill fit between popular justice and the rule of law they were working tirelessly to develop. Maniema's new government was what you would call "mainstreamed" into the speakers' key messages. They'd say: "we, *together with the provincial authorities…*" or: "we, *in partnership with the government…*" It felt like lip service, but the mention had to be made.

Gabriel began cutting clips from Rigobert's interview into a report for Kinshasa so that Rigobert could concentrate on turning around a full package for our *décrochage*. Mamy liaised with Kinshasa. And because Kasmu couldn't be reached, Matthieu started laying down scripts and audio files in the studio — something I hadn't realized he knew how to do.

When finally the last of us closed down the newsroom for the day, the city's kerosene lamps had long blown out. The crickets chirped with slim pauses for the heat, while scuttling cockroaches took the night. Downstairs in the parking lot, two white SUVs — mine and Marie-France's — reposed in the darkness. With Sadala walking just behind me, this might have been the closest I'd ever come to asking him about his taxi. It was truly my one dominant thought. Then, in the course of several steps, the trundling lyrics of Congolese rumba rose above the nightly noise to prominence.

TO MY KNOWLEDGE, no more people were physically harmed for being a Banyamulenge in Kindu. The lynching was the first and last. It was impossible to know whether Radio Okapi had stopped, or had even contributed to stopping, such attacks. But according to the latest national audience survey conducted by the French IMMAR polling institute, it had become the most listened-to information-based station, ahead of the likes of Radio France Internationale (which some saw as an outsider's radio, as it was based in Paris and had no Congolese correspondents) and the lamentable RTNC, which had but one part-time correspondent covering the whole of Maniema. I met the guy one day by chance at Camp Makuta. He was hard to miss: standing there, holding a tape deck in a beige pinafore and too-big trousers. Like a child playing dress-up.

I wrote my number on a sheet of lined paper that he'd pulled out of a shabby faux-leather satchel. "Call me if you ever need anything."

By "anything," I meant anything information-related. Still, it stood to reason that with no one knowing his day-to-day whereabouts, this guy was like a wildebeest ejected from the herd. Where was his Motorola radio? Where was his Sierra—his security—base? Sadala said his nearest colleague was a five-day walk away.

Thank goodness, I thought but didn't say, *the Okapis aren't exposed like you.*

THAT NIGHT, I arrived home with a splitting headache. My hand shot to my head. Malaria! Everyone said it—you don't wait on malaria because it went like this: an infected mosquito bites you and its plasmodium parasites multiply in your liver and then infect your red blood cells, disrupting the blood supply to your vital organs. What came next could kill you.

Mamadou, for one, claimed to have natural immunity. UN doctors, however, said no matter how young or how often you'd been exposed, no one was immune. The thought of it scared me to death. I took my mosquito net, tucked in all four sides and corners, and then used the backlight of my cellphone to scan for bites. I counted eleven. Most were on my ankles.

The next day, Rigobert and Matthieu each put a hand to my head.

"Nope, *ma belle*," said Mamy. "Not hot. But you should still go see Dr. Francis."

"You've had malaria," I said.

Mamy laughed. "Yes."

"And you get it often?"

"Couldn't count the times," said Rigobert.

"Like me and colds," I said.

"Go see Dr. Francis," said Rigobert.

Dr. Francis had a clinic at the foot of the staircase, just off the parking lot, next to Shane's office. I went down to see him, and the man himself appeared in the waiting room and asked his questions right there. We then went into his office, where he did all the things a doctor would do. He ordered a test: a blood test. His assistant, a young Congolese nurse in a fitted white lab coat, pricked my finger and squeezed it. There was no pain per se. But I cried. It was silly—I knew—because it was just a blood test, just a little blood. But it was my blood. And I needed it in my body. I was tired; I was thin. I felt vulnerable—physically vulnerable. I wiped away a tear with the back of my hand. *Where was this coming from?*

"Okay?" asked the woman.

"Okay," I answered unconvincingly.

A plastic bandage henceforth wrapped the tip of my left index finger. I left it there, even after the test came back negative.

The next time I popped downstairs to see Dr. Francis, the nurse smiled widely as I walked through the door. "I know what you're thinking," I said. "There's the crier!"

She laughed.

"But uh-uh! You can forget sharpening your needle! I don't need a test today. For now, all my blood is staying right where it is, thank you."

"Jennifer!" said Dr. Francis, stepping forth into the room. I'd never met a doctor like Dr. Francis before—one so unassuming and relaxed and respectful. I had to remind myself that this was a man who held a medical degree and numerous qualifications. I'd even heard he'd published several eminent research papers. "Good to see you. Are you well?"

I ran a hand through my hair and put my arm down palm up. "Look!" Clumps of hair snarled in the webs of my fingers like yarn. "My hair is falling out!"

Dr. Francis, this big cuddly bear—who was Kenyan, like Jim from UN Security but looked and acted altogether differently—smiled bemusedly as he took a finger to his spectacles to adjust their fit. "Oh, that's nothing! Hair loss is common among *mzungus* in Africa. You're no different. Don't worry."

A kindly sentiment, I thought, yet for all of it, I still worried. Worse, I worried that my worrying might actually worsen the situation. As strand after strand fell to the ground—hundreds of them in a day—I became increasingly desperate to learn how exactly *not to worry*. Incredible no one teaches you that.

"I'm going to be bald like all of you," I quipped to Rigobert, "and I don't have the features to pull it off."

"I'm not bald," Rigobert replied contrarily, scratching the stubble either side of his head. "My hair is grey. I earned every strand. It's wisdom, you know."

RADIO OKAPI KINDU, JULY 2002

The competition was over. The staffing had been completed. So now what? At a time when the radio was still a baby and oral culture was at its most magical, systems and practices had to be set. Practically, it went like this: each day Rigobert and Sadala went out into the field to gather stories. They came back; they wrote their scripts. Eliane, the Lebanese information officer, looked them over. Matthieu translated the reports into Swahili, Lingala and Tshiluba. Jean-Serge, the other translator, handled the Kikongo version. All the reports were sent to Kinshasa, to the national headquarters of the new UN peacekeeping mission, MONUC, where the network aired them nationwide. Eventually, Kindu and other Congolese cities would have their own FM signals and air local news. This was where Kindu's three freelance reporters came in. Their efforts were to supplement regional newsgathering until such time as Kindu began local programming and their UN contracts came through.

No longer free to just stand back and take everything in, Mamy had to come up with her first real story. She found it offside the city's barricaded roads on a hunch. With the war crippling business, local boys were going down to the river, taking off their shirts, lying on their bellies and plunging their arms into the grit of the riverbed. They'd realized they could excavate sediment to sell as concrete in a ratio of five parts gravel to one part cement and sand. Tiny grains to build something hard-wearing and, people hoped, safe as houses.

As the line of confrontation moved farther to the east, MONUC was throwing the full force of its weight into disarming foreign fighters and sending them home, under its third phase of deployment. In the new normal, Kindu was to become a forward support base. An initial deployment of some four hundred troops was planned; soon there would be hundreds more where they came from. For the time being, however, only a handful of military observers guarded the old KFM station, where civilians were busy setting up a UN office, and where Eliane and the Okapis were creating a proper newsroom.

In a recent meeting with the leadership of the RCD in Goma, UN Secretary-General Kofi Annan had insisted on two things: one, that any willing soldier be allowed to disarm freely; and two, that the rail and river connection between Kindu and Kisangani be reopened at the earliest opportunity. In the last month, a contingent of Uruguayans had come in with an engineering company. Their inflatable boats and motorized pirogues would patrol the river. For now, the contingent was working on its gym. Two basketball hoops had gone up, one on either side, and the paint was drying on the blue stripes of the Uruguayan flag. The bright yellow sun. In black letters, two words — *GIMNASIO URPAC-K* — made the space just about complete.

21

JUST WHEN I THOUGHT nothing could surprise me, there was this crocodile. By the time we learned of its existence, the fishermen upstream claimed it had overturned nine pirogues in the course of several months, killing dozens of people. The numbers were doubtful, but the tally kept running. There was talk of a communal croc hunt.

A man-eating crocodile! Here was one story I just had to tell Shane. His droll riposte made mention of that name again, and lo and behold, I figured it out: "Benny Mulengie?" I laughed, not intending to patronize, which unfortunately in my experience had never once excused it. "You mean Banyamulenge?"

Shane reddened some. But because of his ripe laughter and the way he set his lips, I considered the possibility that he'd intended the mispronunciation all along. I took his hand—his palm was warm and sweaty—and gave it a good squeeze. *I may actually miss this man.* It was a fine thought to have as we were combing the markets of the small dirt roads a stone's throw from MONUC to buy the last of his souvenirs.

"So any more word, then, on where you go from here?"

"Dublin. They've confirmed Dublin." We walked with our heads pointed down at the dirt beneath his sandals and my flip-flops. "It's not so bad. It won't be so bad."

"Better than Baghdad." I sniggered. "Or Afghanistan. A tour of roadside bombs in Helmand province."

We arrived at a shop we'd visited before, where Shane was hoping to find one of the raffia-bearded masks he liked. The shop sold countless wood carvings that the old vendor would frenetically dust down whenever he sensed interest. I wondered how many he sold in a day. Up the back wall a column of unfinished wooden shelves displayed a colourful array of the kind of fabric from textile company UTEXAFRICA that Mamy would only wear if she absolutely had to.

It was early May of 2004, and I'd been in Kindu going on eight weeks.

"What am I going to do when you go?" I whined in a way that made the question sound rhetorical.

"You're going on vacation. You'll be living it up in Canada. With your Canadian friends, eh?"

I reached over to pick up a box, stroking my thumb across its top, sensing the fine grains of the pasteboard. "But when I get back. I'll be so lonely."

Shane's attention was drawn elsewhere, after which his words avoided the subject. Someone—*him,* I thought, but it must have been me—brought up the subject of raffia (*What is it exactly—straw?*). And there it was, back again. That fatuous simper plastered across his face.

IF NOT THAT SAME NIGHT THEN a day or two later, as the flying termites outside were wedging their long straight abdomens into my beacon of light, I put my feet on my desk and called Louis. He answered on the fourth ring. His voice sounded disturbed, almost annoyed. I spoke warmly until his hesitation cooled me; then, illogically, his tone turned more affectionate.

"Hey, Jen-Jen. Hey—did you get the latest document I sent you? With the Ontario government's tourism figures? It would be nice if you could look at it. I'm not good at reading that kind of stuff. You are."

By this point, Louis and I had been together for about three and a half years. He was French. We'd met in Paris, in a laundromat of all places. He'd detected my accent and spoke English to me. And things had gone from there.

"Yeah, of course I'll take a look. I should be able to get that done tonight even."

"That's great, Jen-Jen."

My name doubled down like a blackjack hand. "Darling" or "honey" were words that hadn't been spoken to me in so long that I had come to think of them as the sort of careless, impersonal monikers that I never would've wanted.

"Are you eating?"

He meant *now,* at this moment, during our conversation. Knowing he found it rude for people to talk and eat at the same time, I'd been trying to bite inaudibly.

"Sorry." I moved my tongue across my lips as quietly as possible to catch the salt. "They had potatoes today at the cafeteria. It was so exciting! I was almost finished when I called you. I have, like, two or three fries left."

"You eat like crap, Jen. No wonder you're wasting away. I told you you should get that guy who cooks for you at lunch to make you dinner, too. Why haven't you done that?"

"I would, but he has to go home early. It's a long walk. I can't ask him to stay."

"Get him to make more at lunch, then. You could save some … put it aside and eat it when you get back."

I probably ought to have agreed, but because I wanted to tell him he just didn't understand, saying nothing felt like a compromise. "You know, in less than two weeks, I'll be back in Toronto."

"Yeah. That's right. I miss you, Jen-Jen."

"Me, too. I—"

"But fishing season has just started so that's keeping me busy."

Perhaps I could have made some sarcastic comment. But I didn't. *Dialogue entre Congolais* was in the middle of a panel discussion about the schism between the army's tenth military region and that fired Banyamulenge colonel, Jules Mutebutsi, in Bukavu. Host Jérôme had just raised a question in his rich, warm way, about Mutebutsi's comrade in arms, some guy named Nkunda, and I was listening to find out whether he was also a Congolese Tutsi. It felt good, salutary, to take interest in something outside myself.

HEARING PEOPLE SPEAK ON Radio Okapi, it was clear that some of them saw the coming elections as a once-in-a-lifetime opportunity to choose their next despot. One of Mobutu's sons had plans to run and was expected to fare well.

One day, I vented my frustration in the newsroom. "Not everyone here seems to get the idea that democracy is as much about consensus and holding institutions and authorities to account... as it is about holding elections... do they?"

Sadala said Kinshasa was about to start its new weekly show *Okapi Elections*.

"Right." I knew but had forgotten. "Anyway, it's our job to do all that, isn't it? All the time. Inform and, uh—investigate. Disclose facts. It's a good thing there's Radio Okapi."

"And you, Jenni!" said Matthieu sunnily, without a trace of sarcasm.

"Oh, Matthieu," I chided. (You had to shake your head sometimes.)

A few days later, I was sitting with Marie-France in her office. "People here are going to vote for Kabila," she whispered, though we were the only two people there. "Juvenal told me so." Juvenal was the governor's chief administrator. "I don't know why, but he tells me things. I think he's bored here. I mean —" She chuckled brusquely and leaned in to touch my arm. "What is there to do here? I mean... for a man like him. Here with no family – doing that job *here*. Of all places!"

"Yeah, some of them are working under a mango tree, you know."

"I know! I know!" A burst of her laughter forced a fleeting pause. "Infrastructure! Infrastructure! Infrastructure! That's what's needed here. It's a far cry from Kinshasa, let me tell you. And equipment! Well! Let's not get started there! You know, even Juvenal doesn't have a computer? He *shares* one. What takes him three hours to do over there, I could get done here in five minutes. I think I may actually help him. You know, take some of his work and bring it here."

"Maybe you can get them more computers?" By "you" I meant MONUC.

Marie-France scoffed. "And the electricity? More fuel for the generator, I suppose? It doesn't much matter anyway. With all the dust in that place, a computer would be lucky to last six months. If that."

Later, I asked Tumba and Rigobert, both of whom were in the newsroom working on stories for that afternoon's *décrochage*, "Do you think... Do you think that... Will people here vote for Kabila because of... Is it a tribal thing?"

Rigobert's hunt-and-pecking stopped as he looked up from the keyboard. "No, he speaks Swahili."

"Oh, and they like that?" I asked. Rumour had it that Kabila was planning his first-ever trip to Maniema, the youngest of

Congo's ten provinces (having been partitioned from South Kivu I didn't know when). People were excited.

"In Kinshasa, people think he's a fraud," said Tumba. "He grew up in Tanzania. He doesn't even speak Lingala."

"At all?"

It was now that Eibhlin appeared at the door. She wilfully swept her coarse blonde hair behind her shoulders so that even the thinnest strands stayed put. And she was so slow to speak that I quickly ruled out the possibility of her being here to discuss some plan of a send-off party for Shane. Not that she would have brought me into that.

"Hi," I said, when at last something had to be said.

Tumba pulled out a chair to sit back down.

Curtly, Eibhlin asked if she could speak to me—privately—for a moment.

Rigobert reached for his headphones.

Eibhlin led the way into my office and moved to take a seat on the other side of my desk. She said, "I have received very serious allegations against one of your journalists."

It came like a punch in the stomach.

"These allegations pertain to threats and harassment, and it is in the strictest confidence that someone has come to my office to disclose the details of the incident. I—"

"I'm sorry. I have to ask... Who was it?"

Eibhlin sat straighter and tugged at the hem of her patterned cotton shirt. A Zanzibar purchase perhaps? Shane had mentioned that she'd just gone, or was going. "I can't tell you that." Her eyes appeared as blue as ice. "As I was saying, I am obliged to protect the identity of this man who came to me in the strictest—"

"No, no, no... I'm sorry." I'd done it again; I couldn't help myself. "I mean the journalist. Which one? Who was it?"

Eibhlin took a moment before responding. "A… Serge… Shindani. Jean-Serge Shindani."

My relief was titanic. The soles of my feet tingled: she'd actually had my feet sweating. I kicked off a flip-flop.

"Yes, this journalist—Jean-Serge Shindani—could face disciplinary action, and we need to impart upon him the gravity of the matter."

Suddenly, I cocked my head. Shindani. Serge. *Jean-Serge Shindani*. Damn, but the name did sound slightly familiar.

As Eibhlin kept talking, I kept thinking about this name that had absolutely no significance…

Until it did. "Eibhlin," I interrupted again. "Jean-Serge Shindani isn't one of our journalists. Well he is… I mean he *was*. But he was suspended before I even got here. Not for this, but for something else. And between you and me, I'm not expecting him back anytime soon. Which suits me fine."

Eibhlin cleared her throat. "Yes, that's fine. But it doesn't take away the accusation. And this gentleman *may* have been one of your staff members at the time of the incident."

She rose, and I followed suit.

"Here is my card. Please email me. Then I will have your address, so that I can send you the details of the incident and we can proceed accordingly."

I took the card with two hands and looked at it, as if the answer to a forthcoming riddle was embedded in its small cyan-blue print. "But we know each other!" I wanted to say.

WHEN ALL WAS SAID AND DONE, both grievances Eibhlin had raised—first the cholera story and now this—only served to strengthen two things: first, that I was the protector of Radio Okapi Kindu's reputation; and second, that being its *responsable* behooved me to keep watch over the journalists' work and behaviour. For all my heart might've raced—Would I say the right thing? Handle it the right way?—both roles tidily befit *Maman* Jennifer.

This guy, Jean-Serge, must have known who I was. He must have heard things. (From the journalists? Probably.) At some point, he would have seen me—possibly. He might even have sought me out. He must have been curious.

To me, he was like an unplanned pregnancy. If getting a new head of office had worried me, the last thing I wanted was some new—worse, *old* guy—coming in and torpedoing us backwards. Suspended indefinitely. Wasn't that the same as fired?

I waited a day or so before taking action.

"Question for you," I said to Mamy shortly after the others had left for the field.

I was puttering around, and she was working on a story about children scavenging the MONUC dump. Traded in the right places, ten empty MONUC water bottles could fetch 150, even 200 francs. And fifty cents could go a long way in Kindu (and now that stores were again selling Chupa Chups lollipops and Dubble Bubble gum, the richer children held out hope). Mamy's report had used sound to evoke the scene: a heavy truck motor in spurts down a bumpy road; its engine snorts to a stop. Later, above the huffing, children who'd never received a Christmas present squealed as the truck's rear loader compactor hoisted its refuse above a mound of small-boned hands. You could picture the driver emerging from the truck, shouting and pushing the children back, fending them off like dogs: "Eh! Ehhhh! *Dégage!* Move it!" Litter rustling, a number of well-placed strikes landing near the children's bare ankles.

"What's your question, *Maman?*"

"Jean-Serge…"

"Ye-esss," said Mamy with a sibilant *s*.

"Know where he lives?"

"*Bien sûr.*"

I was surprised to learn that Jean-Serge lived in the transience of a hotel – or what once might well have been a hotel, for his building had "Hotel" in its name.

"It's just across the street from Mendes's house. You'll see the guards. With the guns."

"With the guns" confirmed it: I didn't like our vice-governor, Mr. Pierre Masudi Mendes. I didn't like his money – all the dirty bills he must've had zippered away, the source of which I questioned. Tumba said he was in the airline business – a manager or proprietor or some such.

"Are you going to be able to find it?" asked Mamy when she heard my car keys jingling.

"Sure. Of course." Now who was being the mother? "If I have any problems, I'll just ask someone."

"Eh, Jenni —"

I stopped halfway out the door and turned.

"Your hair," said Mamy.

"I know, I know! It's falling out."

"No – it's not that. It looks... healthy. It's shiny."

"Shiny? Well, I do just use cold water... And I certainly don't over-wash it. That water's freezing! I'm in, I'm out..."

"Ah, *ma belle!*" Mamy laughed. The phrase literally translated as "my beautiful one," but in common usage meant "my dear." Everyone said it to anyone female; still I liked when it was said to me. Which I suspected Mamy knew.

I stopped to have a quick cigarette with Shane, then tore out the gate. I rolled down my window as the old police officer waved me through. Magic System's "1er Gaou" was coming on Radio Okapi, so I quickly rolled the window back up. The song was from Côte d'Ivoire; I'd looked it up. I loved it.

Had any of the people toiling outside paid any attention to a UN car manoeuvring around the holes and dips, many would've guessed it was lost. Although I was in close proximity to HQ, what was left of the road led in one of two directions: to a second U-turn heading back from whence I'd come, or onwards to a residential zone. Mendes lived here, among the houses. There were no guns or soldiers in view, yet I recognized the place at once. I pulled up just past it, on the other side of the road.

Children ran to the car before it even stopped. I slammed the door and shooed them away before awkwardly calling them back. "Shindani?" I tried, looking around. "Jean-Serge Shindani?"

The children were leading me across the street when a man no bigger than the oldest child came forth from the glare of the sun. I squinted. Flimsy owlish glasses perched unevenly over a good portion of his face. As he came closer, I could see his eyes were bloodshot and threaded with spider veins matching the reddish-purple undertones of his face.

"Are you looking for me?"

"Are you Jean-Serge?"

He nodded respectfully. I introduced myself needlessly. We separated ourselves from the children to cross a line of pedestrians, plus the wares they carried on their bodies. One man was wearing a Santa Claus hat—in May.

"*Pardon,*" I said, after stepping on someone's heel.

The man—Jean-Serge—led me to the shade of sturdy boughs and palms lashed to roof beams and thick bamboo poles closing the gaps up the sides. Several men reeking of alcohol were lolling in wooden-backed chairs with steel legs when something said in a language I didn't recognize brought everyone to his feet. They picked up cards, bottles and nuts, emptying the space of all but its dirt and two chairs.

"Hello, Madame Okapi," said the last to leave, smiling with gapped brown teeth.

Jean-Serge and I sat facing each other. He was fidgeting.

"Jean-Serge —" We were very close indeed; even in the low light, I could see his fingernails were filthy and bitten halfway to the cuticle. There was dust on his glasses. And his face — his entire head actually — was abnormally small. None of this, of course, was important. "I don't know if it's true," I said; and I didn't care to know the details. "Rightly or wrongly, everyone associates you with Okapi." Which meant his behaviour had better be spot on. "If you want to come back to work with us, you need to keep that in mind."

Why had I opened this possibility, of him ever coming back? Likewise, why did I keep going?

"And the rest of it… the suspension, the drinking, that doesn't mean anything to me. If you come back, you start from scratch. But you'd better be prepared to work — and professionally."

Jean-Serge let out a murmur that sounded like a burp. He realized and excused himself. In the end, this was all he would say. Even though I insisted there was no need, he walked me to the car. Afterwards, I took the U-turn back, first past city hall, then past the metal gates of Kabambe wa Kabambe's old house, and later past Uni-Kin, where Parfum studied. I thought about an impending lunch of goat meat in palm oil and tomato sauce, cubed coconut and mashed avocado — creamy, slightly sweet — before saying "Hmm" over something else entirely.

22

MY EXCHANGE WITH Jean-Serge left me emboldened: it was time I did something about Kasmu. At the very least, I needed to set myself up, in case things came down to that. What was *that?* I wasn't sure. But he was bad at his job—and showed no will to do better.

At the top of a new Microsoft Word document I typed *Performance Review*, then fashioned a few subheadings and fleshed them out.

At the end of the day, I said, "Hey, no one go yet! Everyone, just five minutes."

Kasmu was the last to take his seat. He pulled a chair into the corner and yawned.

"Okay—a few things. First, the two Yves are coming." One was editor Yves Renard, and the other was a man named Yves Laplume, who'd just been brought in as the new head of Radio Okapi—for Fondation Hirondelle, because just as the network had two creators, it maintained two management silos. Fondation Hirondelle was in the news business, which gave it allure. But more than that—practically, operationally—it controlled the radio's deontology, the ethics of duty. It was the moral compass that guided our every action.

Gasps and excited chatter drowned out Kinshasa's headlines.

"Okay, okay. We'll get to that in a second."

Gabriel reached back to turn down the volume.

"I want to talk first about the second thing—the form in your hands."

"Paper," said Gabriel, in English.

"Yes, *paper*."

The performance review, I explained, was a human resources exercise that, if handled correctly, could justify the pay grades and professional opportunities they sought. Matthieu had approached me on several occasions to say he wanted to be made UN staff. He would have had his reasons, money chief among them. For even though Fondation Hirondelle paid salaries on par with what the UN paid its national staff—in the order of US$800 to US$1,000 monthly—a UN position came with benefits and entitlements. Plus, the UN could offer things that a small Swiss NGO could not: the UN could offer the world. We'd seen Vianney from Radio Okapi Kinshasa leverage his national staff job into a UNV position with the peacekeeping mission in Côte d'Ivoire, and although he would be technically *volunteering*, he'd still be making at least three times what he was clearing in the Congo.

"Which reminds me—vacations. I want us to get that done before I go. And it's going to work like Bunia. Priority goes to whose turn it is next."

"*Alors, Maman*, that's me again I think," said Tumba.

He hadn't meant it literally, which I realized, but I still cried out: "I'm not your mother!"

Kasmu shifted noisily in his chair. "It's me. I haven't had a vacation in the longest. It's not like the others—Kinshasa needs to send someone to fill in for me. Maybe you could ask the two Yves."

"Just—" I paused to sigh deeply. "Send it all to me. All of you. I'll deal with it."

"And the performance review is for me, too?"

Kasmu never knew when to stop—or else he knew but preferred to instigate things. Something in him needed to stir up trouble. He must have liked it lonely.

A FEW DAYS LATER, on a Thursday morning, MONUC's direct flight from Kinshasa brought the two Yves to Kindu. The wait to see them walk through the door dragged on terribly. Since the end of our story meeting, we'd been pretending to be occupied with the things that normally kept us busy. Moving our fingers around the keyboard. Putting on and taking off our headphones. Getting up and sitting back down.

When at last the two Yves appeared at the door, smiling broadly, the journalists erupted in bellows. "Mamy!" Yves Renard deduced, cocking his head and beginning to laugh.

"Renard!" said Mamy, with a declarative flounce.

"Jennifer," said Yves Laplume. *"Ma belle!"*

"Les deux Yves," we called them, and truth be told, Laplume didn't look so different from Renard, both being white brownhaired Frenchmen upward of forty. Perhaps Yves Laplume looked more Spanish. His skin was no darker, but his eyebrows were bushier and he possessed a wide girth and stance that came across as stately, as if he belonged to another time. This only enhanced his authority.

THREE YOUNG CONGOLESE WOMEN clustered in a clique, all dressed in going-out clothes, were outside in the MONUC cafeteria when Yves Laplume and I sat down. One of the three—Nicole from General Services—was holding a compact in her hand, putting on lipstick.

Yves dropped a red pack of Marlboro cigarettes on the table.

I'd come armed with the journalists' wish lists but first had my own accounts to shore up; I hadn't even sat down when I started. We needed more computers and Mini Disc recorders. "One per person? I mean, when you're all working at the same time, for the same show, how are you supposed to share? You can't. It's just not possible." We also needed a car and a driver. "We can't go on like this," I said. Above all, I wanted a new technician, using Kasmu's abysmal performance review as leverage. Plus, what was to become of Jean-Serge?

I could hear the girls laughing four tables away. The one wearing the most makeup was constantly squealing; I could barely hear myself think. Yves sat up to take a sip of his Coke, which was already swimming in melted ice. "Jean-Serge is coming back on Monday."

My eyes searched for something to latch onto: Marlboro Red was harsh — way worse than the Gold. I mumbled indistinctly until Yves pushed the package towards me with the tips of his fingers.

"There isn't anything we can do — not if we want to be fair. We can't prevent him from returning. But if he gives us cause again…"

Yves's hot cigarette dangled in my fingers. No promises were made, but I could see his mind was taking him through a thought process. He had an easy way of sitting, relaxed in his hips. And so, perhaps it was his straight shoulders and upper back that put across the impression that he, not I, would have things as he wanted them.

The two Yves were catching MONUC's afternoon flight to Bukavu, where they'd have more choices of places to stay overnight than the slim pickings offered in Kindu. I only knew offhand of one place for foreigners to stay here: the UN guesthouse, which was in the Bolivian camp off the road to Basoko and had a handful of dormitory-style rooms with simple toilets and an outdoor shower trailer.

Before they left, the two Yves took us through plans to revamp Radio Okapi's programming. This included new national shows, a lunchtime newscast and expanded regional *décrochages* — from a half to a full hour. When they announced this — that we would have twice as much local airtime — Rigobert and Mamy pushed out a loud "Ah!" which made Matthieu laugh.

Yves Laplume passed out some Radio Okapi–branded pens, after which we all bunched together for a group picture. Matthieu's skin smelled like OMO laundry soap. Except for Laplume, who took the picture, we all wore MONUC baseball caps. Some of us held up our pens.

ALTHOUGH THE CONTEXT was altogether different, Kindu, like Radio Okapi, was at a crossroads. The network's web desk in Kinshasa penned a series of historical vignettes on several of the country's major cities, and what I learned about Kindu fascinated me. The tale went back to the fifteenth century, when three separate migrations descended upon a small Wasongola fishing village named Kindo: the Basonge, Wazura, Balungu, Kasenga, Nonda, Babuyu, Banyamikebwe and Bahombo moved in from the south; from the east, the Bantu settled the region's north and central areas, mixing with the Pygmies they found there; while Mongo tribes came from the north and west.

Four centuries later, the sultan of Zanzibar earmarked the town for his trading route. Arab-Swahili merchants set up shop in Nyangwe, soon creating large trading posts, most notably in gold and ivory but also in slaves evacuated to western Tanzania and Zanzibar by way of Lake Tanganyika. ("You're close to Tanganyika?" said Louis once. "There's great fish in there, Jen-Jen. Like two hundred different species. Ask your journalists. They'll know.")

Most of the Belgians left in the 1960s after independence. The people who remained dismantled the *mundeles'* stone structures, wooden verandahs and unintelligible metal statues. They repaired only what they felt needed to be. Lawns were scuffed away, the bougainvillea left to grow wild. In time, there was a sense that the past business of appropriation had led to inadequate cultural patrimony and the modern-day impression of a place that had been picked over, and ultimately passed over — so that by the time of the Rwandan genocide in the 1990s, even the Rwandan Tutsi and Hutu refugees would choose to settle elsewhere.

I was aware that history was like journalism — both used select details to cast dramatic stories. I also was old enough to know that life, the world over, was filled with a kind of ordinariness that on close inspection was actually quite extraordinary.

Sadala came tearing into the newsroom the day after the two Yves left. He threw down his satchel and cried, "They've killed the crocodile!"

"*Ah, bon,*" said Gabriel. He sounded disinterested, because he wasn't hyped up, not over a dead animal in the jungle.

"They killed the crocodile? Oh my God! How?"

"They speared it," said Sadala.

"My God!" I said again. *But... but... how did they know they got the right one?*

"When's Mamadou coming?" asked Sadala suddenly, forcing me to think.

"Next Wednesday, I think. The day before I go." *And the day after Shane leaves.* On Tuesday, Shane would be flying to Bukavu to complete his check-out process. From there, to Kinshasa, then home to Dublin.

"And Jean-Serge is back on Monday?" said Tumba. He'd said it as a question, in such a way that I wondered just what he was questioning.

"Yep, on Monday."

I purposefully held silent, trying Rigobert's trick of the incredible entrapping pause. Notwithstanding, the next person to talk would be me.

"Don't forget to call Martin and propose your crocodile story." I headed back into my office. "They aired it the first time. They'll be all over it now."

I GUESS I WAS looking forward to going home on vacation. I say "home," but I was actually going to Toronto, and Toronto didn't feel like home. It felt like an item of clothing I'd had for a while and worn often enough but never seemed to work with what I had or really look right on me, and nowadays, when I'd go to put it on, it would wind up back in the closet.

There were things I definitely didn't want to miss in Kindu, starting with President Joseph Kabila's visit, which would only be officially announced at the last minute, for risk of compromising national security. Just last week, Sadala had reported on sightings of the presidential guard. There hadn't been many of them, but they'd been sighted in uniform and in groups, and on more than one occasion at the old rail line terminus, where it was rumoured Kabila would make a public address.

The guards wouldn't speak to us on air, of course—which proved nothing but nevertheless had me convinced they knew something we only suspected:

Kabila was coming for the Peace Train.

I first learned of the Congo national railway's Peace Train from Eibhlin, at one of the MONUC morning meetings. Eibhlin was leading a partnership of international aid agencies to repair

489 kilometres of the old 1950s tracks, from Kabila's stronghold in Katanga province all the way up to Kindu. The inaugural run would service Kabalo, Kongolo, Samba and various points in between. It wouldn't be picking up passengers so much as it would be dropping off wagonloads of seeds, sugar, iodized salt, agricultural tools and up-to-date medicines.

"We'll have Simba again!" said Rigobert.

"You mean the beer?" I said.

"Eh! We haven't had Simba in… in…"

"Six years," said Tumba. *"Avant la guerre."*

"Where do they brew it? Lubumbashi?"

"Yep. In Katanga," said Matthieu.

"Any good?"

"Delicious," said Rigobert. "It's a pale beer. Malty. Much better than Skol."

I lifted my chin suddenly. "We need to get on that train."

Rigobert took a breath. "Expédit Mwamba Mubi from Kalemie has already arranged to go."

"What? Oh, man! How come I didn't know about this sooner?"

It had been a rhetorical question.

I look back now and can only guess why the journalists never sought to correct my shortcuts or shortcomings. We all play our roles perhaps. It may well be that they saw my face go blank at the mention of a common acronym or bygone event and thought, *One thing at a time.*

SHANE AND I SPENT our last weekend together in Kindu at a house party, drinking marula-fruit liqueur and dancing to Uruguayan songs from my aerobics classes.

The fleetingness of our situation was spared by pure good luck. Some administrative affair of mine had gone askew, and whatever the root of it, Patricia, my boss, recalling her own years in the bush, said the matter truly warranted my presence in Kinshasa. With my Air France flight booked for Saturday night, I would have to leave Kindu on Thursday — when, incidentally, Shane would be leaving Bukavu en route to Kinshasa, after having completed his check-out procedure there. That would give us most of Thursday and all day Friday and Saturday to be together.

"When you go on vacation," said Sadala, catching me during the one and only time I was in the newsroom that weekend, "do you think you could get me a small hand-held video camera? *Vous savez*, one that can film… but also takes pictures?"

"A video camera that takes regular pictures, too…" I thought a moment. "They're expensive, you know. They're like five, six hundred dollars — at least."

Sadala didn't blink an eye, neither at the price or my patronization, and said he'd pay me back with his May paycheque when I returned in June.

Although I duly promised to look for one, silently I was considering. As I'd told the journalists before, I didn't want to mix money into our working relations. I had my reasons. *Good* ones, I thought, as people usually do.

THROUGHOUT THE CONVIVIALITY of the weekend's partying and respite, I was honour-bound to keep thinking of what I'd say to Jean-Serge and the others come Monday morning. Only to find that on the day, there was little to be said.

When I rushed into the newsroom, even perpetually late Mamy had arrived. Wearing a matchy-matchy blouse and skirt in earth tones, she sat laughing next to Jean-Serge, whose head and shoulders were barely visible behind the table.

"They're reunited," yarned Sadala.

I stopped gauchely and arranged a smile. "Who's reunited?"

"Le couple de l'année," said Sadala. The others laughed roundly. "That's what one of our *chefs d'antenne* used to call Jean-Serge and Tumba—the couple of the year."

"Le couple de l'année," I repeated as I surveyed the two journalists: the big face and the small face. "That's a good one," I said. "I like that."

That day, Jean-Serge proposed two perfectly respectable stories before going out to cover them. He returned in good time, sober. Now, for the first time seeing his small oval face subjugated by those big flimsy glasses of his, plus Princess Leia–style headphones—*Was there such a thing as size small headphones? There ought to be*—I began to put down my worry. It had obviously been disproportionate.

"Jenni," said Jean-Serge. "I hear you are going to Canada on vacation. And I am hoping you could find me a watch—and a gold chain." His French boasted clearer diction than the others, probably accounted for by a slight discrepancy in age, which would have put him in school in the 1950s, under the old colonial system.

"You want a watch. And a gold chain?"

"With a small cross on it."

"Thick or thin? The chain, I mean."

"Fairly thin—if you could, Jenni. And the cross doesn't need to be too big either."

I hemmed and blew out a chuckle, resigned by a kind of humour I'd identified but could never have explained. "All right. And the watch?"

"Something sporty," said Jean-Serge.

Something sporty wouldn't have been my taste. But it wasn't about me, was it?

"When the two Yves were here last week, they brought us Okapi pens," I said, off the cuff. "You want one? I have a few left. In my drawer."

SHANE LEFT FOR BUKAVU on Tuesday, which turned out to be the last thing to go according to plan. On Wednesday, Mamadou failed to show. I looked into the matter and discovered his name wasn't on Movement Control's passenger manifest. Whatever was going on, he hadn't cancelled at the last minute.

"Mamadou's not coming today," I told the journalists, after most of them had returned in a sweat from the field and Sadala had asked. "And maybe not tomorrow either—we'll see. I still have to go, but you guys are okay on your own 'til he gets here. And until he does, I'm leaving Mamy in charge of dealing with Kinshasa."

Rigobert glanced up quickly, then turned away. I supposed my naming Mamy hadn't surprised anyone, especially if they indeed thought that she and Matthieu were my favourites. I would have hardly picked Matthieu.

"You can all send your scripts to Kinshasa—to Martin, Leonard or Noella. Or Étienne—he might have more time. I should drop him an email now. At any rate, do *not* let Marie-France or anyone else tell you what to report or who to go interview. That's not their call. Suggestions are fine, but…"

Would our colleagues outside the radio actually try to interfere with its affairs? Given the chance, I thought they might.

The UN tended to attract a certain kind of person: *Do it like this; do it like that. This is good — say this. This is bad — denounce that.* It's how we were trained to think. With a world of good intentions. It was why we were paid.

LATE THAT AFTERNOON, Shane called from Bukavu.

"They're shooting, Jen. Can you hear it?"

I pressed the receiver tighter against my ear. "No. *Who's* shooting?"

"I don't know." But it had been going on for a while. He said people lying on the floor around him were starting to complain of bruised knees and hips. "I've barely had the time to get up to take a wee." He wasn't laughing.

Out in the newsroom, Sadala was talking on our internal landline.

"Is that Bukavu?" I mouthed.

He nodded.

Gabriel walked in the door.

"They're shooting in Bukavu," I said.

"Ah, bon." He didn't sound surprised, and perhaps he wasn't, as Bukavu was so close to Rwanda and there was a history there. I pointed to Sadala on the phone, after which Gabriel crept over and the two of us hovered.

Two. Three. Four minutes passed.

"What's going on?" said Gabriel, in a projected whisper. Sadala turned his head.

Tumba came in, soon followed by Rigobert, who headed straight to the radio. He kept the volume low. It was just a song.

When at last Sadala put down the receiver, Tumba declared, "It's Mutebutsi."

"And Laurent Nkunda," said Sadala. "It's their forces. They're behind this."

"Why?" I asked quickly. "What are they trying to achieve?"

As someone who came from a culture of breaking news, even when there was nothing ascertained or weren't any verifiable facts to report, the silence was killing me.

"When is Bukavu—or Kinshasa—gonna say something?"

"They were checking," said Sadala.

"Checking what?"

"The facts," said Sadala.

"Well… how long will that take?"

It was obvious why we had to wait. In the current context, misinformation carried serious consequences; what had happened when people in Kindu had somehow heard there were two Rwandan soldiers in town was proof of that. People here didn't have the luxury of saying things first and retracting them later. This was especially true for us at Radio Okapi, knowing that decision-makers from government officials to fathers would take our news as fact and act accordingly.

Over the next few hours, my cellphone zigzagged across the room. Periodically, Marie-France would poke her head into the newsroom; she'd glance over at our dry-erase board, see that it was unchanged, and then grill the journalists for information, checking what she'd heard against their understanding of events. At one point, she paced the floor a good ten minutes before leaving and coming back. When she went away again, she took Tumba with her.

Throughout, Radio Okapi maintained its programming schedule, with feverish electric guitars, synthesizers and jaw-dropping vocals, which in normal circumstances would have evoked national pride.

The next day at dawn: news from Bukavu. Radio Okapi journalist Serge Maheshe reported the shooting was connected to infighting among newly integrated elements of the Congolese army, pitting those loyal to the government in Kinshasa against renegade soldiers from the ex-RCD. Fired Congolese colonel Jules Mutebutsi was part of a posse headed by Laurent Nkunda, a Congolese army general from across Lake Kivu in North Kivu. Nkunda, another Banyamulenge, had purportedly rejected the transitional government's authority from the start.

Serge's report had worked in a sound bite from one of Bukavu's MONUC public information officers who said that at least two people had been killed. They'd been found dead in a market in central Bukavu late on Wednesday, both wearing military fatigues. A third person — a civilian, a judge — had been seriously wounded. Also, a stray bullet had grazed the leg of a foreign aid worker. I wondered if I knew who it was. MONUC was sending units from Goma, the capital of neighbouring North Kivu province — plus some units from Kindu, apparently — to reinforce patrols.

Although Serge didn't say the words "civil war" — and he wouldn't have, not at this juncture — his script spoke of heavy artillery, advancing troops and rebel forces that had captured the city's Nguba neighbourhood.

So this was Thursday. I didn't fly to Kinshasa, and Shane didn't either. I offered to push back my vacation, which Marie-France appreciated. But given that Mamadou was still due to replace me — and that the clashes, though fierce, could be seen as contained (as MONUC wished them to be) — I proceeded to Kinshasa on the last Friday of May, en route via Paris to Toronto.

By the time I reached Paris's Charles de Gaulle Airport, a path of villages had fallen. Watching the report on the news, as I did in a hall full of people, all of us slumped on stiff plastic seats not knowing whether we were coming or going, I could suddenly imagine myself as a refugee. Weary and at a loss, I just wanted to get to wherever it was I was meant to be, in one piece.

The story I'd been waiting for first appeared in a banner onscreen, underneath the anchorwoman's tabletop:

CONGO REBELS ADVANCE

The finest print read: *Government troops, former rebels clash in eastern Congo.*

The anchor said the UN was reporting eight dead and more than twenty-five wounded, as more soldiers loyal to General Laurent Nkunda and Colonel Jules Mutebutsi advanced to the outskirts of Bukavu. They were closing in on the city. According to Human Rights Watch, marauding government soldiers were searching homes for Banyamulenges and opportunities to pillage and rape. File video of Mutebutsi flashed up, during which there was more talk of the Banyamulenge and Mutebutsi's fight to prevent an alleged state-sanctioned genocide against them.

The next thing I knew, the anchor was back onscreen, saying something more—some line to tie up the story, to put it in context. I didn't catch what it was exactly.

The next plane I boarded was bound for Canada.

Pearson airport Terminal 1 in the summer was cold, thanks to air conditioning. I jutted through, head and body first, with a nubby suitcase and one tanned arm behind me, shivering in desperation to find out what was happening in Bukavu. (This being the time before everyone owned hand-held devices.) Had Mutebutsi taken control of the city? Had the fighting spread outside the region? Who else had been hurt?

I asked Louis after having kissed him in Arrivals. He didn't know. He said: "Forget your little African village in the bush, Jen-Jen. You're back in the real world now."

But all the way home, on the marvel of fourteen lanes, I kept thinking about Rigobert and Mamy and Sadala—even the Okapis I'd never met in Bukavu. What would happen to them and their families? The prospect of an all-out war went beyond my belief. If worse came to worst, the journalists would be safe in the MONUC compound. I supposed they could stay in there for days if they had to.

These were the thoughts running through my mind as we took the corner onto the Gardiner Expressway running parallel to Lake Ontario. After a dip, the downtown core of constructions as tall as the sky came into view.

NKUNDA WAS COMMANDING about four thousand fighters; Mutebutsi, several hundred more. Between them, they succeeded in dispersing government troops throughout South Kivu like slash-and-burn farmers. In response, MONUC called on belligerents to canton their soldiers. Several arrests were made. UN peacekeeping troops in Bukavu (with the redeployment that had begun several months earlier, there were about eight hundred in all) then moved to secure the city, knowing it to be a strategic centre, as the Congo's trading post to Rwanda and beyond. Losing it would be the biggest setback to the peace process since the setup of the transitional government.

There was evidence of targeted killings like the kind seen in the war. Hundreds of people were dying. Serge Maheshe reported from Bukavu general hospital, rendered a place of screams. Survivors of sexual assaults and other violence lay one against the other on the concrete floor, perpetrators on all sides. The place was filled beyond capacity. President Kabila said he'd initiated a process that would lead to a state of emergency.

On paper, MONUC had authority to act. UN Security Council resolution 1493 had recently strengthened a previous resolution, giving the UN a mandate to protect civilians under imminent threat of physical violence. The directive had raised expectations: surely the people in their big white cars, the same ones who were driving up local prices and lunching at fancy foreign restaurants and cavorting in clubs with pretty girls at the weekend, would come to their rescue when the time came.

Public protests against MONUC erupted in Kinshasa on the second day of June. Riotous demonstrators numbering in the thousands accused MONUC of being complicit in South Kivu's deadly mutiny. Some people burned UN vehicles; others despoiled any UN asset or installation within reach. When people began scaling the walls of MONUC HQ in Gombe, in downtown Kinshasa, right across from the Chinese embassy, UN troops opened fire. Two demonstrators were killed.

Within hours of the violence in Kinshasa, rumours spoke of a planned protest in Kindu. So Marie-France tasked the South Africans to post an armed personnel carrier next to the MONUC Security reception, at the intersection where the old police officer directed traffic.

The next day, Bukavu fell. On air, Serge Maheshe spoke of UN troops having failed miserably. Though of course he didn't say "miserably" – he didn't have to.

That same morning, Uni-Kin students and others gathered outside MONUC Kindu in protest. People threw their weight against the cyan-blue gates, rattling the metal to the point of collapse. Stones – the bigger, the better – bricks – anything heavy close to hand – lobbed through windows. Smashing it all to smithereens.

Nkunda, Mutebutsi and their renegade forces occupied Bukavu for a week, with Rwanda denying any involvement. The UN and international actors set to negotiating, while more than thirty thousand people fled to Burundi and Rwanda. At least two thousand civilians sought shelter at MONUC Bukavu.

It wasn't clear what made the insurgents withdraw in the end. In any case, they had made their point.

24

A YOUNG MAN KITTED IN A neon-yellow pinafore that was catching eyes like sunflowers to light welcomed me. "Madame Okapi! *Karibu!*"

After three weeks away, I was back in Kindu. In one sense, my time away felt like an intermission. The time elapsed had been brief. The stage was still set, the characters and storyline more or less unchanged. You pick up where you left off.

Mamadou had taken the day's flight back to Kinshasa and left the car in the parking lot. As porters hauled in a bellyful of goods... products – *things* – the car's smoothness glared through the wide aperture of the terminal's entrance. It was sooty around the hubcaps, but its tires hadn't been burned and its body was still intact. Strange how I felt mollified by the perceived loyalty of an inanimate object, which, stranger still, seemed to be reassuring me that I would never be left out or behind.

The city and its people looked little changed by events. Still scraping by. The trees stood upright, densely leafed and green, imposing their rigidity. The light was buttery and bright. Driving down Airport Road, I approached a woman hauling cut bamboo travelling in my direction and toyed with the idea of stopping and offering her a lift, knowing that UN insurance policies strictly forbade giving non–UN staff a ride. The old tennis court was coming up on the right. As always, weeds sprang forth through its cracked asphalt, and the day hadn't yet come when someone had decided to take a ball and racket to a court without a net.

I beeped twice at my house. Lumumba, our security guard—back working days or having swapped—swung open the gate and waved both arms widely. I waved too, then glanced to the left to where Rigobert's place (which I had never seen, not from the inside) was tucked behind yellowed ground cover. I drove past the Shabani residence as Sadala's voice came over the radio. He was interviewing two teenagers in Swahili for *Okapi Jeune*.

Through the windshield, the main drag was coming into focus. After so many kilometres journeyed, I braked to take the corner slowly.

From a distance, MONUC Kindu deceived in its standing—no outward damage, no debris or charred ash. I drew near the intersection and rolled down my window to wave at the kindly old traffic cop. Then I noticed it: reinforced barbed wire—coil after coil—taking MONUC's barriers higher, so that now even a pole and a vault couldn't have hurled you over. As I sat and waited for the cyan-blue gates to part, contracted muscles raised my shoulders anew.

The inside of the building smelled like the bleach the cleaning ladies used on our blue walls and floor. My nubby black Samsonite wheeled down the hall in clear recognizable bumps and spurts; in my anxiousness to see the journalists again, how easily prior events could be forgotten. I twisted back to look upon the suitcase, and like a mother on Christmas morning, became filled with doubts that the things I'd bought weren't dear enough to make everyone happy. Someone would be disappointed.

Rigobert saw me first. "Eh!"

"Ree-Go-Bear!"

Mamy, Matthieu and Jean-Serge rose to their feet and laughed from their cores. Rigobert leaned in to touch the side of his head against mine. When he pulled back, I could see.

"My God," I said, motioning towards what had once been our window. Where had it gone? It was so dark. By some stretch of the imagination, with the newsroom as dim as it was, it *was* Christmas morning. As if the sun had not yet risen and the curtains were still drawn.

"Be careful," said Jean-Serge when I began to walk over. "There's still glass about."

"They boarded our window. Oh my goodness, they've put... plywood planks over our window." I'd perhaps had to say it aloud to make sense of the cool darkness where our dust used to gambol in the light.

Gabriel reached behind him to turn down the radio.

"After the protests," said Matthieu, "engineering"—MONUC Engineering he meant—"came in and knocked out the pieces of glass. Then they nailed that on."

I walked forward, eyeing each step before setting down a sandaled foot. I turned my shoulders and peered into my office.

"Your window, too, *ma belle*," said Mamy.

I stupidly asked what had happened, as if the answer couldn't be seen: a boarded window, a wooden door opposite that was dented and split. Someone outside—a protester—must have picked up a very heavy object (*a brick?*) and chucked it with such force that it had smashed through the window, the one directly to the right of where I usually sat. From there, it would have sailed onwards to the door that led onto the hallway, a door we never used.

"Good thing you weren't here, Jenni," said Jean-Serge.

I indulged a whim and brushed the plywood with my finger-tips. The grains pricked, and I recoiled.

"They don't have any glass left," said Rigobert.

"But they're bringing it in," said Matthieu.

Mamy tapped the tight braids of her wig, jet black all over, but that was only the dye.

After a moment, Jean-Serge said, "It's great to have you back, Jenni."

"Me, too... I... I got you things—just little. Come look."

We went over to where I'd left the suitcase. I flipped it flap side up, but the zipper was stuck. After much tugging, a high-pitched *whiz* sent out a mess of clothes. Matthieu, Gabriel and Tumba laughed, and Matthieu said, "Wow!"

Sadala looked down at the clump. You could see—*I* could see—he was trying to judge shapes and depth.

I squatted down and moved aside a pile of cotton T-shirts. "I got your camera." I fished out a square box and handed it to him, and he promptly spun it around back to front. "I got it at the airport—duty free."

The picture on the box was labelled with print so busy and small that Sadala flipped it back to its particulars in French.

"It takes video and photos, like you wanted."

Jean-Serge, who'd been quietly inching closer to the suitcase, put his hands on his hips such that his thumbs were pointing forward. "And the watch, Jenni?"

"Yep, the watch... *and* the cross..."

Plus, there were earrings, nail polish and a costume jewellery necklace for Mamy. Also, Louis and I had cased Toronto's Yonge and Bloor dollar stores for Canadiana day planners, pens, note-pads and key chains; these items I gifted to the men. Everyone examined their presents long enough to be polite, and in some cases for longer.

Matthieu was the first to break away, jolting his chair backwards abruptly in an apology of laughter. "I have to go start loading our clips. Thanks for the gifts, Jenni."

"Of course… Oh, God, no — they were nothing."

It seemed to be the moment to say something. But what? I wasn't their mother any more than we were family; there was only so much I could ever say. And so, almost twenty-four hours went by before I was able to put on a good face and address… *it*… in so many words, in a way that made me come across as the nice guy. (I'd never been into charity and wasn't about to start now. But it seemed the professional thing to do.)

"I was thinking we could all put some money together, for Kasmu. He worked with us — he was here from the start, no? And… well, there's no pension or… unemployment cheques in Kindu. So…"

Everyone agreed without hesitation. We settled on $25 each, so that on the day we went over to Kasmu's house after work, I had an envelope of $200 in my purse. We couldn't have bought a card, of course, because there weren't any at that time. Besides, what would I have written in it? *Sorry to have had you fired — and not even to have had the decency to have done so myself?*

I was angry, but more than that, I was personally slighted that Mamadou had gone ahead and done something that, by all rights, the station's *responsable* ought to have done. When Yves Laplume had told me that Mamadou had fired Kasmu while I was away — Fondation Hirondelle had decided not to renew his contract, he'd said — I'd gulped and given myself over to bursts of nodding. "Oh," I'd uttered, in the place of feelings I couldn't articulate.

After all, I myself had said it: I wanted a new technician. It shouldn't have surprised me.

Now we were walking under the orange band of sunlight linking MONUC HQ to Kasmu's house. To our right, a boxy structure—a new store—was being painted red. Before I'd left for Canada and he'd left for Bunia, Tumba had written a short script announcing that telecommunications giant Celtel was setting up shop. Merriment had hit the streets: another phone tower was going up in Maniema! I'd always been amazed that people who couldn't afford three square meals a day could somehow manage to cobble together the means to buy a cellphone.

Kasmu's house was concrete. It was hard to tell how big it was, because it appeared to be part of a bigger, irregular building. Its entrance was at the back and marked by a faded paisley cloth tucked to one side where cobwebs of dust motes had settled. Kasmu appeared before any of us had knocked. When he saw us, he smiled, as did the baby in his arms, whose dinner was mush on his chin. Did he, this innocent little person, bear any family resemblance? I really didn't see babies then.

"Hello," said Kasmu warmly, inadvertently brushing against the drape, causing me to sneeze. "Come in."

Gabriel went first, ducking his head.

The one room in view was a parlour filled to the rafters. The Ramzani family had *things,* including woven mats, pictures in bronze frames and artificial flowers on doilies similar to the ones I'd seen in Mamy's house. A woman about Mamy's age hurried to pull together cushions and chairs and arrange them in a circle.

Suddenly, from behind a corner, a kitten leapt onto our feet.

"Oh, meow!" I said, reaching forward and scooping it up.

Beside me, Mamy squealed and tittered. "Jenni!"

"What?" I pulled the little brown bundle so close to me that its fur felt as though it were spawning from my skin. "You don't like cats?"

"Not to pick up," said Mamy, scrunching her nose. "Germs!"

"No! It's domesticated! It's clean enough."

Kasmu's smile took on softer lines. Someone at some point had taken the baby from his arms so that his hands now fell easily on his lap.

I don't know who spoke first. It was probably me. Regardless, Kasmu was now sitting up to receive our envelope with both hands. He then put it on his lap. It sat there throughout the entire ten minutes of our small talk, placid and unmoving. Like a brick at rest.

We stayed and talked long after the kitten had scampered away. Kasmu thanked us with a soft, gruff voice. Rigobert touched his arm.

"Do you know what he's planning to do now?" I asked Rigobert, once we were safely outside. Although we were well out of earshot, I was mindful of the level of my voice relative to the smacking of Sadala's cowboy boots against the stones.

"I believe he's going to start driving a taxi," said Rigobert.

"What?" My voice jumped an octave higher before I caught myself. "A taxi?" *Where were all these supposed taxis in Kindu?* I sure as hell hadn't seen any. I looked up for Sadala, but he had drifted too many steps ahead of me. I could see him whispering with Gabriel and Mamy.

"You know Caniche?"

It was Matthieu, walking beside me.

"Yes," I said. Caniche produced *Radio Okapi Sports* in Kinshasa. Matthieu had never actually met Caniche in person. But I had.

"He has twins, too, you know." The way Matthieu smiled, the way his eyes peeled back, it was as if his new twins—a boy and a girl who'd been born while I was away—gave him membership to an exclusive club. Or perhaps not an exclusive club, for exclusivity wasn't what a man like Matthieu would have wanted. I suspected I knew what he was after: the belonging part.

I could relate, because not only was I happy to be back in Kindu, I was almost sad to have missed the things that had happened while I was gone, as terrible as they had been. They were the kinds of things that you were better off not seeing; at the same time, it was as if yet another experience I hadn't been a part of was consigning me to the outside once again.

We carried on through the bruised twilight. The barbed coils stood out like above-ground power lines. With Matthieu still in step beside me, I said, "That's it? Just you and Caniche? With twins?"

Then Matthieu lit up once again. No, he said, there were others—two or three. He named them—no one I knew; they weren't from Kinshasa. At any rate, it was then I knew for sure. That I'd been right about Matthieu. That he and I had that in common.

25

AFTER THE BUKAVU CRISIS, as everyone called it—never being clear on whether they were talking about Nkunda's incursion, or MONUC's screw-up, or the protests, or all of it—things changed. For Radio Okapi, it was a moment of triumph: the radio had served as an accessible, neutral platform that had helped diffuse tensions. *Dialogue entre Congolais* had done everything it'd been set up to do: moderating lively discussions based on fact and mutual respect. Jérôme, its host, was like a god now. I thought about that radio station, that one in Rwanda (Mille Collines?), whose top executives had been convicted of crimes against humanity for having used their airwaves to propagate hate during the genocide. Now people were seeing the opposite was possible, that responsible media was noble. The journalists said people had noticed how objective Radio Okapi had been in covering UN stories. Unafraid of biting the hand that fed it. As a result, people's heads were filling with ways to get on air or otherwise collaborate with us.

At the same time, the Bukavu crisis had laid bare our limitations and vulnerabilities. What Nkunda had managed to achieve had raised the stakes. It was clear now: the transition could come undone, and there was no clear panacea. Not even the formidable Radio Okapi could prove to be a simple cure.

One bright and sunny morning, Gabriel came in holding a sheet of paper with a piece of tape stuck to it.

"Paper," I said in English, pointing.

Gabriel hiccupped a stunted laugh. *"C'est un tract."*

Sadala stood from his desk and reached for the paper. It was just a regular unlined sheet, which had been taken over by black marker. Gabriel said he'd found it taped to a tree.

Mamy walked through the door, also with the tract, and then stopped to take notice of the paper in Sadala's hand. "Oh, you saw it, too."

"*I* found it," said Gabriel.

"Where was yours?" Sadala asked her.

"Security." Mamy set down the paper and her purse. "Robert gave it to me downstairs. He said his brother found it over by the Banque commerciale du Congo." She was referring to the building and not the bank, which had closed its doors around the time that people had lost confidence in the country's economy and trust that their neighbours were bondable.

Although it didn't look it, Mamy's copy must have been damp, because when Jean-Serge picked it up, it failed to flap musically as a crisper paper would have.

Matthieu came over briskly. "Let me see."

"So… what *is* it?"

Matthieu broke away (*Had he even had the time to read it?*) and quickly passed me the paper. I recognized the word "Banyamulenge." That, plus another word—*"gutahuka"*—seemed to jump off the page, as if the person who had written them had depressed his pen harder, accentuating the brimstone of their otherness.

Gutahuka was Kinyarwanda. It meant "Go home." I knew because it was also the name of a program broadcast in collaboration with MONUC's DDRRR—disarm, demobilize, repatriate, resettle and reintegrate—division that aired weekly on Radio Okapi's eastern relays. The DD-triple-R people in Kinshasa believed there were twenty thousand Hutu rebels living in the Congolese bush: they were the Interahamwe, the militia viewed by the Rwandan authorities as the force behind the genocide's worst atrocities. Now, ten years on, they were also the Interahamwe's children and, in some cases, the Congolese women and girls that the Interahamwe had forcibly wed. By now, I'd come to understand that DDRRR was one of MONUC's main reasons for existing.

"Someone should take this to Marie-France," I said, in the millisecond before Jean-Serge volunteered. "I'm not going to let them manipulate us like this. No way, no how. *Not gonna do it.* Somebody—*God knows who*—tacks up a few sheets to a tree and gets their bullshit hate message…*propagated*…on our airwaves? *Fat chance of that!*"

Whistling from the kettle summoned Rigobert to our last coffee grains from Canada. My package of blueberry cereal had already been gone for three days, having stubbornly outlasted my ultra-pasteurized milk.

"We have to cover the story!" said Sadala, with discernible urgency. "The tracts aren't secret. They're everywhere! If we don't cover it, people will accuse Radio Okapi of bias."

"We *are* biased!" I retorted. "Radio Okapi, the frequency of peace?"

The journalists went quiet. Beyoncé was singing: "Got me lookin' so crazy right now, your love's got me lookin' so crazy right now…"

"What I meant…" I crossed the room to turn down the radio. "Of course we're not biased. What I meant to say is that we have a mandate. We can't disseminate hate messages over the air, like… like… Jerry Springer."

Jean-Serge's eyes flicked wide like an owl's.

Rigobert came towards me with the calmness needed to handle a hot mug. "Why don't we do a talk-tape?"

"Thank you," I said, parenthetically as I reached for my cup.

Rigobert's idea was to interview several people and then craft a story by cueing in select tape. "We could make it about what the governor... MONUC are doing to improve community relations... you know, after the killing of the two Banyamulenge soldiers and the Bukavu crisis. We can mention the tract—and put the question to Governor Sumaili—without making it the focus of the story."

"We could even interview some Banyamulenges," said Matthieu.

"Where are you going to find Banyamulenges in Kindu?" said Gabriel.

"The military—"

"Who *aren't* in the FARDC, because the FARDC hierarchy doesn't authorize soldiers to speak."

I brought my hands together and snapped open my palms; I was becoming Congolese. "Wait a second—if you're saying there's no Banyamulenge in Kindu, then why the tracts? Does that make sense to you?"

But there *were* Banyamulenges living in Maniema—at least enough of them to organize a sit-in outside Sumaili's office. When we learned of it, Mamy and I got into the car and drove over—and there they were, numbering about a dozen, squatting under the mango trees, chatting among themselves. They were wearing the same vibrant geometric-patterned wax-printed clothes and ill-fitting trousers fashionable in town, and some of the women and girls had their hair braided into short twists shooting from their head in all directions, which was common for Kindu. So in short, everyone looked perfectly at home.

I shook my head and sighed. First the tract and now this protest… What was I to make of it? Were Banyamulenges here really in danger? It sounded crazy to say so, since two Banyamulenge soldiers had already been beaten to death, but I really didn't think so. I just didn't think people in Kindu would actually plan and execute mass murder.

Years later, people would say to me, "The Congo? Was that… did you feel safe?" And the truth was, on a conscious level at least, *yes*, I did. I felt love. I felt curious, and alive and attached to every living thing around me. At the same time, a feeling of dread was creeping in. Which I looked at the way I wanted to. And whenever things got uncomfortable, for me or for anyone else I worried for, I sent my fears gullying down the river like some brave soul moving downstream, clutching a hand at the river's edge. To be swept away and deposited elsewhere.

WHILE I'D BEEN AWAY in Canada, I'd thought of all the things we could do, and do better. Now it was time to implement them.

"Let's create regular features! We could have, like, variety shows. Local musicians can come in and play their music, live in our studio! Do you guys know of anybody? Any bands?"

Ideas would come to me in the car, during MONUC magazine runs or later, when the sky was so black you could lose yourself in it, after I'd come back from the cafeteria to sit at my desk with a phone to my ear, half-listening to Louis discussing what we should do to prepare his fishing travel show for the day I was home for good. Nine weeks remained on my contract.

In the end, I never saw Shane before he left. I hadn't tried to contact him since, perhaps for the same reasons he hadn't reached out to me. And although I remained vigilant against living in the past, my fear of falling victim to its seductions was fast diminishing. I wondered what he was doing and how he was.

Shane, I typed—tilted my head—and then hit delete. *Hi Shane,* read better.

Just then, my landline rudely rang.

It was Eva, an American about my age who ran Radio Okapi's station in Kalemie, some eight hundred kilometres away on Lake Tanganyika—the one with all the fish.

"So Expédit is on his way, not this Friday but next."

"What? Already?" The Peace Train wasn't supposed to arrive in Kindu for at least another two weeks.

Eva agreed—"I know! Crazy!"—and asked if there was anything I needed from my side. Expédit was obviously in touch with Rigobert and everyone.

I drew a long breath. Were there any pictures I could use? I would have to write an article, for MONUC.

"No... nothing that I can think of. Not offhand. You remind me, though, I have to get on that."

Between dealing with the tracts and trying to pin down a permanent replacement for Kasmu, I'd been procrastinating. There was still talk of Kabila coming, and although we'd had nothing concrete to go on (and thus had never engaged in public "Will he or won't he?" banter), our listeners would've had the benefit of certain facts. For one thing, Kindu was now overrun by soldiers of the special presidential guard—some of whom had enough time on their hands to loiter and filch. Just today, Sadala was working on a story about a civil servant who'd been on his way home from work when he'd crossed paths with one of them. It was the last thing he remembered before waking up a wallet and a watch lighter, bleeding from the head.

"Hey," said Eva, abruptly changing tack. "Do you want a cat?"

"A *cat?*"

Her cat had had kittens, she said. Apparently, they were the grand-kittens of Michel's old cat. Michel was another MONUC public information officer, who was also Canadian but far sharper than me—as in, sharp like Mamadou, such that the two of them didn't normally get along.

"So it's like…" She laughed again. "It's like we're running some kind of cat farm here."

I laughed, too, and told her, no, sorry, I couldn't just *take a cat*.

"They're good for mice."

When I asked what would happen the day I left, Eva said someone would take it. She didn't know—how could she?— that it was unconscionable for me to take on something with a plan of abandoning it. To ever turn my back on responsibility.

The conversation changed as Eva and I tendered our gripes. A markup of the new *décrochage* had just been circulated: the thirty extra minutes we'd been promised had been confirmed, *but* we were supposed to allocate those minutes—and more—to eight songs of our choosing—*eight!*—as per a schema of item then song, item then song. Marie-France and I had done the math, and under the new expanded format, we'd actually wind up with *less* time for news and information. A paltry seventeen minutes! Plus, they were going to scrap the press review— *the press review!*

"Don't they realize there're no papers outside of Kinshasa? No Internet?"

"It's the way Étienne does it in Bunia," said Eva. "The Okapis call it *La Bible St. Étienne.*"

THE FOLLOWING DAY started badly when Bérénice announced she was moving out. The hollowness we lived in amplified my indignation. *I should've known you would do this to me,* I thought. Was I scared to live on my own? Perhaps. There was no reason for me to be upset otherwise—I could easily handle her share of the rent.

Bérénice, who possessed the kind of fleshy lower jaw that appeared stronger when set, drew a noisy breath that lit her eyes. After more than two years in Kindu, she said, she finally had the chance to live in a decent house — with a garden and furniture and an electrical line connected straight to MONUC HQ. For her, it was clear, and given the chance, I'd choose the same. And if I didn't, then I was dumb.

THEY WERE FUMIGATING when I walked up the stairs at HQ. I heard the noise, like a small propeller-driven plane, buzzing like a super-mosquito. I looked down near Marie-France's end of the building and saw the man with his mask and his long siphoned-cylindered fogging machine. The chemicals raged: they didn't actually smell, but you could certainly catch a good whiff of them.

I wasn't supposed to be in here. The note had been sent; it was one of those Saturday mornings. When the grey haze would start seeping down the hall, irritation would scratch my skin, water my eyes and turn them red in pain. We were supposed to wait at least an hour before re-entering after the spraying. Most times I did. I wondered how long the mosquitoes waited. It certainly seemed as though they just kept flying in. Having the MONUC cafeteria just outside, completely in the open, might have been great for aeration, but it was a joke when it came to these things.

Nicole of General Services flounced into my office not long before noon, sometime after the tickling sniff of lava had wafted away. She thumbed through a deck of squared-off parchment of a higher, thicker quality than the stuff we used for our scripts. She stopped at a page and placed it on my desk. "Mmm," she whirred.

"Madame MONUC Public Information/Radio Okapi" it read. A date, time and place were indicated in ultra-bold purple-inked font.

"We're holding a Miss Kindu contest—and we'd like you to be a judge." She paused to tug the bottom of her skirt, slithering to pull it down past her knees. "The winner will go on to represent Maniema in the national Miss competition." It would be the first year the competition had been held in Kindu since the war, she said.

I looked at her hard, her big black lashes flitting like a butterfly. I suddenly realized how little makeup Mamy actually wore. "But—" This Nicole of General Services, she looked so pleased with herself—why? "Shouldn't you be asking Mamy? She'd be better for this, I think."

"No, we want you to do it."

I looked at her again. "Right," I said finally. "I see."

I very nearly yielded to a sense of... *partisanship? loyalty?* but in the end did my bit and sat with the other judges on the panel. There were four of us. I was the only woman. I didn't know who the other three people were, but they knew me. (Though not by name: "Ah, Madame Okapi!" they said. "What a pleasure!") There were perhaps eight or nine contestants. They wore strapless dresses or tube tops and skirts that showed skin but nothing scandalous and had all had their hair, nails and makeup done. They took turns parading around the space: we were in an interior courtyard, the kind I never would've thought existed in Kindu, darkly lit by lamps courtesy of a noisy generator. Some plastic tables with wax-printed overlays had been set up off to the side, where people—men and women—were drinking soda and beer.

We judges sat shoulder to shoulder behind a long narrow stand, just above the action, enough for us to be looking slightly downwards as the young women spoke in turn about Kindu and the war and their dreams for the future. Honestly, they all looked and sounded lovely.

When it was time to choose a winner, I did something rather unlike myself and let the other three judges debate their points. At times, one of them would huddle in and ask for my opinion; I simply restated a simplified version of whatever had just been said. Surprisingly, I felt emotional.

Once a decision had finally been made and we had a name to read out, the winner sprang into the air as if a weight had suddenly been lifted. Nicole of General Services stepped forward with the crown.

To be fair, I never heard Nicole say anything bad about Mamy. But there were rumours. I never approached Mamy regarding anything I heard, for a host of reasons. First, it was none of my business. It was no one's business, but the reality was, if Kindu had had a tabloid magazine, the very woman to have put herself in harm's way for the sole purpose of dispelling rumours would've been the first to see her truths crooked into some baseless cover story. Mamy was that kind of popular. And, in my own way, I could relate. Neither of us had wifely ways.

26

ABOUT A WEEK AFTER the Miss Kindu contest, Mamy arrived at the radio—late—dressed to the nines and chipper, with an announcement. Rigobert was the first to react: "You bought a motorcycle? *You?*"

"Yes, *Papa!*"

"Eh! And you're going to drive it? Yourself?"

"Nah!" She set down her purse and Motorola radio. "I'll just get one of my brothers to drive me around. But... Well, maybe... I don't know. I might learn. We'll see."

"Mamy Halili Tshibangu!" exclaimed Rigobert, with a slap to his knee. "What made you buy—"

"Mamy, you've bought a motorcycle?" I said, coming out of my office. "That is *so* cool!" Not even the men had one.

Rigobert, Matthieu and Jean-Serge shook their heads incredulously, and at once, I knew they saw it the same way: you just didn't see freewheeling women going around riding motorcycles through Kindu. Why not? wasn't even a question. You just didn't see it.

Sadala, Gabriel, Rigobert and Tumba, who was just back from Bunia, all took advantage of the moment to get in more questions about Mamy's new motorcycle: What make was it?

And which year? Which model was it exactly? How many cylinders? Where did she even get it? And how much did she have to pay?

Eventually, Jean-Serge invoked Rigobert's lost question about what made her think of buying it.

"Nothing," said Mamy, almost in retort. "I just wanted one."

From behind his computer on the room's far side, Sadala sounded off fractiously: "You're going to have to get that registered. City administration has started up the licensing bureau again. They'll fine you if you don't."

"Vraiment," muttered Gabriel.

"Well… well…" I said blithely. "That's a story! That they're doing that again. Motor vehicle registration, I mean."

"I know," said Mamy. "I didn't forget. I was at city hall just now. With *this*." She reached into her handbag and thrust forward a Mini Disc recorder. "I interviewed the clerk. And I just spoke to Martin in Kinshasa. They're expecting a clip for noon."

Matthieu said he could help, and I stopped to smile again. "So…" I said, almost singing the word. "We're getting a new technician!"

There was an audible gasp in the room. "It's José, isn't it?" said Rigobert.

I was about to shush him, when Sadala's phone rang—once. He'd been beeped. He reached for my cellphone just as Marie-France appeared. Her face was wan. "Bad news from Kasongo. Armed men burst into Radio Sauti ya Mkaaji yesterday and beat its station manager. Badly."

"Eh! Shabani!" said Rigobert, looking truly horrified.

Gabriel's face froze.

"That's Modeste Shabani," said Tumba. "From the community radio station. How is he?"

Marie-France said he was in the hospital in intensive care.

"Eh! Eh! Eh!" said Matthieu. Beside him, Jean-Serge's eyebrows sailed above his glasses.

I turned towards Sadala. "Shabani? Is this guy related to you?"

Sadala said no. But you could see from their silence they all knew the guy well.

"Which group?" asked Gabriel finally.

"Old RCD," said Marie-France. She paused to swallow. "But let's not forget—" Her arm shot up with her tone. "They're all one glorious army now!"

KASONGO'S HOSPITAL, some 230 kilometres from Kindu—a two-day walk at least—was a cement building left unpainted that had taken on the colour of oatmeal. Its structure held forth without the benefit of a foundation, standing self-contained on an even lot, smack dab in the middle of a field of red hibiscus and the weeping willows of a monastery. The Congo lacked serviceable ambulances, so no laneways led to the hospital's door, no signs indicated the location of the emergency entrance or admissions parking or what have you. The building itself was an astoundingly nondescript two-floor walk-up with an L-shaped staircase running along its exterior and continuing as an outdoor hallway, like at a motor inn. And the way Kasongolers carried on unceremoniously around it, the entire hospital could've been put on a flatbed truck and plunked down in some other clearing just as easily. Fancy equipment—*Don't make me laugh!* But the place reeked of sterility. "Arm muscle," said Gabriel, was put into its daily disinfecting.

Gabriel, myself and Fernanda of Human Rights had come as fast as we could raise a flight. We'd all been profusely grateful to AirOps, MovCon, the head of office and the DoA—the director of administration—all the way up to Kinshasa, when the requisite forms had been signed, approved and tasked into action within less than a day, a real rush compared to the hard and fast seventy-two-hour rule.

The day our helicopter blew about long yellow grass to set down in a field of children's squeals, we broke into three groups, with Fernanda taking a third of our military escort to the town's civil and military authorities; the second third staying behind to keep watch over the helicopter (and smoke with the pilots); and the remaining third – three Bolivian soldiers – accompanying Gabriel and me to the hospital. The five of us, all trailing a nun, had just turned the corner down an open-air hallway when I looked over a low wall into the monastery's gardens: they were still and sprawling green – messy but visibly tended to, if only to be lovingly cut back from time to time.

We found Modeste Shabani with bloody bandages wrapped around his head and an intravenous needle hooked into his hand. He was in a small, sparse private room, curled up on a toddler's cot with his back towards us. A mosquito net had been knotted out of the way above the wafts of a rickety standing fan angled in the bed's general direction. Apart from a drip bag, the room held only a Red Cross calendar on the wall. I made a mental note to pass on one of the new MONUC electoral posters Kinshasa had recently sent.

Yesterday, as Gabriel and I had been printing off our MOPS, Rigobert had said that Modeste Shandani was one to speak out but never one to complain, and the sister who nursed him now didn't waste a minute in telling us how much she appreciated the difference. It was a good thing Modeste was so pliable, because his injuries were not. For instance, having become aware of our presence, he'd attempted to turn over to face us but couldn't, for his hip bones protruded like apples. He couldn't lie on his back either, because the flesh of his buttocks was exposed. I had never before seen gashes of this nature and so had nothing to compare them to, but I was astonished by how deep and pink they looked against the darkness of his skin.

Given how he was laid up, we spoke under the strain of not being able to see each other. Modeste was better at this than me. He introduced himself before asking me a series of generous questions about where I'd come from and what I'd seen of the Congo. What did I think of Maniema? How were my friends and family back home? They must miss me. What did they make of me coming to the Congo? Somehow, before I knew it, I'd broken down and confessed to how much I missed the family cat—since it wasn't a person (I said to state the obvious), the nature of our relationship—mine and the cat's—required physical proximity: pats and cuddles and the like. And without these, I explained, the relationship was, for all intents and purposes, dead. "Even my three-year-old niece, Emily, can pick up the phone and talk, you know?"

Modeste laughed as best he could without busting a gut. He thanked me for coming and said it was good of me to have organized the flight so quickly.

Gabriel and Modeste spent the next few minutes conversing in low voices, using tones, accents and syllables that sounded like English but without the breathy puffs of *t*s and *p*s and with more vowels clusters. Given the similarity, it almost seemed as if the two were talking in a code that could be broken if only I listened hard enough.

In time, Gabriel took out a recording device—(not *his*, because his had been stolen during the Bukavu protests). After they'd finished, Modeste asked if I'd brought a camera.

"Do I have my camera?" *Good question*. "Oh yeah, yeah, yeah." For some reason, I had to think a moment. Then: "I've got it," I said frantically, rifling through my bag. "It's right here. It's just here…"

Taking his photo required getting in close. One, then both

of my knees went up on the edge of the bed, which rattled and squeaked as I found my centre of balance. I shifted oafishly, and then put down a leg to bear my weight. Of all his wounds, a deep caning on his upper back, just underneath his shoulders appeared the freshest, layers of tissue perceptible to my lens. At the same time, his body was putting out the brackish odour of healing—nothing too stinky, but it was there. As he pulled up the corners of his dressing gown to reveal his haunches, I wished Gabriel had swooped in and offered to take the photos. It was too late to ask him now.

Modeste cricked his neck so as not to talk into his pillow. "You getting it?"

"Yeah, yeah. It's good," I said hastily. "I mean—it's not good. You must be very uncomfortable."

"You would think," said Modeste spryly, "and actually you'd be right! Someone go out there and pick me some opium."

"Oh!" I said, perking up. "You mean those flowers out there? The red ones... with the petals that look all papery? I thought they were hibiscus!"

Gabriel laughed. "No, Jenni. Those are hibiscus. He was just joking."

When Modeste chuckled too, the bed began to wobble. "Yeah, but on second thought, a mouthful of plants couldn't be any worse than what they pass off as grub in this place."

"Hospital food," I said.

"*Vraiment,*" said Gabriel.

Quiet returned to the room. I had taken six, maybe eight photos, and had the back view covered. "So..." The fan's dull fluttering suddenly seemed to be getting louder. "Gabriel!" I said, affecting a jocular voice. "I'm going to leave the frontals to you!" I backed off a leg cautiously, so as not to cause further disturbance. "I got to worry about my reputation here. You know the

UN . . . the whole sexual exploitation and abuse deal." At the time, MONUC was building up a new section, called SEA, to address and prevent future allegations of abuses by its peacekeepers. The workload had gone far beyond the capacity of Gender or Human Rights or Rule of Law to handle.

Gabriel and Modeste let out a few gurgles, probably not because of what I'd said but because they realized why I was trying to be funny. Taking the camera from me, Gabriel travelled around the bed to capture the recto view. I took another step back, and like a *maman* with her *pagne,* slid out my ponytail holder several times before putting it back in.

The standing fan jangled as if on its last legs. My eyes held steady, my head cocked to one side. Like a portrait, Gabriel was bending down, snapping photos into the backlight. And over here, closer, was Modeste, holding up a corner of his hospital green in one hand, with a needle stuck down the back of the other. Outside, Kasongo's goats baaed. Trucks honked. People went about their day. While here inside, it was a quiet crying shame: I knew we all felt it, this cursed shame—which belonged to none of us in the room, and we had no reason to feel ashamed, damn it. The monastery's bells tolled. Gabriel and Modeste twisted uncomfortably to capture the right angle, at some point dislodging the Mini Disc recorder that had been sticking out of Gabriel's shirt pocket. I thought about the testimony in that tiny silver machine, testimony that risked another beating, or worse. I thought about Mamy and Rigobert, and the others working diligently back in Kindu . . . Matthieu taking on all the technical stuff, in addition to his daily reporting.

Something made Modeste laugh, and his squeak of pain made Gabriel laugh, too. For once, a more dominant emotion had whittled down my sense of responsibility. It wasn't fear. It was something else. Honour sprang to mind.

AFTER WE LEFT THE HOSPITAL, Gabriel went to buy pineapples while I walked about, disseminating MONUC magazines and T-shirts and introducing myself at the school, the mayor's office and the police station, all of which were single-level *béton* structures built with no other code than a thought for ventilation. All I had to do was mention the Peace Train and the products it would be bringing, and there went everyone's faculties:

"*La population du territoire de Kasongo souffre!*" A man holding a cup of something I suspected to be moonshine flung out his free arm and asked me in an agitated voice, did I know that *avant la guerre,* the territory of Kasongo used to be one of Maniema's biggest producers of white rice? *Big factories!* produced corn, cassava and peanuts for export to Rwanda and Burundi and beyond.

"That's interesting," I said, and meant it. (I'd never studied history in school: an astonishing omission, I now realized, for someone whose livelihood traded on current affairs.)

Gabriel and I joined up near 1 PM outside the nutritional centre, where I'd left the last of my handouts. From there, we flagged down two motorbike taxis, whose drivers beamed when they saw us as if they'd just made two new friends.

We mounted the bikes.

"Where were you?" I asked as Gabriel changed his grip on two flimsy charcoal-coloured bags. He'd been gone for quite some time for just pineapples.

"I went over to Modeste's offices at Sauti ya Mkaaji."

"Oh, it wasn't shut down? What did you see? Did you get to talk to people?"

Gabriel said he had. His driver booted his kickstand. The engines revved.

"What does that mean? Sauti ya Mkaaji?"

"Voice of the farmer," Gabriel yelled.

His driver shifted gear from neutral to first, then second and third, rolling on the throttle. As we pulled away, I squirmed to find the least intrusive space I could without sacrificing my view of the flowering red hibiscus bearing forth in the yellowing fields like a citizen's army. Freshly worked dirt padded the road, the air's warm blue lens moving across my face and through my hair. I inhaled deeply, taking in strong floral notes and a tinge of manure.

We increased our speed. I briefly removed a hand from my driver's waist. He had the waist of a dancer. I waved and Gabriel smiled as we overtook them.

"*Les Chinois,*" my driver called back as three large trucks passed in the opposite direction. *Progress?* I thought. Who was to say? The farmers, the Kasongolers, I supposed, who probably prayed to God for renewed economic activity—be it thanks to the Chinese, the Americans or men from Mars.

Barrelling around a corner, our helicopter came into view. Where were the children who'd run to see us arrive? Was there no fun in watching us go?

Our bikes slowed in approach. Almost as soon as we got off, Gabriel's eyebrows arched in and his cheeks drooped like an old man's belly.

"What?" I said, with a mix of surprise and concern.

"During the war…" The death of the engines had reduced Gabriel's voice to a murmur. "I was reporting. A soldier—a Mai-Mai—accused me of spying. He grabbed my arm and led me into the jungle at gunpoint."

"My God—"

"He was going to kill me. I stood there, facing him, with the gun pointed at me. His finger was on the trigger. But at the last second, his commander appeared. And he yelled, 'What are you doing? That's a Radio Okapi journalist! You can't kill him!'"

For a moment, I lost my breath.

"He just… let me go."

Our drivers were hovering. We'd agreed to a flat fare of five U.S. dollars, which I now settled with a generous exchange rate in francs, forgetting as I always did to get even a scribble on a scrap of paper to serve as a UN receipt.

Gabriel and I walked in silence, the grass sweeping our calves. Fernanda of Human Rights, our Bolivian escorts, the Indian crew, plus two Congolese army officers who'd come along as part of the seventh military region's investigation into the brutal attack against Modeste were all waiting for us at the foot of the helicopter. Colonel Bokeone, former RCD-Goma, now of the Kasongo garrison, had been dismissed of his duties and may well have been looking at a court martial. Or maybe not. Say what you will, but justice had never been the fulcrum upon which the Congolese army turned. That was the reality we were dealing with.

27

THE DAY THE PEACE TRAIN arrived in Kindu, it was terrifically sunny—a day for opening the door and letting the children run wild. Once again, it was hot like gangbusters. We were packed shoulder to shoulder in a block squared by the restored rails on one side, a built-up stage on another, plus two incurved paths that led to the grounds of the freshly painted station. Very few people had come as families. Instead, Kindu's mass-tailored, vibrantly patterned *pagnes* and short-sleeved shirts were out in full force in a show of political and civil society colours. Some groups had had special T-shirts printed, and at times the ripe smell of armpit sweat cocked my neck back. A boom box belted out Congolese singers JB Mpiana and Werrason.

That day, we Okapis were all there in the fray, at least in turns, given the various angles to cover. President Joseph Kabila hadn't come. In his stead, the one vice-president whose name I could never remember—Arthur Z'ahidi Ngoma—had made the trip, alongside four transitional government ministers, including, aptly, the minister of transport. I was disappointed Kabila hadn't shown (Juvenal, Marie-France's friend in Sumaili's office, had told her the president's team had felt they couldn't adequately secure Kindu), because people did want to see him—and besides, weren't we good enough for a presidential visit? I figured Kindu didn't have enough voters to make it interesting, and the Kabila people knew that when there was an election — *if* there was an election — Kindu would vote for their man regardless.

A hum, a slight vibration, rippled through the ground. Here in the thirty-five-degree heat, my vinyl hobo was sliding in sweat off my shoulder. I let it fall and hugged it like a rugby ball so that I could make my way out of the crowd, to move more freely along the outside.

At the track's wooden railroad ties, I found Sadala already in position.

"Hey! Sadala!"

At the sound of his name, Sadala promptly lowered his new camera — the one I'd picked up for him in Canada. "Get ready. It's coming!" he cried.

Excitedly, I rose to my tiptoes but couldn't find a line of sight. It would take considerable manoeuvring and a loud triumphant whistle for everyone to jockey in such a way as to allow my MONUC lens to see. The train whistled again as its lead cab braked into the station. The humanitarian aid was in boxcars at the back. At the front, hundreds of heads and hands formed frenetically waving triangles. The band began to play. I panned my camera, zooming into the joy.

I felt I would've recognized Expédit at once, even had Rigobert, Tumba and Sadala not been running alongside the train, trying to catch up with a set of arms reaching out the window. When I saw the four of them place their hands upon each other and laugh like schoolboys, I put my camera down and ran over immediately.

TUMBA'S RECENT RETURN from Bunia had me convinced of two things: one, that he was the newsroom's most prolific reporter, which I'd already surmised; and two, that his presence actually bolstered Kindu's urban football league. On match days, he would take my cellphone to file a hit from the field; José would patch him through the boards so that Rigobert—it was usually Rigobert hosting—could inquire about the score, prompting Tumba to give a live play-by-play. The segments worked so well that Tumba began to do the same on weekends for Kinshasa. I only found out because I heard him on the radio one Saturday, talking over whistles and roars when he was supposed to be off.

Of all the journalists, I probably knew Tumba the least. He and I rarely talked one-on-one. He appeared to gravitate towards Sadala, who was his drinking buddy (Jean-Serge still drank, but he drank alone, or at least well out of my sight), and he and Rigobert shared a plethora of Maniema references; together they knew just about everyone in the province. Overall, Tumba was a calm, agreeable person who I guessed had never been able to capitalize on looks, even as a younger man; perhaps this point alone went some way to explaining why he was able to see people's characters and the situations they got themselves into so clearly. It was hard to imagine anyone not liking him, and I would say, from his perspective, he had different uses for us all.

One morning, halfway through our story meeting, Tumba said there was a story we should cover: "People were scared to hear the helicopters today."

"You mean, this morning?" I said. "The MONUC helicopters? That... training exercise?"

"Oh yeah," said Sadala, sitting up in his chair. "They were scared. Someone asked me if I knew what was going on."

"Yes, especially after Bukavu," said Gabriel. He was standing at our story board, marker in hand.

"Yes, Jenni," said Jean-Serge, nodding solemnly, as if he were the wisest of the group and I needed convincing.

We discussed it some more, the ways we could make it right. I told my story about the day I heard the Congolese army running up and down the street and was afraid we were about to be attacked. And I noticed that no one laughed, even though I'd laughed a bit myself, for whatever reason.

So Tumba wrote a short news brief that day that summed up what the helicopters had been doing. I learned my lesson and shared the story later at the MONUC morning meeting; I asked all contingent commanders present to be sure to inform us in advance of their exercises—at least a couple of days before, I said. That would give us enough time to draft and read out a public service announcement during our *décrochage*. From then on, they always did.

TUMBA, AUGUST 2002

Before becoming a journalist, Tumba Dieudonné Mobile was, not surprisingly, a teacher. He'd taught junior high school for thirteen years at the Collège de l'Enano, where Mamy had gone, though by the time she'd got there, Tumba had already left for l'Institut Imara.

To hear Tumba tell it, junior high school presages a man's calling and things that happened in school twenty, thirty years ago might as well have happened yesterday. He'd often say, some students you remember: the ones who learned from your tutelage (and acknowledge as much) nicely fill the weakest parts of your mind at the most sensitive of times and places. As if you'd raised a kind, sage child who will preserve you in your gentle old age.

Gabriel Amisi Kumba definitely wasn't one of those students. He was something different. You could tell him the same thing three times and he still wouldn't be able to say it back to you. Most tests he took he failed. So he was a poor student; that was the first thing. He didn't get his diploma. But he was memorable, and particularly more so now in hindsight, when the passage of time connected previously isolated dots in a way that made Tumba say, "Of course! I should have seen that coming." For despite Kumba's lacklustre grades, no one could deny the boy his ability to run, to anticipate and to rally a team. On the football pitch, he was something fierce. And they didn't call him "the fighter" for nothing.

One day, when the journalists were about a month into working for Radio Okapi, with the RCD still controlling Kindu, Rigobert filed a report saying three RCD soldiers had been injured in a battle with Mai-Mais some sixteen kilometres down the road to Kasongo. As with all Okapi reports, the version that aired had been thoroughly vetted and—if war as a subject could be described as such—was factual to the point of being bland.

That same night, with a yellow moon high over the eastern hills, the RCD-Goma chief of staff, General Gabriel Amisi Kumba—Tango Fort he was now called—came knocking at his old teacher's house. Tumba opened the door in the clammy darkness, expecting a brother or one of his wife's sisters, because with the security situation as bad as it was, only a neighbour would come visiting at this time of night. As it turned out, he'd forgotten one major exception.

The door flung open, Tumba was spooked to see a wide and protruding silhouette. "Where's Yuma Ndwani's address?" rumbled a voice gruff like the ultimate tough guy.

Tumba knew the answer but said he didn't. Amisi puffed, then peered ominously into the light streaming from the house, as if he were a smarter man—one with the ability to think things through and realize that any man who valued life would have always replied the same.

Later, after Amisi skulked away, back to his metal and men, Tumba asked his wife to quickly get word to Rigobert's wife that Tango Fort was looking for Rigobert.

Two nights passed without incident. Then, at nine o'clock the next morning—on the kind of day that drenches your undershirt and makes your skin sticky as glue—just as the schoolchildren across the street were settling into class, heavily armed soldiers in cheap sunglasses turned up at Rigobert's house, saying the RCD's chief of security had sent them. (If their old neighbours and classmates excavating sand from the river could be seen as Kindu's local entrepreneurs, these boys—none older than nineteen, surely—were Kindu's taxi drivers, operating other people's guns to drive the war.) At the sight of them coming up their grassy-patched lawn, Rigobert's wife started screaming.

Rigobert dashed into the back room for his two-way Motorola radio.

MONUC Security rushed to the scene—they were civilians, not military, and not even armed, because the UN Charter limited MONUC's Chapter VI mandate at the time to the "pacific settlement of disputes." In a firm and righteous tone, one of the *mzungus* explained that Rigobert couldn't be summoned, for he was UN staff, working for an observation mission that had been set up at the invitation of the Congolese government with the full support of the international community. The *mzungu* spoke several minutes more, uninterrupted, before recapitulating that all UN staff, whatever their nationality, were to perform their duties unimpeded.

A lull suddenly fell upon Rigobert's front garden, like the death of a hailstorm. Rigobert's wife looked up in a stunned, anticipative haze and stopped her sobbing. The calm had settled but several seconds, long enough for MONUC Security to shepherd Rigobert into one of its shiny white vehicles. Anger shunted to violence. The soldiers had their orders: they grabbed for and caught hold of Rigobert's wiry leg, which on instinct he thrashed about as if an animal trapped in a snare. The posse of hunters pulled and pulled as the UN defenders lunged. Rigobert's grip on the back seat was loosening. Then: a slip. Weakened core muscles or a decisive yank, and the tug-of-war was lost. The RCD soldiers hoorahed like frat boys pantsing a freshman and threw Rigobert like a sack of rice into the back of the army-green pickup they'd come in. Then they sped off down the road.

Rattling, rattling and repeated rattling made it impossible for Rigobert to distinguish the louder sounds of the old assault rifles the soldiers held in their hands banging against the pickup's edge or the half-on, half-off mechanisms that clunked underneath the Jeep's belly.

The vehicle stopped where General Byamungu, the head of the RCD forces in Maniema, lived. Immediately, someone—two someones, at least—clutched Rigobert by the arms, as one shouted, "Go! Go!"

Inside. Through the foyer—his legs still in spasms—Rigobert was taken directly down a flight of stairs to the basement and a cave. There was blood everywhere. It was spattered on the floor, on the walls, in the cracks. It was human. It smelled fresh. Rigobert had been scared from the start, but now came fear, *that* fear, with its symptoms and reactions. Pools of sweat turned his white trousers into swimming trunks, which he also soiled. His hands, fingers and toes throbbed. His face was on fire. His shins, kneecaps and elbows stung as if he'd been whacked upside them and large contusions were forming. Quadriceps, calves and hamstrings became petrified tree trunks.

So this was how it would go. He would die here. In this cave. At not even fifty years of age.

In an eyeblink—that fast—three soldiers gripped him steady as a vice while another took out a long wooden baton. They stripped him down and started lashing. The strikes were rhythmic. They struck the spine in the small of his back where there was bone and stinging skin. They hit his buttocks and kept on coming, one after another.

How he didn't want to die! *And like this… goddamn it,* over nothing. Three injured RCD soldiers: everyone had heard there'd been a fight, so what that he'd put a number on it? Hot tears ran down his cheeks. That fear, that shrinking fear that was holding its grip on the muscles and organs and joints of his body. For how much longer would all these be his?

The whipping intensified. He began to choke for air.

28

THE DRY SEASON CURLED banana trees from the stem. Produce and grains whose time had come had to be picked or perish. I ought to have told Roger to give up his fruitless search for oranges but still held out hope.

With school on summer hiatus, active children who could have benefitted from vitamins and minerals, from something other than cassava, were out on the streets stoking wire hoops in circles, dribbling a ball or shooting hoops outside the Salle Champagnat.

Perhaps it was seeing the children playing, coupled with a healthy dose of Peace Train Fever, that inspired MONUC IT's Samuel and Rashid. I first learned of it in an office-wide email and proclaimed to myself, "Yes, what a great idea!"

"What's a great idea?" asked Matthieu, his face scrunched. He was sitting on the other side of my desk, where we were going over one of his scripts, which with Matthieu was seldom a straightforward affair.

"The MONUC Kindu Welfare Club, the one that Samuel and Rashid run—you know... IT? They're collecting money to have the tennis court fixed—that one by the airport. They're getting it done over so that people can actually play there again."

"Ah bon," said Matthieu. "That's a great idea. *Vraiment. Vous savez,* there's a great tennis instructor here in Kindu. He's been out of work since... since —"

"Since *avant la guerre,*" I said, deadpan.

Matthieu held silent in thought. After a moment, he chuckled.

The healthy birth of his twins had made Matthieu far happier than any of us had expected. He'd seemed especially pleased when Sadala had loaned him his video camera. Matthieu, who never swore, averred these two would be his last; and there was no reason to question him. Increasingly, Congo's middle-class families were considering family size, citing pricey school fees and inflation. Yes, the country was slowly stabilizing. But social welfare? Job creation? That would be a long time coming.

OUR NEW TECHNICIAN — I'd met him once in passing — was getting married in Kinshasa. He'd invited me, but I'd declined. Time, not money, was at issue, for although I'd used my vacation to evacuate my cash from Kindu, June's mission sub-sistence allowance once again flushed my desk drawer with U.S. hundred-dollar bills. And Sadala had repaid me for the camera and Jean-Serge for the watch. Both reimbursements had been remarkably uneventful. "Jenni — your money," they'd simply said.

Two days after his wedding, José Ekofo N'djoli whirled into the newsroom in a trail of static cling. I looked at him, all bright and hyper-alert, and thought, *This level of energy can't be sustained.* But time showed it could: José was a worker bee. Although he wouldn't be paid a franc more for it, he came with story ideas and translated and recorded all our reports into Lingala for Kinshasa. It was impossible not to see him as the complete opposite of Kasmu. For one thing, José liked people — to the point of giving them airs. He was forever dropping the names of his old Radio Okapi Kinshasa colleagues, not to impress but to recall dear friends he was missing, as if to keep them alive. He had a story to tell about each voice that aired. "That's *just* like Rahma," he'd say. Or, "Jérôme *always* does that!"

José was tidy in appearance, with an oval face framed by neat eyebrows and closely cut black hair that almost looked painted on. He had pink lips that seemed too full, too defined to belong to anyone over forty. He was perhaps thirty-seven, thirty-eight? The woman he'd just married had made him a stepfather, and I had the feeling it was a real novelty for him, because he talked about his stepdaughter a lot when none of the others ever said a peep about their children (Well, Matthieu occasionally did—but never Sadala, never Tumba, never Gabriel).

Most importantly, every day when the *décrochage* began, I now felt that our work was in secure hands. For his part, at last unbound by the studio's sliders and controls, Matthieu indulged in rambling tales that he at least seemed to think were funny. I said: "I bet you're happy now," and he just laughed.

Having José also greatly improved all the sound elements and transitions that our listeners heard on air. But there was more: Radio Okapi Kindu had a few tricks up its sleeve. Production, which had suffered from lack of attention for all our focus on editorial rigour, suddenly flourished.

Thanks to Mamy, who'd brought him in, a young student who headed up a local theatre troupe called Light of Life began writing short comedy skits that the group would perform on air.

The guy's name was Peter. "That doesn't sound Congolese," I said to him. He replied that Peter was his stage name. This was when I put two and two together and remembered that Mamy had done an Okapi Portrait on this guy: he was an orphan—both parents murdered in the war (or one of them stricken by disease?). Somehow, Peter had managed to keep himself and his brothers and sisters in school, and now in university, he'd started a community theatre troupe in the conventional Congolese style, where actors donned elaborate wigs, poured white chalk over their heads and stuffed large padding under whatever colourful costume most veered towards the ridiculous.

Peter and I decided he would write skits — about teachable things like army integration, disarmament, the elections… peace. I had a small budget for these things. We agreed it would be a waste of energy to translate skits that would eventually air in Swahili, just for me to be able to read them. Instead, I delegated oversight to Rigobert, who was showing interest and aptitude in producing. Ultimately, the skits aired once a week, on Fridays, and they must have been a success because even José, whose Swahili was barely passable, would laugh throughout and quip, "These guys are funny!"

Some of our best new segments came from Rigobert. For instance, one day he came into the newsroom with a lawyer who wrote songs in his spare time. He had a guitar with him. José led them into the studio, and the man spoke to Rigobert about what music brought to his life and played some of his songs. Weeks later, I was still singing his catchy refrains, blunt as they were: *"Refuser de soigner ou de tuer, c'est la même chose."* To refuse to treat or to kill, it's the same thing. The man's name was Maene Nzulo, which I am sure of because Radio Okapi's *Fête de la musique* CD produced the following year featured two of his tracks.

Rigobert was also the person responsible for immortalizing Monsieur Pays-Capital. The man himself, Mr. Capital Cities, came in one day looking old and poor in brown thick-ribbed corduroy pants and an acrylic sweater the likes of which I hadn't seen since the early 1980s; the arms had been stretched out, which scarcely seemed possible, the man being so short.

Rigobert rolled two chairs over and set them face to face. "Canada?" he then said, in his serious radio voice.

"Ottawa," said the man, easily.

Rigobert turned over the top card. Correct. "Australia?"

"Canberra."

"Chad?"

"N'Djamena."

Monsieur Pays-Capital returned each challenge promptly and neatly. He had confidence; he had panache.

The game kept going as Rigobert gradually removed any trace of a question from his tone, as if to put them on more even ground:

"Botswana."

"Gaborone."

"Fiji."

"Suva."

Only once did Monsieur Pays-Capital answer incorrectly.

"Tonga."

"Tongatapu."

And although no listener would have ever been any the wiser, Monsieur Pays-Capital recognized the foible instantly. "No, no, sorry. It's Nuku'alofa."

"Yes," said Rigobert, with pressed lips upturned. "Nuku'alofa. That's right."

And this was what Rigobert was able to do: highlight Kindu's poignancy in the revelatory details of its people. And because he possessed this rare bent, I'd begun to think of Rigobert not as a *mwami*, a wise man, but as a curator, leading us towards an understanding of some new thing. He was like the kindly sculptor down the street who'd sold me my family of wooden elephants: Papa, Mama and baby. Eyes go here, mouth goes there. Crafting the space in between.

Although he and I had never spoken of it, one of the others — Matthieu, I think — mentioned once in passing that Mamy had known nothing about journalism when she was hired, and that Rigobert had personally trained her. I thought, *Oh my God*. How deeply offended Rigobert must have been the day I'd left Mamy in charge. I actually hoped he'd thought I was stupid.

RADIO OKAPI KINDU, AUGUST 2002

Eliane, Ulli, the head of Political Affairs and all the MONUC heads of section present in Kindu descended en masse on General Byamungu's house. They scooted past a line of boys donning the tatters of freshly ironed military fatigues, through the gate and up the scrubby turf.

The general eschewed protocol and went to the door himself. He stood sneering in the doorjamb, the remains of peanut shells and a cut of meat encrusted in his dark-pink gums. His breath reeked of stale tobacco.

Eliane, a no-nonsense woman at the best of times, for whom professionalism called for a cold form of seriousness, said (her voice hoarse from her latest pack of cigarettes): "We know you have Rigobert Yuma Ndwani. He is a UN staff member. If he is dead, give us his body. If not, let us see him."

Beside her, a satellite phone was produced from a hip, because this was a matter that couldn't be settled by a group of dusty, anxious people standing either side of a door. To resolve what was happening required higher-level diplomacy. From New York, or Geneva. From Goma.

Tango Fort took direct military orders from a man who was unlike him, a man with a nose spread flat like a boxer's, who'd once been on a path to being one of the Congo's tallest doctors.

What would patients have thought if, in another life, they'd looked up from the operating table to see Adolphe Onusumba Yembe towering over them holding a blunt and rusty scalpel in a giant's hand? But as it happened, Onusumba had chosen a different course—one that had taken him to South Africa and had turned him political. He rose through the RCD ranks in no time flat, and now, when MONUC Kindu called UNHQ for support, at just thirty-seven years of age, Onusumba was the counterpart the UN Secretary-General needed to get ahold of.

By this time, hours had passed and still Rigobert lay curled up in the cave. Was he dead? Was he alive? Without knowing anything about the current state he was in, all anyone who cared about him could do was keep busy writing reports and making calls.

When at last Annan and Onusumba established a line, Annan repeated: "Hand over Rigobert or produce his body." And perhaps Annan carried some sway with Onusumba. Or perhaps Onusumba had doctored the whole crisis so that he might scoop up his giant scalpel to come and save the day. Whatever the reason, Tango Fort, Tumba's old student—the man they once called the fighter—was summoned to Goma and told to release the UN journalist at once.

At noon, Rigobert was propped upright like a baby who couldn't hold up his own head. He would not be able to manage the most basic humanoid functions for days. Men had whittled his top and bottom in places that would never heal. He was marked. He was changed. But he was alive.

Out in the blinding light of day, Eliane carried him directly to MONUC Kindu HQ, where he stayed a full week before venturing home. His wife and their ten children were waiting.

29

"ARE WE GOING?" asked Jean-Serge, looking and sounding alarmed, as if there was a risk of me forgetting my word and leaving without him.

"No, I'm just gonna scan this. And then I'll be back. And then we can go. You'll want me to get this done," I added, giving the sheet in my hand a shake. "That is, unless you're all sick of me and want me gone."

This — the sheet in my hand — was an amendment to my contract. It had three boxes, marked: *No extension*; *Six months*; and *A year*. I ticked *Six months* — it was the one in the middle, after all. It felt like a happy medium. But between what and what? I couldn't say.

Jean-Serge and I set off just before 10 AM. Rigobert and Gabriel came, too. We first dropped off Gabriel at the Belgian development agency, La Coopération technique belge. Rigobert got out at Governor Sumaili's office ten minutes down the road. Jean-Serge and I drove onwards past the tennis court, where three men were down on their knees painting yellow and white lines. I couldn't believe how fast the work was advancing.

"What colour will your cat be?" said Jean-Serge, looking up.

I had said I wouldn't, but I had. It had become a practical matter. Fear had set in. Somewhere along the way, little things like my own shadow had begun to startle me. I would think I saw a snake but on second glance would realize it was just a stick. I was looking behind me more often and watching where I stepped—and not just on thick, sticky nights when my flip-flop would arbitrarily land on some scuttling cockroach. Mosquitoes were the worst; anything black attracted a swarm of them. I felt sick at the sight and sound.

After one of the last times I dropped Rigobert across the way, I had to honk for Benjamin to come and open the gate. He appeared after several seconds, shining in my headlights like a hunted impala. Hot as he must've been, with his hood up and skin covered, he was shivering. He rolled up his sleeves, then twisted behind him to fetch a kerosene lamp to hand me. I later left it on the table to burn out.

That same night, somewhere in the middle of it, I awoke to a noise loud enough to solicit my screams.

This was the turning point.

Benjamin came running to the window.

"Something's banging on my door!"

Benjamin said to let him in, but I refused. I had to keep the door shut. He said it was just rats, but how could he know? If I let Benjamin in as he wanted me to—and he was wrong—I would get hurt.

The noise endured and I kept on wailing. At some point, I called Louis, just to maintain a line. Time I wanted to be spending sleeping had become painfully bellicose—until ultimately imagination and reality blurred to such a point that my bedroom door began to rattle.

I watched, stock-still, as the doorknob turned.

As soon as it stopped, I went to the door—fear be damned! —unlocked it and walked down the hallway. There was no one. Feverishly, I removed the wooden bar across the front door.

Benjamin, who'd been there waiting, entered with his flash-light.

"Relax!" he begged of me. "Stop screaming. Go back to sleep. Everything is fine, Jennifer." His address of me by name felt significant: a reprimand perhaps? "I'm here. It's okay."

Eventually, I fell asleep. The next morning, I woke up yawning until my ears popped, with no recourse but to call Eva.

"What colour is the cat? Good question. White—I think."

Jean-Serge's face relaxed into tenderness such that I could suddenly picture him loving a woman or feeding a child; for the first time, I could actually imagine his sensitivity not wasted on a bottle—that was, I *could have* imagined it, had he not already been old and if the world hadn't changed in ways that had long played out against him.

He and I had had a brief conversation about it the week before:

"I'm not going to ask you to quit or even try." His personal life was none of my business. "But if you drink during work hours, you're gone."

He had replied soberly, as if he were wishing an end to his thinking and an end to his problems.

I knew Jean-Serge wanted to muster the willpower to curb his drinking, just as I knew his willpower wasn't the question. So I decided to make him our regular French news announcer.

"Your French is the best we have, and your diction is strong." This was true. "We need you for this, Jean-Serge. Can you do it?"

Jean-Serge nodded earnestly. "Yes, I can."

"Good," I'd replied, curtly for me.

And that had been my attempt at purveying structure—forcing the early return to the office of a man who couldn't keep his hands still long enough to keep them away from a flask. And when, now and then, I couldn't help but notice the reddening of his eyes, I looked the other way. I never could tolerate the sight of a bloodshot eye.

We were now approaching the airport, Jean-Serge still talking about the cat. Eva had arranged for someone—some guy—to stash it in his carry-on bag on board a MONUC flight from Kalemie.

"Let's see him, Jenni," said Jean-Serge eagerly, after he'd finished interviewing the manager of the airport authority and returned to the car.

"It's a she," I said, unzipping my purse.

The cat that wiggled out was smaller than my palm. Like a gremlin, her ears were the biggest part of her; from base to tip, they were the same size or even larger than her face. Her fur was white smoke with patches as black as her nose.

Jean-Serge said she was very cute.

I grew to love that cat and ended up naming her that—Cat—after *Breakfast at Tiffany's*. And often I sang her the Bill Withers' song "Just the Two of Us," changing the words to "Just the two of us, me and Cat." Roger was fond of her, too. Twice a day, her ears would prick up as he called out "Cat! Cat!" and set down her food. Usually, it was a rice mixture on a plastic saucer. She would pick out the sardines. Goat was a treat.

Very quickly, Cat and I established a routine. Near 8 AM, she'd start playing with the netting as I lugged myself out of bed. She'd trail me like a puppy out the door, and then greet me at the gate at noon. We'd lunch together (when sometimes, shamelessly, I let her eat off the table), after which we'd nap—or else I'd nap while she frisked around the bed. I'd return to the office somewhere between one thirty and two and stay there until at least ten o'clock. I'd come home to find her meowing for food—which we didn't have—nipping at my ankles.

So there were two mouths to feed now. But I did sleep better.

THE MORNING AFTER I discovered that the showers at the MONUC guesthouse ran hot water, which felt downright motivating, like it could change everything, I came out of my office sometime after eight thirty to find Gabriel slumped over, looking drawn and battered as if he were about to sigh and say, "That's it, I give up."

"Oh, you're all here," I said, looking at Mamy and meaning, "Even you, Little Miss Late." "You're so quiet. How unlike all of you!"

Sadala said it first. Which, regardless of what came after, could only have been a coincidence. "Jérôme Ngongo is dead."

José began shaking his head wildly. "No! No, no, no…"

"Jérôme," said Rigobert wistfully.

"*Vraiment…*"

José remarked that Mamy, who had just returned from vacation in Kinshasa, was the last of them to have seen Jérôme alive.

Our Jérôme? As in, Dialogue entre Congolais *Jérôme?* I'd seen the emails but hadn't read them properly. The language had been too flowery, too insider and all mixed up in Lingala, with every second or third sentence evoking God or eternity or the soul.

I asked what had happened, only to get an answer that was frustratingly factual in the place of a lie that might have made more sense. Apparently, Jérôme had gone home the night before, after hosting DEC, to his wife and their two young daughters. Then he went into cardiac arrest. And died. He was thirty-five years old, said José. Sadala said he could have been president.

In a short time, crowds amassed at the MONUC Security container downstairs, engendering a poem of *Okapi Messages*. Kinshasa produced special programming, and we in Kindu prepared a special *décrochage*. Officiated services were quickly arranged in Kalemie, Bukavu, Mbandaka and Goma. William

Lacy Swing, the Special Representative of the Secretary-General, presided over a multi-faith service in MONUC HQ's courtyard, which, now having the capacity, Radio Okapi streamed live.

A day or so later, we walked from the newsroom to chiming bells. Mamy, sniffling, reached forward to place her hand in mine. At the steps of the church on the corner, the officiating minister excused himself from a conversation with the mayor and Marie-France to drape his sleeve of silk around José's shoulders. José wept openly. It was a public memorial, running about an hour, including scripture, orations, an organ and a choir. I sat on a pew without a thought for how I'd gotten here or why the death of someone I barely knew hurt me so deeply.

In the days and weeks following Jérôme's death, I reacted angrily each time someone off the street suggested something sinister had befallen him. It would start off fine, with harmless condolences and prattle; and then, *whammo!* they'd slip in words seeking confirmation of whichever rumour they'd heard and had chosen to believe, of poisoning, state-sponsored assassination, HIV/AIDS … even witchcraft. Over and over, until I was blue in the face, I'd sermonize: "Don't give me such nonsense. Rumours are disrespectful — and to Jérôme, of all people!"

I thought about Mamy's poisoned grandmother, the monster crocodile that ate fishermen for sport… about society's general atmosphere of mistrust and people's penchant for determinism, where accidents and the misfortune of a string of bad decisions were virtually unheard of. And I thought I understood.

In Kindu, you never heard of anyone having a doctor's or dentist's appointment. One day, Matthieu proposed a story about an itinerant ophthalmologist coming to town. "He specializes in cataracts. You know, when people —"

"I know. I know what they are. We have them, too."

Then, feeling quite pleased with myself, I said: "So I suppose people think it's a miracle when this guy comes out of nowhere and suddenly they can see again."

Rigobert looked up, his face characteristically appreciative. "No, they know he's an ophthalmologist and not a diviner. They just think he's good."

HAVING DECIDED TO extend my contract, I was due for another vacation. It seemed sensible that this time Louis come to Africa. We could go to the beach, see the view from Table Mountain. Go on safari.

When I made the suggestion, Louis drew a loud huff. "What? Are you crazy?" He said: "You might have your cushy UN job, Jen-Jen." But he'd have to keep slogging away if his show was going to be a success.

I sighed. No was no, I supposed, but didn't he realize that Kenya was Kenya? His show would work—I was sure of it— but when again would we get the chance to see the Maasai Mara? I very gingerly broached the subject for a second time.

Another army of bugs had recently hatched, these on the smaller side, like ants with wings. They crawled, they trudged, they footslogged, all to reach the promise of whatever it was that was attracting them to partially obscured light. Poor little self-destructive creatures. The wood was way worse than the glass. It never fit right from the start.

A sudden light tap on the door brought my feet off the desk to the floor. "Just a sec," I said to Louis, as the door pushed in. I flicked up my eyes and smiled. It was Gabriel.

"Ah, you're still here," I said. Then: "Hey. I'm talking to Louis, *mon ami*" (a conveniently ambiguous term), "the one in Toronto I told you guys about. Here —" I stretched the receiver as far as its twisted cord would take it. "Say hi."

Gabriel's side was to me, making it impossible to tell whether he actually wanted to speak to Louis. *But why wouldn't he?* He seemed happy enough when he took the receiver, nodding at my smiling face and saying very clearly, *"Oui, allô, c'est Gabriel."*

Then something changed. I realized at once what must've happened, why the conversation had turned. And I hated myself. Gabriel was good about it, though, still polite. He even attempted to smile after handing me back the phone and before clumsily whispering that he'd "just be in the newsroom."

For a second, I stared at the limpness of my hand. I was mad at myself, but *shit!*

I put the phone back to my mouth. "Louis, what did you say to him?"

"Nothing! I just asked him if he was the one you told me about who imitated a woman on air. Told him I thought it was hilarious."

I knew it, I thought. Goddamn it, I knew it. "*Jesus*, Louis, why'd you have to go and say that? He felt really bad about that. And now... Now not only does he know that I told you... *Ahh!* He must think we were laughing about him behind his back. *God*, you *never think.*"

"Jeez, Jen, I'm sorry, but don't you think you're being a little bit over-sensitive here? He seemed pretty cool about it to me."

"No! He wasn't!" You don't know him like I know him. He's extremely conscientious, and sensitive. And capable! He really thinks about the consequences of what he writes. Way more... He's way more professional than most journalists I've met... outside of Africa, actually! And now he's going to feel... *denigrated*... like, like we think he's some kind of a joke."

Louis said he was in no mood to hear me go on about my Africans and our little radio. "What do you want me to say? I said I was sorry—if somehow I upset the guy."

It was too much. Or it ought to have been.

"Nevermind," I said finally, with an air of resignation. "It's my fault." Which it was, for having betrayed Gabriel's trust. "I never should have told you."

"Yeah, well, you did," said Louis shortly. "Anyway, can we get back to the document? It would be great if you could send that to me tonight. Do you think you can do that, Jen-Jen?"

WHY HAD I moved to the Congo? Was I running away from something? If so, I didn't want to think about it. I was exceedingly privileged—I could suddenly see that so clearly—and it sickened me to think that with all I'd been given I could still be dissatisfied. As if—nope!—a loving home, meaningful relationships, clear job prospects and security weren't enough; no, not for Jennifer.

It was late now. Had Gabriel left? I was wondering, when he poked his head in to announce his departure. I started to apologize, but he wouldn't hear of it (which brought on new awkwardness).

As I shut down the computer, two things suddenly occurred to me, both of which should have been obvious from day one: One, how little I knew—for a fact—about the lives of a group of people who, despite us not really socializing or confiding in each other, I'd come to care for very deeply. (How could you explain that?) And two, the journalists didn't need me to teach them anything; who was *I* to teach *them?*

The *chef d'antenne* position was a go-between for MONUC, the radio and its staff. My role was about getting the journalists what they needed to do their work: feeding them UN stories, securing their equipment, fixing seats on UN flights. Like how I'd been able to help Matthieu finally get his UN contract. He'd been so happy about that. With tears in his eyes, he'd thrown his hands on my startlingly bony shoulders and said, "Ah, Jenni! *Maman!* I love you so much!"

30

ONE NIGHT IN MID-AUGUST: it was just another night for us in Kindu, nothing out of the ordinary. I would have just been arriving home to Cat nipping puckishly at my ankles, when across the border in Burundi, throngs of soldiers and civilians wresting traditional arms, small-bore bombs and gas encircled the Gatumba refugee camp, where hundreds of Congolese families had sought safe haven, many after the Bukavu crisis. Children were woken from the long breaths of sleep to witness their fathers and mothers doused with gas. The assailants went ahead and incinerated them and many others, murdering 166 people within the space of two hours.

The next day at dawn, when the news came out, the journalists read everything they could get their hands on. The survivors all said the same thing: that the perpetrators had ring-fenced Burundians and Congolese ethnicities other than the Banyamulenges—they were the targets. Sadala, Gabriel and Rigobert were all keyed up, as if the news had shocked them, yet for all their "Eh! Eh! Eh!"s, it seemed as if they weren't nearly as outraged as they ought to have been. Perhaps the worst of it was that the Burundian soldiers stationed outside the camp had not acted to try to stop the slaughter. If that wasn't enough, the camp was just three and a half kilometres from South Kivu, yet neither the Congolese army nor any of the UN soldiers on patrol had heard (or had signalled that they'd heard) anything.

Almost immediately, fighters from the Hutu rebel group Forces for National Liberation, formed almost twenty years earlier in Burundi, said they were behind the attack. The FNL was one of the undesirables that the MONUC DDRRR section was seeking to disarm, demobilize, repatriate—and yes, reintegrate and resettle, if anyone would have them. The international news-wires used the words "claimed responsibility," as if there was any chance that the assailants might have to assume responsibility for the crimes they'd just committed. It felt obvious no one would pay—not with the kind of impunity that left even a man like Sadala (who'd never been blasé about any form of social injustice) pretty close to just throwing up his hands.

I WAS SOMEWHAT SURPRISED the day Maniema's vice-governor in charge of finance and administration left a message on my cellphone. He said he'd like to see Sadala Shabani. I didn't call him back straight away, because we were working to deadline.

At 3:30 PM, Tumba came into my office:

"Jennifer, His Excellency Vice-Governor Masudi Mendes called, asking to see Sadala urgently."

I cringed. Where I came from, a journalist would never have allowed herself to sound sycophantic. "Mendes? Again? Well, he'll just have to wait. He should know we have work to do. We can't just drop everything because he calls."

I expected Tumba to go back into the newsroom. Or at least say something. Instead, he just stood there.

"Yes?"

"I think… maybe… it's better if you talk to him."

"Is he still on the line?"

"No."

"Well, then!" I sighed dramatically. "If he calls back, just pass him to me and I'll deal with it."

And so we carried on until, despite my best efforts, our last script was done and dusted at five minutes past four.

"Anybody need anything?" I tried. Then: "All right, Sadala —" I rolled my eyes, as if to soften the concession while reminding myself that maintaining a good relationship with local authorities was first and foremost a matter of security. "Let's go see the vice-governor. Let's go see what's so damn urgent."

In the end, Sadala, Tumba and I all went. We pulled alongside what ought to have been a curb in front of Mendes's one-level residence, which was long, like a strip mall. On the lawn, a man in military fatigues stooped under the weight of one of the guns that Mamy had been talking about. Stupidly, I said hello. Two more armed guards stood at the entrance; several others were just inside. *(M16s?)* With nowhere to go, no place to sidestep, my shoulder accidentally brushed against someone's gummy arm.

"Excuse me," I said, because it couldn't be helped.

I twisted back, still moving forward, to cast a surreptitious look at Sadala and Tumba but regrettably had no time to get my message across, for Vice-Governor Mendes was arriving in the living room from somewhere deeper back. I was caught off guard by how gargantuan he appeared at this range, in his domain.

The living room possessed a boxy wide-armed sofa and chair set in an ostentatious leopard print. The walls were white and smelled of fresh paint. Mendes took one of the chairs, imposing his forearms one on each flank like roadblocks. I sat sandwiched between Sadala and Tumba, whose weight was dragging me to his side.

At first there was silence, Mendes's mouth a tight line.

"Hello," I said, I hoped graciously.

"Good day, My Excellency," said Tumba.

One of the security guards coughed over whatever form of verbal reception Mendes deemed fit.

"You're late," he scolded, glowering at us.

"We're not late," I retorted. "We didn't have an appointment. And we were unavailable until now."

Mendes didn't argue the point. "I want to question Sadala over the false and injurious news story he reported yesterday. Had he approached me before reporting such a lie, I surely would have told him that the allegations are unfound—"

"I'm sorry—" My voice cut in sharply. *(Too sharply?)* "Just to be clear, you're referring to the story about the territorial administrators who've been suspended from their functions?" Sadala's story had been four lines at most. I hadn't thought of them as contentious.

"They haven't been suspended." Mendes's brow was furrowed with anger. "The governor and I are simply investigating and deliberating their functions."

"They claim they've been suspended."

"It's not true," said Mendes hotly. "And I demand that Sadala explain himself."

Sadala shimmied to the edge of his section of the sofa. "Sir, I..."

Mendes snapped his head, envenoming a look of hate. "I didn't authorize you to speak."

I suddenly became aware of a distortion in my breath, before dropping my hand to my thigh. It was clammy. "I think Sadala is best... *positioned* to talk about his own story."

"Yes, he is," said Mendes smugly. "In my office, this evening."

For the briefest of moments, my body shut down. *How—when*—had the conversation turned so badly? Three armed men stood an arm's length away. They looked terribly young, and soulless. Those dead eyes. *Would they shoot?* No, they wouldn't shoot. Not right here in Mendes's own living room.

Would they?

"It's out of the question that Sadala will come see you this evening. I am responsible for Radio Okapi, and if you wish, you're always welcome to come to my office to speak to me about anything you'd like to bring up about any of our stories—" I had run out of breath five words shy of the end of my sentence—"no matter who the reporter is." My mouth had gone dry.

"Madame," said Mendes loudly, after too long a moment. "You may be a foreigner, but Sadala is Congolese and he answers to me."

"No, he doesn't! Not when it comes to the radio—which is democratic, and works under the guise of freedom of the press. When he is working for the radio, Sadala answers to me, and to Kinshasa."

"How dare you! Lecturing me on democracy! He will come see me this evening. Or he will be arrested."

The underside of my thighs sensed Tumba squirming; although our bodies had been touching the whole time, I'd forgotten he was there. "I'm afraid Sadala won't come to see you this evening. Or any evening. And we're leaving now."

Tumba and Sadala rose. So I guess I did, too. The next thing I knew, we were climbing into the car and the automatic door lock was making its gruff swallowing sound.

"Oh, boy," I croaked as we drove away. "This isn't good, is it? Are you guys okay? I ask you, what was I supposed to do? I had to say that."

"En tout cas," said Tumba from the back seat.

I turned my body to where Sadala sat, cross-belted, and told him we'd work something out. "But you're not going to go see him—out of the question! It's not gonna happen." My mind was running away from me, imagining Sadala trapped inside Kindu's central prison. In a grey cement tomb with no windows… Or maybe *one* window, high up like in a public toilet, barred like in a jail. The whiff of festering wounds, urine and breath that smelled nauseatingly fruity from the breaking down of fat. And Sadala reduced to a thing of putrid, emaciated misery, stinking up a paper-thin mattress on the floor. There were those new mattresses that MONUC had given out, but they'd looked cheap, mediocre—not good enough for Sadala. They'd be dirty by now.

It felt strange to be standing in the newsroom, hearing Sadala tell a *tracasseries*-style story in the first person, knowing we weren't going to cover it. Mamy and Rigobert had stopped listening to him and started a side conversation with Tumba in Swahili. And of all the faces Matthieu had worn, the tightness around his eyes and him biting his lower lip was new and not nice to see.

There was just one thing to do. I did it. I went to see Marie-France. If nothing else, her friendship with the governor's chief administrator could help.

"Yes, we have a problem, a definite problem," she said. I was close to finishing the story. "Let me call Jim. We need to plan for this evening, and Sadala should not go home tonight. Security! Security! Security!" She picked up the phone, but with no one responding, reached for the Motorola radio on her desk: "Sierra One, Sierra One. This is Hotel Oscar. Over." Static filled the room. "Sierra One, Sierra One. This is Hotel Oscar. Over."

"Hotel Oscar, this is Sierra One. Send your message. Over."

"Sierra One, Sierra One"—she hung up the phone—"we have an urgent matter to discuss with Romeo Oscar. Please come to my office—now. Over."

Within minutes, Jim was with us, his eyes obscured by his photochromic lenses, seeing right through Marie-France, and right through me, I suspected. Pacing and fidgeting, her hands on her hips, Marie-France recounted facts I couldn't remember having told her, such that I had to remind myself that she hadn't actually been with us at the time.

At her first true break, Jim spoke up with a soundless imperturbable wave. "I'm sure there will be no problem." Jim was never one to get flustered easily—confidence maybe but more likely something else. "But let us lodge this gentleman tonight at the Bolivian camp—simply as a precautionary measure. No harm in that."

Marie-France immediately nodded agreement. "Yes, good," she said, "so let's do that, then," in an undertone that seemed to claim the idea. "I'll make the calls."

FOR ALL I COULD GO ON about the importance of keeping our *décrochage* to a standard beyond reproach, Matthieu came into my office later that day with a script about a public health seminar on getting a *Rhabdoviridae* virus from canines, and I said, "That's fine, that's good, record it."

At six o'clock, I jumped up, keys in hand, and called Sadala's name. Outside, the sky was a mix of blue, yellow and red reflections on a white canvas of suvs; by the time we'd reached the car, it was purple fading to black. We advanced down the main street, the small hairs on our arms raised in the air conditioning that was turned up too high. Sadala sat listening to the national Swahili newscast. I listened too, understanding the most important bit: that there was no point in me saying anything. I could say I was sorry, but what for? He would end up trying to make *me* feel better, when I was about the last person to have anything to be worried about.

We stopped in front of the ghost of Sadala's punch buggy. Sadala got out. Tracy Chapman was singing. "Baby, can I hold you tonight..."

The engine idled.

Sadala returned to the car after a time and sent a quilted drawstring duffle bag plunging into the space by his feet. By this time, the modern urban anthem with the words "Nelly, I love you" had changed the tone considerably.

"All set?" It appeared that it was. "Was your wife there?"

"Mmm, she was there. I told her about Mendes and *ça va*."

"She's not worried, I hope?" I'd met her once. Only once. It had been a month or two back. I had invited the journalists, with their wives, over to my house. The Uruguayans had made us pizza, and Bérénice had helped with the arrangements and hosting. So she had still been there. Thinking on it now, I realized that had been very good of her. To help.

"No, she's fine. I told her it's just for one night and I'll be home tomorrow."

Sadala was funny. He could get so angry over politics, but when certain activities associated with those politics touched him personally, how starkly his behaviour opposed the world I knew best, a world where people insisted they would never give up the slightest shred of themselves, where anger trumped fear and sadness, no contest. Anger was just so much *cooler:* Throw a hissy fit, blame *that* guy and *that* guy for your problems. Be mad. Feel entitled.

I honked at the gate of the Bolivian camp, and after a moment, a darkly clothed figure of an average size appeared through the bars. Something about him — or about the common man he represented — made me reflect again on the spectre of anger in a world where all forms of life had to fight to survive. *Just think,* I said to myself. If poverty didn't get you, if disease didn't get you — if war didn't get you — how stupid would you feel when you were dead and buried six feet under if you could suddenly somehow realize your own anger had done you in?

THAT NIGHT, what I feared most came true when Mendes showed up in my dreams, scaring me so much he had to be real. Harm would come to my friend. And it would be my fault.

The next day, as early as I could (which felt as late as I could leave it), I rang Sadala at the MONUC guesthouse, who said he was fine—just like that, somewhat pat, as if I'd simply asked him how he was. I let out a long sigh that sent my head back and thanked my lucky stars, as if it were the stars that made our decisions overnight.

Cat and I went out into the living room. "Not now, Cat," I muttered.

If Sadala wasn't to bunk with the Bolivians forever, the *responsable* had to sort out the mess. I quickly got ready, picked up Sadala and brought him to the newsroom. I called Mendes's office, but he wasn't there. His secretary told me he'd caught an early flight to Kinshasa on business. Lucky stars again.

"Where are you going?" said Rigobert, seeing the keys in my hand.

"Governor Sumaili's."

I dropped off Rigobert—and Gabriel—and then ended up waiting outside the governor's office for ages. When at last he received me, he did so courteously, inviting me to take a seat on a padded wooden chair that was still warm from his last meeting. Our seated positions very neatly split the difference of our standing height. Compared to Mendes, Koloso Sumaili was short and dumpy.

After hello, I lifted my chin and thanked him for making time to see me. It was true the circumstances were different from the last time we'd met. That had been just weeks ago, at a party Sumaili had held to mark his wedding anniversary. I'd been surprised my name had made it onto the guest list but attended and danced with strangers. Sumaili himself hadn't asked.

"I feel very badly over the… *situation*… that… transpired between Radio Okapi and the vice-governor. And of course I would tell him if he were here…" Cautious not to be too wordy, I touched on the radio's overarching goals and methodology, treading very gingerly over the issue of the freedom of the press. I didn't apologize—though part of me wanted to—because I didn't know how to say sorry without conceding anything.

For his part, Sumaili was positively epigrammatic. "I understand. There's no problem here."

And that was it: with one giant outbreath, and the relieved expression that went with it, I'd managed to deflate any further arguments—just by, essentially, showing my face.

"But the next time you treat a matter directly related to the workings of the government, I would ask that you contact us for our version of the facts—before airing your story. For balance."

So I wasn't to be let off entirely scot-free.

Sumaili escorted me to the door. He didn't seem eager to get rid of me, not exactly. But he was wearing a metallic-faced watch and glanced at it now. "We have no problem," he reiterated and extended his hand.

It was now I realized I was forgetting something. "Oh wait!" I said, rummaging through my purse. "I brought you something…"

Seconds later, the governor's fingers were wrapped around a Radio Okapi pen.

"You can keep it," I said.

Sumaili clicked its spring twice with his thumb. His barely-there eyebrows arched slightly.

That he hadn't fawned over it, that he hadn't made more of my gesture, made me want to snatch the pen back up and say, "Nevermind! I'll just take that back, thanks." Didn't he know how in demand those pens were?

Once I was safely back in the car, I pictured myself swiping the pen right out of the governor's hand and running off with it. Which had me laughing loudly to myself.

31

AFTER WHAT HAD HAPPENED with Mendes, I couldn't help but think about how I could have handled things better, how lucky we were and how wrong I'd been to think the Okapis weren't exposed like the RTNC correspondent I'd met by chance that day at Camp Makuta. Was some little thing like a UN radio check going to stop anyone from attacking the journalists if they really wanted to? Would they actually stop and say to themselves, "If I throw this guy in prison or even have him killed, the international community is gonna come and get me"? Radio Okapi had had its honeymoon phase; that was over now. Innately, I knew there was real reason for concern, that we were operating in the realm of equipoise, mitigation at best. The thought of it terrified me.

A map with a special name was leading Radio Okapi into the future. *La pérennisation* (as in, sustainability) envisaged MONUC's demise, either through the lapse of its UN Security Council mandate or because the Congolese government had rescinded its welcome. That day was unlikely to come soon but still needed to be planned for. On the editorial front, Fondation Hirondelle was spearheading a process of baby steps. The two Yves, the triumvirate and Saint Étienne were busy sketching up September's new national programming schedule, known as *la nouvelle grille.* Our new-format *décrochage* was part of that. There were also new segments: Okapi *this,* Okapi *that.* My favourite was a Q&A called *Professeur Okapi,* with a wonderfully *r*-rolling Laval University–educated, Kinshasa-based professor who had a way with words and an answer for virtually everything.

Talking about the triumvirate, Leonard was promoted to deputy chief editor. The announcement was made in *OKAPI exPress,* the internal newsletter produced by Fondation Hirondelle, which we'd wait for every Friday night, even though it sometimes didn't come out until well into Saturday.

"It's great about Leonard," I heard Sadala say. Tumba agreed he was very good, to which Gabriel added, *"Vraiment."*

One day one of them — someone in the team — would be named *chef d'antenne* for Kindu. In other words, our goal was my obsolescence, even if none of us ever saw it quite that way.

Because Sadala kept insisting that Étienne's *Question of the Day* segment was extremely popular in Bunia, and sure to be mandated into the new-format *décrochage,* I said, "Fine, then. Why wait?"

We started our own daily question-and-answer segment, which I called *Question from a Listener.* To do so, I drafted a public service announcement soliciting listeners' questions, which we then engaged to answer, *not ourselves* but by interviewing the most apposite official or local personality. The author of each question answered on air would receive a MONUC T-shirt or a Radio Okapi pen, so long as we had them in supply.

"Jenni?" said Jean-Serge one afternoon. He was sitting at one of the computers with his shoulder to the screen, reading a handwritten letter. Since we'd started our new *Question from a Listener* segment, Jean-Serge would rarely come upstairs empty-handed. "This one's a good one," he said now, with an arcane smile, shaking the paper as if an edge had caught fire. "Somebody wants to know who painted all the tree bottoms white, and why. I think we should do this one. We can ask Governor Sumaili. It would put him on the spot—to comment on Kabila."

"Good idea!" We'd been looking for a way to freshen the story. For the last few weeks, the protracted presence of the presidential guard (GSSP for short) in Kindu was our sole means of broaching the topic. Of course, the GSSP had become a story in its own right, the sad truth being that the acronym had replaced FARDC in almost every last *tracasseries* script we wrote.

Sooner or later, it was all fair game for Peter and his disguised civic education skits. One Friday when their segment was on, I ran back into the newsroom to fetch something and thought Matthieu was listening like everyone else, because he wasn't wearing his earphones. But then he saw me and pointed at his computer screen: *"Maman* Jennifer, I found two women for my streeters!"

"Good!" I said. I was always after the journalists to seek out women for their on-the-street interviews; I hated the idea of us broadcasting the views of five men back to back. *(We're just perpetuating the notion that only men can have political opinions! We're probably doing more harm than good. People'd be better off if we just... threw this whole tape in the garbage!)*

I walked over to Matthieu and looked at the waveforms on his screen, as if I could actually make out the voices on sight, as if I were reading sheet music. "Is one of them Bijou again?"

"No—real women!" He made a face. "Two of them!"

I made a face, too—a sort of good-humoured eye roll. I moved away towards my office, calling back over my shoulder, "Don't tell Bijou you don't think she's a real woman!"

NOT LONG AFTER we'd started our new *décrochage*—and in the end my modifications were few: we cut two songs to make room for Kinshasa's daily press review and cheated a few minutes to flesh out the French and Swahili newscasts—Marie-France appeared at the door.

"Get ready for a guest!"

"What guest?" I said. "Who?"

A representative from the British embassy in Kinshasa was in town; if I ever knew why, I instantaneously forgot. But he wanted to sit in on one of our broadcasts. If permissible, he'd said.

"Wowza!" said José, loudly.

We couldn't have said no (though we wouldn't have, anyway), because at the time the U.K. government was one of Radio Okapi's major funders. We always prepared our *décrochage* diligently *(Otherwise, what was the point?)*, but it was fair to say we prepared our program extra-diligently that day. Rigobert took on a coordinating role: I'd also just designated him our regular host, because I knew he'd set a good example, and because old habits die hard. I'd come to believe that day one mattered, that it was important to get things right from the start, so that what came after might find an allowance for forgiveness. And for once, I tried not to be overly neurotic about the whole thing—until I came upon a story Matthieu had written about an elementary school reopening, and there was no question that I had to call his name.

"Who wrote this?"

"I did!" His tone was sharp, though it hadn't been a snap, not exactly. Matthieu was incapable of true snapping. "What's wrong with it?"

Cautiously, I slid my eyes over his shoulder, as if to make one final check. "Nothing's wrong with it," I said finally. "It's simple, clear… direct—even thoughtful."

Matthieu's face relaxed, as if he'd suddenly lost ten years. "I told you to keep correcting me. I told you I was listening."

I smiled and guffawed affectionately. But this wasn't enough for him.

"Didn't I? Didn't I?"

I laughed; you had to laugh. Lovely Matthieu. "Yes," I said. "Yes, you did."

THE BRITISH DIPLOMAT turned up just before five, wearing a bespoke suit and leather-soled shoes. His cheeks were rosy red, and he was too quiet to be anything but shy. I led him into the studio, showing surprising forethought by asking about his family. His face glowed. He had a daughter named Kate and a picture of her on his phone, which at the time was quite rare.

At five o'clock, as Kinshasa began its newly expanded five-minute hourly newscast, he put his phone in the pocket of his jacket and sat discreetly in the place I'd indicated, between José and me, eyes straight ahead. I would have asked for his opinion on things—things about our show—but he was a diplomat and wasn't about to disclose anything adverse. So I tried to read his mind. Several smiles, plus a look of active listening, which is normally hard to fake.

Étienne had said it: eight songs in an hour-long program would help with pacing. He was right *(darn it!)*. Still, I missed our old Maniema song, the one we used to always play in the middle of the program. I said this to José, but he just laughed quickly. It wouldn't have meant anything to him; he didn't share the memory. Kasmu would have agreed.

Mamy strolled in just as techno-soukous star Awilo Longomba was singing "Karolina." José and I were chair-dancing. Soon, Mamy was out of the studio and Jean-Serge was in—more smiles—before greeting our English dignitary with exceeding courtesy: if there was such a misguided thing as a set way to speak to a European, Jean-Serge would have known it. I'd heard he'd once been married to a white Belgian woman. (They had a child? That she took back to Belgium? Who had told me this? Sometimes I thought I was dreaming up these things.)

"You ready to go with your *Question of the Day?*"

"You know, Jenni—" Jean-Serge's voice carried over my head, though ostensibly he was talking to me. "People on the street stop me to ask how they can get their questions on air, or to ask if I've received the ones they've already left for me at the security gate."

"You're doing a great job, Jean-Serge."

José chose James Taylor's "Handy Man" as our last song, as if he could somehow see into the future, to this day when I'd be looking back. Rigobert could never manage to get his tongue around the name. "Jams Tie-lor," he would say.

When the song was over, Rigobert said goodbye and José handed back the signal to Kinshasa. I stood, trying not to look proud. "So, there you go. Another program completed." I wanted to ask for feedback; and I guess in my way I was. "It certainly wasn't the smoothest…"

I had just told a lie, which was all right, so long as the diplomat didn't tell one, too. "Frankly," he said, his eyes looking clearer, "I am genuinely impressed. I've actually been inside the BBC studios witnessing a similar exercise, and I must say this production was every bit as strong as that—in all aspects."

I paused a moment. I didn't want to come across as too— I don't know—surprised or… *eager* for his approval.

"That's nice to hear," I said finally. "And it's certainly nice of you to say."

"I mean it sincerely."

I think I danced out of the room. *As good as the BBC! Wait until I tell everyone,* I thought. Victory!

32

IT WAS VACATION TIME AGAIN, and all through it—in Canada, where it had grown blustery and cold, the stuff of chapped lips —Louis spoke of the day I'd be home for good. He said for all the time we'd been together, it was great that *at last!* Jen-Jen had money. I couldn't disagree but emphasized the irony that my newfound means were coming from the one job I'd ever had that wasn't about the money. Money: I'd spent more of it in two weeks in Toronto than I had over three months in Kindu. "A cash hemorrhage," I called it.

My first week back in Kindu, it rained and rained, water dripping off the tips of droopy palms. Damp husks. The ground was soppy again, but still no oranges, no mangoes. The rickety old train ran at its rickety old pace: I didn't love Simba like Rigobert and Jean-Serge loved it but thought it tasted okay for beer.

One Sunday morning in November—it was very early, as always—I woke up aching all over. Cat was kneading my face. I pushed aside the mosquito net to let her out, and she darted up the netting to its top, sinking it down like a hammock.

At 11 AM, I lugged my throbbing body into work. Matthieu was typing at the keyboard.

"Jenni! I'm sending Jocelyne the introduction to my magazine story on the latest WHO rape statistics. You know, the story that talks about the number of boys who are raped? She wants to use it later today for her best-of-weekend programming."

"That's good," I said, insipidly.

Matthieu jumped up to grab my arm. "You're yellow!"

"Matthieu, I'm not good."

His fingers shot to my forehead. They were cold, or I was hot. "Jenni, please!" he said, with his long-suffering pout. "Go home and rest."

I soon saw that Benjamin was worried, too. I hadn't even stopped the car in the drive before he was charging to hoist me out. "Madame! What do you have?"

I just needed some sleep, I said, shivering in the squally rain, warm like the Bolivians' showers. I hadn't been to those showers since before vacation—when I'd nicked myself with a plastic razor and fainted over the blood. The cleaning ladies had found me passed out, with the water still running and me, naked as a jaybird.

Benjamin made me promise to go see a doctor. I said I would, *after* sleep.

I must have tossed and turned for more than an hour. Cat thought we were playing. I'd get up and put her outside the door, but then she'd scratch it until I let her back in. I watched her climb to the top of my mosquito net and saw the holes she'd previously left. I knew it was my fault for not disciplining her. I thought: *Lariam or no Lariam, a girl is bound to get malaria at this rate.*

Which of course explained it.

Benjamin heard me come to the door and pulled his jacket up over our heads to shield us from the rain. He draped me over the steering wheel, and soon the windshield wipers were whooshing at full speed. The Chinese Level II hospital was about nine-tenths of the way to the airport, down a dirt cul-de-sac. I turned. The hospital was in sight, though the struggle of two wiper blades against a gushing stream made it hard to see anything beyond a horseshoe of prefab containers. I got out of the car and rushed inside... then went back out and in another way. Water rushed down my face. Eventually, I found a small red cross marking the main entrance, which led to the corridor of another section of containers. Here, a spectacled Chinese man in a white lab coat with a stethoscope around his neck happened to be walking in my direction. He looked up with mild curiosity but didn't respond to English or French.

At the reception desk, two young nurses in full makeup and high heels loitered near a telephone. A third woman sat behind the counter, using the Internet.

Suddenly, a second male doctor approached. "No doctor's note?" From Dr. Francis, he meant; it was UN policy that sick staff see him first. When I told him, no, no doctor's note—it was Sunday, after all—he said, "You must come back tomorrow."

I now became hysterical.

The doctor turned away but must have passed on some manner of instruction because one of the nurses put her hand on my shoulder and led me to a small room off the corridor, where two small cots grazed the walls. The nurse nudged me onto the closest one. Then a needle out of nowhere jabbed me into tears. With my arm feeling like a ton of bricks, I used my tongue to lick them dry. They tasted like salt—and something else. Disease, I feared.

The diagnosis came back as cerebral malaria. Bad case, said the doctor. The nurse surged a second needle deep into my butt cheek, then lifted my hand: she was looking for a vein on its dorsal side and had to slap it several times to find one. It took her five or six attempts—replicated on both hands—before, clearly frustrated, she reverted to her first try.

Once pinned into place, the IV felt terribly uncomfortable. Beyond reason, I yearned to rip it out.

The nurse was good at her job (and went so far as to fluff my pillow). But I just wanted Mom. I wiped away tears to mime a telephone. The nurse helped me to stand, as redness collected in the tube jutting out from me. I panicked, but then the nurse set my hand flat beneath the drip bag and the tube ran clear again.

Rather than dialling my parents, I dialled my sister, thinking she'd take the news better. In the end, my brother-in-law was the only one home, which, when I thought about it afterwards, was one more person removed and just as well.

I punched in my PIN again. Louis answered on the fifth ring.

"Malaria? Wow. I thought you were on drugs for that."

"Yeah, well…" My voice sopped with the pity I was hoping he'd bestow upon me. "I'm in the hospital."

"In Kindu?"

"Yeah. A UN one."

There was a pause. "Oh, my poor sick little Jen in Africa."

I whinged—just enough, I thought, to garner more attention. But Louis's patience for my theatrics had long ago worn thin.

"I told you you had to take better care of yourself. I told you you should get your cook to make you a proper meal in the evenings. All you ever eat are those crap french fries."

"Yeah," I said pathetically. "I know."

"Are you going to be okay? What did the doctors say?"

"I don't know. They're Chinese and we can't communicate."

"Jen, maybe you should leave the Chinese and see the Africans. They know about this stuff."

I liked his point and liked him for making it, but said no anyway. "They seem to know what they're doing here. They have me on IV. They've given me shots. It's all good."

I could hear the rise and fall of Louis's breath on the other end. "Go rest," he finally said. We agreed I'd call him back later. Tomorrow, we said.

AT DAWN THE NEXT DAY, my temperature had fallen from 40.7 degrees Celsius to 38.6, such that mere existence was no longer taxing. Within minutes, I fell back asleep.

When my eyes opened again, a wide, round and earthily red-tinged face was centimetres from mine. "Ah, *ma belle!*" Mamy was sitting on a chair pulled up beside my cot. I writhed around to see Gabriel, Sadala and Matthieu crouched down.

"You're all here."

At the sound of my voice, Marie-France came rushing into the room. "Ah, there you go! Good! You're awake! You're our third malaria victim this week, you know."

She and Gabriel took a seat on the empty cot, causing it to dip sharply. Mamy moved from the chair to steal a corner of my bed. "If you're thirsty," she said, motioning towards a box of apple juice on the night table. "I got it from the South Africans."

Matthieu stroked my hand.

Marie-France had more to say (of course), though goodbye came relatively quickly, prompting the others to stir. She must have been their ride.

"Don't worry," said Gabriel reassuringly. "We have everything covered. I ran today's meeting and we've distributed all the stories."

I lifted my hand – being sure to keep it flat and even – and set it on Gabriel's bare arm. "I'm not worried," I said tenderly. "But it had better be good, because I'll be listening at five!"

ON MY SECOND DAY RECOVERING, I looked out the door and spotted two South Asian men in the same pale-blue and white-striped pyjamas I was wearing, one of them snacking on a spring roll. So there were other patients; I knew that. What I hadn't realized was the *food*.

I got up, careful to keep my hand low and flat, and wheeled my drip bag into the hallway, where more pyjamas were coming from a container at the end. I turned and walked hopefully and — *Thank you, God* — it was a meal room. Another person in faded blue-and-white stripes was just finishing up. Beside him lay a compartmentalized tray — untouched — of lush green broccoli florets, white fluffy rice... some kind of marinated meat. And a spring roll. I approached and read *Bakody* on a sticker pasted to its side, followed by what I was told was my bed number in Chinese.

I sat and for a moment gazed upon the tray as if it were a present dropped from the sky. Then I took a bite. The tray had had time to cool. I took a second forkful, then a third; and for the life of me, I wondered how anyone could've ever complained about food like this. I made a point of talking it up when Mamy came back, this time with Rigobert and Tumba.

"Ah, Jenni! You look so much better!"

"Thanks!" I felt better. The Chinese had saved my life; I knew that. "The food is yummy. Ridiculously good! So fresh! And one of the guys here has a laptop with a built-in DVD player. I've seen so many movies!"

Rigobert jittered in excitement before straightening his spine.

"No, not Nigerian ones. Hollywood ones — and ones I haven't seen. We saw a really good one yesterday. It was about an Arabian horse race. Hilda-something or other..." I squirmed to make space on the bed. Rigobert and Tumba sat but said they couldn't stay long. Dispatch was waiting.

Mamy gathered my mosquito net and tied it in a large floppy knot overhead. She was mothering me, which I suddenly realized was something she tended to do. I never knew whether she was dating anyone. But her older brother, Esther's father, didn't seem to be coming home from Kinshasa, and something told me there was no mother in the picture.

"There still electricity?" It was a question about President Kabila. For two weeks straight, authorities had rerouted lines from the Lutshurukuru hydroelectric power plant in Kalima. Also, he—the president—had just made a trip upriver to Kisangani. So it felt as though it ought to have been our time.

Rigobert said they'd heard Kabila might come on Thursday. Or perhaps next week.

Tumba spoke up in a monotone. "The head of the Coopération technique belge has been arrested in a police raid on his house. A trial has even started."

I immediately envisaged a man my father age's riding a motorcycle with a Congolese girl on the back. I'd never met the man but had seen him like this at least three or four times. "A trial? You're kidding? What's he accused of?"

Mamy and Rigobert exchanged a look. Tumba wriggled on the cot and said they didn't know exactly.

"What do you mean you don't know—exactly?"

"Marie-France said it wasn't a Radio Okapi story. She told us not to go to court."

"Or to follow the proceedings," said Rigobert.

I drew a breath. If I didn't swear, I wanted to. Their quietness helped. Because of course they would have seen the hypocrisy of Radio Okapi boycotting what appeared to be one of the rare carriages of justice that the UN was incessantly advocating for. They knew I knew they had no choice but to follow a direct order from the head of office. And I was irate at Marie-France, even though a part of me could understand why she would've told them to stay away from what was by design a very messy affair. Obviously, I thought she was wrong.

I turned to face Tumba. "Here's what we're going to do. Tomorrow, you go to court. Get all the information. Take notes. Do your interviews. And *then* discuss with Kinshasa. If Marie-France says anything to you—*anything whatsoever*—you tell her to call me here in the hospital."

Rigobert nodded approvingly. He had an excogitative look, as if he were considering the actions he would have taken in my place.

When Mamy slid her handbag down the crook of her arm, I remembered. "Please—someone," I said, reaching for my wallet. "Give this to Roger." I took out a five-dollar bill. "It's for Cat. Tell him it's for her goat."

I LEFT THE HOSPITAL on Thursday, when the rain had stopped and started several times over. The incident I'm thinking of—the one that changed it all—came several days later. Another *décrochage* had ended and the journalists had all gone home to their families. The radio was on low. I had just finished eating—an omelette, because the MONUC cafeteria was again out of potatoes—and was on the phone with Patricia, my boss in Kinshasa, whom I'd called.

"Of course, nine months in Kindu is enough," she was saying through an exhalation of smoke.

I thought: How late would she be staying in the office? And then what would she do? I wondered what kind of food she ate. Whether she was able to cook at home. I bet her place had air conditioning.

33

AS I'D FEARED, Yves Renard and Étienne lambasted us (me) over missing the Coopération technique belge story. Yves said we'd let down our listeners. Étienne said people were asking questions.

"I know," I said insistently, as if insistence could absolve blame. "I know. I don't know what to tell you. I was sick. I was in the hospital. I had no idea."

As it turned out, by the time Tumba had made it to court that Wednesday, the Belgian embassy had already intervened. The worker in question had been hastily repatriated to Belgium. And the case was now closed.

About a week after my release from the hospital, we all piled into the car and drove down to the university for another of Marie-France's town hall meetings, which was one of the more positive things to have come out of the Bukavu crisis. The idea was for MONUC's so-called substantive sections to brief the students on mission activities in the context of its overall peace and security mandate. The action was happening in the centre of a large rectangular hall, well away from the broken windows running the length of the room. Ignoring the extra space, the section in use was chockablock with young men and a few women, squeezed together on hardwood pews.

When it was my turn to speak, for both Public Information and Radio Okapi, I scoured the room for Peter of Light of Life and Mamy's younger brother, Parfum, but the sun was in my eyes. I spoke for maybe ten minutes, everything off the top of my head. Then it was time for questions. After five or six people, all of them neatly dressed and tidy, had pushed their way to the front, Marie-France reminded, "We're only taking two," loudly from offside. She was perched like a bird on the edge of a stackable plywood chair, as if deciding whether to fly or leave it at a simple squawk.

The first person in the line slouched aggressively with his hands in his pockets but still waited for a nod before introducing himself. In a hot voice—José had set up a microphone—the young man asked why Radio Okapi hadn't reported on the Belgian who was arrested and—in his words—deported last week. Was the radio censored? And if so, by whom? Because if it was, he said, Radio Okapi clearly wasn't the impartial medium it claimed to be.

I should have expected the question—that we'd be raked over the coals. And perhaps I had.

Indistinct keyed-up chatter shook the room, the scorching sun streaming in, cradling us in the balance: six hours had passed since dawn; six more would come before dusk. My eyes fell to Matthieu, who was wearing his *I Heart Jesus* baseball cap. It was softly wrinkled, the kind of cotton cap I liked. If you asked me, even two-worded T-shirts were hard to pull off with dignity, but Matthieu wore his cap easily. He loved what he loved and never questioned his right to. I looked at him and thought, *Here is a man who pays no heed to the cynics who give him every reason not to believe.*

The young man banged into the microphone stand accidentally. He cheeks were pinched tight. But he wasn't fooling me. He too believed, or else he wouldn't have asked the question.

"You're right," I said, thanking him by name. "We should have covered the story. It was a mistake that we didn't."

The room went quiet. Sadala, opposite me, looked watchful. It was the first I'd noticed his high cheekbones. After all this time.

"I was in the hospital with malaria when the story broke. There was a misunderstanding. I don't know how it happened. But anyway... the story didn't get covered. It was my fault. I'm sorry."

The hall remained quiet with expectation. I thought: *This is the chance I've been looking for...*

"The other part of your question — if I understood you correctly — has to do with our editorial line and the issue of censorship."

I can fix this...

"Radio Okapi works for you. It doesn't work for anyone else. It's not for my interest... not for the government's" — here I motioned towards Marie-France — "not for hers — and not for MONUC's."

I didn't mean any disrespect and hoped this was known.

"The radio was set up this way because democracy is about bringing power to the people — about giving people well-sourced, factual and impartial information... to allow you to make decisions for yourselves. So I can't promise you we won't make mistakes with the radio, but I can assure you that we won't allow ourselves to be censored. In fact, we did do a small story yesterday about the CTB and its plans for a permanent replacement, and we were able to get some information about what happened last week. We'll keep at it."

Marie-France-the-bird, now deciding to take flight, placed her palms aside her legs to propel herself off her chair. She hadn't yet found her balance before saying: "Okay, okay, just one other quick question for Radio Okapi — please."

But no one either sitting or standing in line made any attempt to step forward. I squinted to meet Mamy's gaze and slowly digested the fact that everyone had sought to raise the same question. The crowd retook their seats. My apology had been accepted. The matter was behind us.

A COUPLE OF DAYS LATER, in a brewing storm, Patricia called to confirm my reassignment. I set down the can of Fanta I'd just opened, as if preparing to interrupt her. She said "can you," but she was actually telling me to be installed at Radio Okapi Goma by the middle of next week. As we were talking, I consciously stopped thinking; I was too tired to think—and too scared that I might talk myself out of this.

I was just coming back from the cafeteria, after Tumba had finished a sweaty turn at the market and was talking to Rigobert and José. He was saying Kindu had the cheapest cement. José shook his head knowingly. "In Kin, it's *hors de prix*." In the absence of an official means to gauge inflation, a new Radio Okapi segment, *La Mercuriale,* compared prices across the country: a kilo of rice, a litre of kerosene, a three-pack of condoms—that sort of thing. Each week, Kinshasa would send a spreadsheet and the journalists would run around filling in the sheet, and then send it back to Kinshasa.

About the price of cement, the chunky heels of Sadala's cowboy boots coming back from the field interrupted whatever it was I was going to say.

"Ah Jenni," he said, seeing me. "Martin called. He says they're ready for Kindu in Bunia."

I nodded, not surprised. Sadala more than anyone kept track of the rotation. He had an uncle—Uncle Morgan—living in Bunia, who'd used to be a colonel in the old Mobutu army. These days, Uncle Morgan ran the guesthouse where some

UN staff and all the Radio Okapi station managers stayed, even though the place had thin walls, no running water and a cost of $800 a month. I assumed Uncle Morgan had the decency to put up Sadala for free and that that was why Sadala always wanted to go.

"They're waiting for us to send someone to Bunia," he said again.

I coughed a tickle out of my throat. Lying by omission felt… *constricting.*

"Nobody leave after the *décrochage*," I said, skirting around Tumba and José. "I want to talk to everyone. Just quick."

HOW SLOWLY the evening came, yet once it had, how fast the time seemed to have gone. Even as I was standing there, telling them I was leaving, it seemed as if this was just another one of our crises. And that I could fix it. But again, I was too tired to think.

"I know it seems sudden," I paused, "Patricia just called me." I didn't necessarily mean to lie but did so because the truth, as I knew it then, seemed illogical and incomplete.

Matthieu's face shrivelled. *"Vous partez?"*

"But the two Yves promised us you would stay here! That they wouldn't reassign you," Rigobert cried.

On another day, Mamy would break out and exclaim, "*Maman* Jennifer! Leaving us for Okapi Goma!" Today, however, she like everyone else took up the rituals of farewell with talk about how much I'd be missed.

At one point in our song and dance, Gabriel looked away, but not before flashing a look of wan regret that verged on dejection. In that one gesture I couldn't have felt worse than if he'd said, "Jenni, you've failed me. *Me* in particular." Of all the stupid things to think, I thought: *Have I not done enough for Gabriel? Did I not pay enough attention to him?*

BY MY LAST DAY IN KINDU, most outstanding matters had been resolved. Benjamin and Lumumba had found new bamboo fences to guard; I didn't know whose. Roger suggested coming with me to Goma, but I couldn't take on that responsibility. He offered to keep Cat, but that issue had already been resolved. The cat would be smuggled again, this time to Goma. She was still small enough for a purse. As for Roger, he was scheduled to start working at the MONUC cafeteria, of all places.

Near four o'clock, Rigobert and I were alone in the corner office. He wanted feedback on his work, and I'd given it to him, hard as it'd been to find something critical to say. Now we were looking through the binder of *conducteurs* I'd kept from the very beginning. My left-hand fingers anchored the pile, while my thumb lifted the corners of May.

"Ah!" I said breathily. "Remember this? The story about the crocodile that was eating all the fishermen in the Congo River?"

"Oh, yes," said Rigobert seriously. "In Salamabila. In the end, one of the fishermen built a large spear and killed it."

"Yes... I remember. He'd built a spear. That was quite something. Sadala covered it. I loved that story."

Mamy called out my name about something and my thumb let go. Rigobert and I returned to the newsroom, consigning the heavy black binder to the dust balls. Rigobert sneezed.

By this point, the newsroom could have used a good cleaning. Not of the kind that three young ladies with their blue buckets might undertake but of the *straightening* kind that can only be done by someone who knows what goes where, what can be thrown out and what must be saved. That role, I supposed, had been mine. At least it was something I'd always meant to get around to.

I stopped to look around the room: strewn loose-leaf on the desk, maps of places where Radio Okapi Kindu had been or would one day be. The paper marked *Bunia Rotation* showed Jean-Serge (for his first time) would be the next to go (and then Sadala). Jean-Serge would travel over Christmas, when, seen from the air, the Lualaba swelled with runoff.

Dog-eared as they were, the radio's editorial values adhered defiantly to the wall:

We are **professional** and work with rigour.

We are **independent** from political and economic powers, which is crucial for our impartiality and credibility.

We have the **integrity** to report **facts** as accurately as possible, taking into account our biases, prejudices, life experiences and personal perspectives.

We **respect** pluralism, the dignity of each individual, and that human rights are **universal**.

Mamy said my name again. She wanted me to look over one last change she'd made to a script on the Maniema government's assessment of how the province's poverty reduction strategy paper was being implemented—("half-measures," Governor Sumaili was calling it, vowing to flesh out the next one). I leaned in to read Mamy's screen and noticed she'd kicked off one of her sandals under her desk. "Ha!" I said. "I do that, too."

Okapi Jeune was just starting. Gabriel reached behind him to turn it down. Rigobert pushed back his chair and got up to go over to the steaming kettle on our white plastic table next to where Ulli's *I Love My Dad* mug was dripping from having been rinsed clean. At the back, our old Nescafé tin of sugar sat closed to the ants; beside it, thanks to Matthieu, duct tape covered the broken corners of our coffee pot. "You'll get cut!" he'd said in a syrupy voice—meaning: "if I had not intervened."

34

MY MOTHER OFTEN SAID there was no geographical cure. She'd say, "Jen, the problems you have in little old Dartmouth will follow you everywhere." I believed her. But being honest with myself, me leaving Kindu was absolutely an attempted geographical cure in its most literal sense. I was afraid of getting malaria again. I was terrified of it. The reality was that there were just too many blessed mosquitoes levitating around. Drugs couldn't hold them off. My physical resistance was down to zero. I couldn't go on not eating, getting thinner and thinner. I thought, *Next time, I die.*

But I couldn't leave the Congo. Not before the elections. They were due to be held within eight months, though Sadala said there was no way in hell they'd be organized in time. The Independent Electoral Commission (IEC) was just getting set up in Maniema — late, said Sadala. He said l'Abbé Apollinaire Malu Malu was going to have to ask parliament to push back the date; he wouldn't have a choice.

José had agreed and said people in Kinshasa were saying the same thing. "When Claude Buse interviewed Vital Kamerhe" — who was the leader of Kabila's political party, PPRD — "on DEC last week, he all but said it. There's no way they can register everybody... get the machines... and distribute all the ballots in time."

By April, the elections had been pushed back, just as Sadala had predicted, and just around the time that a special MONUC working group had come together to draw up a series of key messages that would eventually be marked *Confidential*. The big thing was no one was supposed to say the elections had been pushed back. No. The correct phrase was "the transition has been extended." I learned the language very early on, being part of the working group—in Kinshasa. Goma hadn't worked out. Not between me and Goma's nervy journalists, who reported as they lived in the Congo's most traitorous city: in a spectre of general distrust, questioning everything.

Of course this very idea of questioning everything made them fine journalists, you could see. And I liked them all *individually*. The problem was the lot of them. And me. They weren't joyous; I wasn't serious. I lacked authority. Michel, the smart Canadian, later said that if I'd been a man, things would've been different. But he'd said it in a tone of voice that had felt as though it had been his way of saying something else, something I wouldn't have liked.

And so I'd come to Kinshasa in March of 2005, three months after I'd left Kindu. I wasn't working with the radio anymore. I'd tell people, "Well, at least not directly"; I'd even say it to people who hadn't asked. My new job—still with MONUC—was to rally international support for the coming elections and get the Congo in the news (with op-eds and fact sheets and things like that—there was no social media back then; not there, not anywhere). And as I'd said before leaving Goma, in front of the journalists but to no one in particular—"How naïve would you have to be to expect that one day at a poll could bring about true democracy?" For now, at least, people where I came from would have to do more if things were going to change. It wasn't about charity or kindness.

Already I could talk for hours to my friends and family – anyone who would listen – about the Congolese radio station called Radio Okapi and how its impeccable, responsible newsgathering was inspiring a nation that had long needed a good news story. I'd become passionate about the radio's role in the peace process and dared to imagine *real* stories coming out of the Congo. Stories where people were real and were allowed to have real problems. Enough of these sweeping one-dimensional caricatures!

My new title was special assistant, public information division. My new boss was Algerian. Patricia was gone; Kemal had replaced her. Kemal's wife and teenaged children – it was a second marriage – lived in the family home in the U.S. Midwest. He was a Green Bay Packers fan; he had a key chain. I saw it sticking out of his pocket once. He drank endless amounts of coffee from the cafeteria downstairs (in paper cups left trailing in the soot and papers on his desk – no *I Love My Dad* mug). He had a flask and at least two shot glasses, which he kept in the top right-hand drawer and often resorted to using. And he had so many stories! Some of them he was in but many of them not. In the evenings, on the weekend or over a long lunch at Cercle Elaeis or La Piscine, he could weave a tapestry off the back of any flyaway remark. The art of conversation. He was a history buff and was never as sharp as when the topic was military-related. I thought, *Boy, would my dad like you.* More accurately, he would've been impressed.

Kemal was a yes man. "Can do" – he would say it like that, with a twinkle in his eyes, as if he (unlike everyone else, those lazy bums!) could make magic happen. At first, I had thought this was something he and I had in common.

Because of space issues, I sat at a spare desk in the Photo/Video Unit, pushed up against the back wall beside boxes and the office printer. Sitting there, no literary masterpieces were being crafted. No: there were spreadsheets and talking points. Dictated memos. With each grunt, Kevin, one of the video editors, would snigger and point: "Ah! Bar-code-y! Not having fun doing Kemal's dirty work?"

One afternoon in late July, Kemal called me into his office. I didn't feel the need to knock. He asked me what I was working on and didn't feel the need to look up.

"God, I don't know anymore… That memo about deploying an Okapi to Kikwit and Bandundu… Finishing the press kits… the ACABQ stuff, I don't know."

Kemal coughed in a swirl of smoke and said okay—as in, drop it all—because we had to start working on an RBB document (as in Results Based Budgeting) for the fifth floor. The fifth floor was a nickname people used for the Special Representative of the Secretary-General and his two deputies, whose offices were on the fifth floor. One of the two deputies was Kemal's direct boss.

As if he were half asleep, Kemal fumbled through a stack of papers heaped messily between two ashtrays. "A lot of the information can be found in here…"—a USB memory stick—"I'll send you… an example, so you can see how it works."

Kemal alternated between talking and coughing until he hacked something up and had to stop talking altogether. My stomach growled; it was almost lunch. I realized I hadn't accomplished anything I'd wanted to that morning. All the emails I wanted to send… Over lunch, I was going to run down to the travel agency on the Boulevard du 30 Juin to plan my next vacation. I was going home. To Halifax. Louis and I were through; he'd left me for some woman from Quebec who was old enough to make his mother uncomfortable. She—this older woman—was going to produce his show and had grand plans to distribute

it across Quebec and into Europe. So Louis was out of the picture, which brought about mixed emotions, including relief, for
our split freed me up to go see Cat, who now lived in Dartmouth
with my parents, and the other cat I'd previously given up. I'd
ended up taking the cat back to Canada over Christmas in a
birdcage on a flight via Uganda.

"Bakody, are you listening to me?"

"Yes," I said, sitting up sharply. I was.

"So. As I was saying…"

It was now that I saw it: a scrap of scribbles. One name.
And a place. Not just any place. "That note you have up there.
You need someone to fill in for Bilamekaso?"

Bilamekaso was the person who had replaced me in Kindu.
He was from Togo.

Kemal cranked his head. "Oh, yeah, right. That's another
thing." He reached for his Zippo lighter. "We'll have to find a
replacement for Kindu, for three weeks, while Bil's on vacation."

I paused, and said I could go.

Kemal said, "You?" And then he paused. "Someone else can
go. I need you here."

"No, you don't. I mean… not really. I can still work on all the
stuff you need me to from there."

Now came the dreaded "We'll see." I knew it well from my
mother, who used it tirelessly as an alternative for no. I supposed there was no use but still pleaded my case as Kemal set
the last ashes of his cigarette aside the tray. He didn't extinguish
it, which is a different thing.

"I'm sending you that example right now. We need to get on
this RBB today."

VOTER REGISTRATION STARTED in Maniema in late August
2005. The day before, MONUC's Electoral Assistance Division—

in partnership with the IEC, so everything orange and blue — led various sections in a motorized convoy through Kindu's main axes, past Celtel and Vodacom scratch card vendors and the new *cambistes* sitting behind elastic-bound money wads on the side of the road. Dozens of orange-capped motorcyclists in blue and orange T-shirts, the collars still tight, all of whom were day hires courtesy of international funds, wove their bikes in and around the procession. Some people had megaphones. Matthieu looked out from under his orange rim onto the tires of an IEC-branded pickup truck and the whiteness of the road. Feverish shouts, in broken and accented French — "Registration tomorrow! Yay! Elections in the Congo! Yay!" — drew him back inside the car.

"Jenni! *Nakupenda sana*"; he'd missed me, he said. He was laughing; I was laughing. Mamy was in fine form, too. She was in the back with a Mini Disc player. Marie-France was two cars ahead.

Civic education. How happy I was to be driving around here doing it. Delighted to have gotten my way, Kemal be damned.

Matthieu poked a large IEC flag out the window into the blazing heat. When the pole slipped in his grip, he jerked in panic and then laughed at himself. People from the slum apartments on the corner (which Rigobert said had once been a luxury hotel but which I knew as the place where FARDC soldiers lived) stood leaning over the balcony's cast-iron rail, waving enthusiastically. Gone was laundry besmirched with river water hanging out to dry; the exterior walls were washed clean and painted limoncello.

On the day of voter registration, the journalists fanned out across the province, bearing in mind political tendencies, economic importance and potential trouble spots. Rigobert and I were to man the desk. I was staying at one of the humanitarian affairs officers' place while he was away. My old house had been taken over by the electoral commission; it was now their headquarters in Maniema. And when I arrived in the newsroom with an onion omelette and fries from the cafeteria—a real Congolese-American breakfast—a pot of filter coffee was already on. It had been strange to see Roger in the cafeteria, standing next to the tall lanky guy and Bijou.

"Rigobert! Good morning!"

"Good morning," he said. Then: "No problems," when I asked. "It's slow, though. Tumba says where he is in Alunguli it's taking thirty-five minutes to process one person. One of the machines has broken down. They only have two."

"Two left?"

"One left."

Sadala called in later from Kalima, saying enumerators were struggling to verify people's nationalities. At issue were the adult children of Burundian and Rwandan men who'd come to the Congo before independence to work in the mines, a fact that had been disclosed when their personal referees had shown up. Ironically (or not), many of these people had never set foot outside the Congo.

Sadala told the story so gaudily you would've thought he was somehow caught up in it. Or that he knew someone personally who was. But I knew him; he was just being Sadala. I interrupted him to pass him over to Rigobert, who reached for a notebook and pen.

NOT TWO WEEKS LATER (because I was still in Kindu when it happened), *OKAPI exPress* announced Radio Okapi was appointing senior news editors at the regional level—staff who would take over daily assignment from the radio's expatriate *chefs d'antenne,* who would themselves be relegated to oversight.

The news—with the names—came out that Friday night after our *décrochage*. There were no hollers or whooping, just thoughts left agonizingly unspoken. Almost immediately, Rigobert put on a poker face of sorts, betrayed by the corners of his mouth.

"Congratulations, Rigobert," said Gabriel finally, with a detectable trace of good manners.

Mamy was the most zealous: "Chief!" she ragged, patting him on the shoulder. "*Ree-go-bearrrrr!!*"

Jean-Serge stood and gathered his briefcase. "Okay, well, see you tomorrow, Jenni. I'm the one working *permanence* tomorrow."

The sunlight was fading, the darkness throwing small beasts against my window. MONUC Engineering had finally removed the boards. Of course, every last insect crowding this light had never known anything different.

Rigobert was the last to pack up and go. He peeked into my office before leaving.

"Congratulations again," I said. "I know you'll do a fabulous job."

"*Merci. Merci…*" His voice trailed off in the way voices do when a person has more to say about something related but different. "Jennifer? I'd like us to sit down when you have a moment so we can discuss how you expect my new role to work." He was holding a hard copy of this week's *OKAPI exPress*. He'd printed it to take home. "Also, I'd like my own workspace, if possible."

"Of course, that's mos—"

"Apart from the main desk."

I waited. Perhaps he wasn't done.

"Rigobert, of course we'll sit down and work through what role exactly you'll be playing within the newsroom. More or less, the way I see it, you'll be responsible for story assignment, coordination with Kinshasa and making sure that Kindu's subjects shape up as they should. That's what I was doing, anyway."

Rigobert relaxed, almost fully. By now, I loved seeing him like this, so it's likely I smiled when he said, "I see it that way, too."

He seemed to like what I suggested next: that he set up a workspace, for now, in the corner by the window, opposite Sadala. "Tomorrow, contact IT to help you move one of the computers over. Get them to give you a form to install your own phone line—and we can get Supply to give you a cabinet or shelves or something to organize your stuff."

Rigobert left shortly thereafter, walking back to his house, where his wife, their children and his sister's children were sleeping for the night. Cameroonian jazz angel Richard Bona sang in the blackness enveloping my little old office. Bona was cool as a cucumber (or was that the air conditioning?) but sounded a bit melancholic. Lonely even.

CONGO'S GENERAL ELECTIONS were held on July 30, 2006. At the time, I was the *chef d'antenne* and head of public information in Bunia, where there were enough problems to keep us busy but scarcely more. The transitional government had negotiated a deal with the region's militias in the run-up to the polls. The terms weren't disclosed, but the pot must've been sweetened enough, because Kasai, where Matthieu's daughter was living with his brother, was the only province were things really got out of hand. Even then, it was limited to riots and looting. The violence was caused by veteran opposition leader Étienne Tshisekedi's decision to boycott the polls; Kasai was his home turf.

The presidential election took two rounds to decide. It was down to President Kabila and Vice-President Jean-Pierre Bemba. On November 15, the Independent Electoral Commission released its full provisional results, handing victory to Kabila.

This was the first time I'd ever heard mortar fire. I was in Kinshasa, checking out of the mission, when it started: deep, burrowing explosions vibrating though a vehemence of machetes, boulders and flames. How violent would things get? I figured I'd make it out just under the wire.

A ceasefire deal was struck in good time, all things considered. Bemba took his grievances to the courts, claiming irregularities. By November 27 – so within days – the Supreme Court confirmed that Kabila had won the election. I was gone by then.

IN SOME WAYS, my story only began after I left the Congo — when things became quieter and there was distance and, as Rigobert would have put it, I could look up from my life.

Work-wise, I just kept going. First, I went to London, to work for a charitable arm of the BBC, then called the BBC World Service Trust. My job was to manage media development projects in Africa. For instance, I was in charge of an initiative that sent Sierra Leonean and Liberian radio reporters to The Hague to cover the war crimes trial of former Liberian president Charles Taylor.

I liked my new job — or rather, aspects of my job, starting with the idea of it. But it was no Radio Okapi.

London was cold. The bottoms of my feet cracked and bled, and all the foot cream in the world couldn't fill the fissures. It was dark by 3 PM. Grey-scale figures outside the window of Bush House's southern facade scurried head down the 1,200-metre thoroughfare known as the Strand. No one ever slowed for any reason — all these solitary figures with some place to be, somewhere to go, other than where they were, hoping to escape the darkness. Come 5 or 6 PM, I was one of them.

I met someone: another Frenchman, another neighbour. Without necessarily being the man I was looking for, he was

every bit that person, plus a great deal more. He was so genuinely likeable, so exemplary, so complete, that immediately
upon meeting him, I said to myself, "That guy would make a
great catch for somebody." Of course, I was somebody. Once we
started dating, we saw each other every day.

Throughout this time, I called the journalists in Kindu the
odd time or two. Everyone had their lives. There was social media
now, plus I found it impossible to make out anything said over
the phone: either I was going deaf or the connection was that bad.

Then came the sad day I found out about Serge Maheshe. The
story had been prominently placed; as in, I hadn't gone hunt-
ing for it on some obscure site. I later said to my husband (we
weren't married yet but would be) that Serge Maheshe's death
fit the bill for international news coverage to a T, because 1) he
was a UN staff member who was 2) working for a UN-backed
radio mandated to help bring about peace in one of the world's
most dangerous places. And on top of that, 3) Radio Okapi was
seen as a huge success story, and of course 4) Maheshe was the
first Radio Okapi journalist murdered.

I had come to know Serge in Bunia. He and Stéphane
from Kinshasa and Ascain from Mbandaka, who were on the
same rotation, often hung around the prefab container where
we worked, watching France's game show *Questions pour un
champion* on the Internet, their sprawling limbs draping over
each other like rag dolls. I called them the Three Musketeers.
I'd be cleaning up the *conducteur* or polishing off some press
release when one of them would suddenly shout out something
like – "Quick! Jenni! Women's lacrosse ball: what colour?" Or:
"The national bird of Canada?" And I'd scream back in panic,
"What? Umm… Oh!… I don't know!" I never knew, but they still
kept asking. You'd think they would've figured out I was a lost
cause. Afterwards, Ascain would say something as gratuitous

as it was dubious, like, "Tell me, Jenni, am I not the most handsome black man you've ever seen?" Because he and Stéphane and Serge were jokers, yes, but they had me figured out.

Serge was murdered in Bukavu. On the street. He'd just been with friends, planning the logistics and cost structure of someone's wedding (they were the wedding committee, which was how it frequently worked in the Congo), and was about to get into a UN vehicle when two men in plain clothes stopped him and said, "What's your name? On your knees!" They then shot him in the chest and legs, leaving his companions unharmed.

As soon as I found out, I picked up the phone and called Kindu.

There were a number of reasons why I'd left the Congo. My attempt to outrun death had been one. And not just my own. We'd all known this day was coming and would come again.

"Jenni!" cried Jean-Serge. *"Oh, c'est Jenni! Jenni! Quel plaisir!"*

Damn, I thought. The line was still bad.

"Jenni! How are you? We miss you! Eh, Jenni! Where are you calling from?"

Jean-Serge and I talked a long while. Everybody was well, he said. Things were good at the radio. Bilamekaso had left— he'd been reassigned to Bunia. It was just Martha now (she was a UNV from Cameroon who'd been brought in for the elections and had stayed on). And Rigobert, of course. Sadala was now in Bunia, too—permanently. Jean-Serge said he'd been transferred the year before, though I myself had been in Bunia until almost that December and hadn't heard anything about it. It was one of those things that didn't add up that was hard to work through because of our poor connection.

And Mamy had gotten married? Jean-Serge said something about her having met a doctor from Goma. I said, "What? Married? Put her on!" But apparently she wasn't there.

"Did you hear about Serge Maheshe in Bukavu?" he finally asked.

I drew a breath. My head turned out the window to the Strand. "It's why I called," I said, scarcely above a whisper. "What happened?"

"Jenni! *Jenni?*"

"I'm here. Jean-Serge? Can you hear me?"

"Jenni, yes, I can hear you. Wait—Matthieu wants to say hi."

Matthieu sounded just like Matthieu. He said Serge had been looking into old RCD stuff—military stuff—and his murder had probably been politically motivated, which was exactly the sort of thing I didn't want to hear.

"Jeanne is pregnant again." Matthieu might have thought he was changing the subject, when to me, in my frame of mind, it was all related.

"Pregnant! I thought you said you weren't going to have any more kids!"

Matthieu had been right; it felt good to laugh.

The next time I called Kindu, perhaps a year later, was to speak to Gabriel. There had been a blurb in the news: "DR Congo: Radio Okapi journalist in Kindu receives death threats."

Gabriel picked up. And to tell the story, he had to take things back—to after Koloso Sumaili had won a seat in Kinshasa with the new government and a member of Kabila's ruling PPRD had replaced him as governor. That man, said Gabriel—Governor Didier Manara Linga—had become the subject of many Okapi reports.

"So the other day in Lubutu," said Gabriel, sounding dry and factual, "a businessman from South Africa came and deposited $10,000 into the public treasury. I did the story." There'd been a record of the deposit, he said, but no money. Apparently people had been quick to denounce the alleged crime and had implicated two men. One had been the local head of the Congolese Business Federation, Séverin Kizozo; the other, Governor Manara.

Gabriel said his report had just aired when he'd received a phone call from an anonymous number. "A man spoke. He sounded Congolese. He said, 'Wamenya? Watch out. We're going to kill you. Just like Serge Maheshe. And Radio Okapi will still go on.' Then they hung up."

I said something like, "My God!" or "Jesus!" and asked him what he was going to do. "You can't stay there and keep working. Did you talk to Kinshasa? What did they say? They have to do something for you."

Gabriel said as a first step he would go to Kinshasa. Then they would take it from there. I had to ask him again: "What are you going to do?"

"Jenni…" He knew what I'd meant was, "For cripes' sake, quit! Get the hell out of there!"

He was slow to speak but finally said, very softly but unmistakably, "This is what I do."

THE NEXT FOUR YEARS saw many people tied to Radio Okapi die, as I learned things about life that can't easily be reconciled as lessons. At the end of 2008, another Radio Okapi Bukavu journalist was murdered: Didace Namujimbo—and there was no justice for him either. Soon, I would stop counting the number of Radio Okapi journalists elsewhere—in Kinshasa, Goma and Bunia—dying young of heart disease, HIV/AIDS or other health-related complications. Perhaps there were six or seven.

One day in early 2010, Mamadou, who'd been redeployed to MINUSTAH, the UN peacekeeping mission in Haiti, was on the fourth floor of the mission's six-storey headquarters in Hotel Christopher, on a tour in east Port-au-Prince, when an earthquake struck. He died. He'd been in a senior management meeting. MINUSTAH's newsroom was located on the ground floor, so the radio's staff, including at least four or five former Okapis, had been able to run out, though they'd only had seconds.

Mamadou was in his mid-forties then—which was about the same age that Michel was when he suddenly died a couple years later at his new UN posting in Cyprus. I actually fell to the ground when I heard the news.

In 2011, the new UN peacekeeping mission in the Congo, MONUSCO, tarnished MONUC's faultless air safety record. A Bombardier Canadian Regional Jet travelling from Kisangani crash-landed in heavy rain and high winds at N'Djili Airport. Twenty-nine passengers and four crew members—everyone on board but one—died on impact, including Maniema's former vice-governor Masudi Mendes. Later, Tumba told me that he'd actually gone to school with Mendes. Tumba said the news had hit people in Maniema hard; he said with the passage of time, Mendes had come to be seen as the best authority the province had ever had. He was sociable—charismatic, certainly—and was known to be generous. People admired his support of Uni-Kin students, Tumba said. He'd even donated to orphaned children.

I was in Beijing a year later when I found out about Sadala. I hadn't even known he was sick. Matthieu knew, though; he'd seen Sadala in Kananga, in Kasai. He said he'd gone to check on his daughter and had left worried about Sadala, who'd been transferred, again, from Bunia to the Radio Okapi station there. As Matthieu later said to his wife back in Kindu, clearly something was wrong with Sadala. He wasn't himself. He'd lost his corpulence, he was black; they were all black of course, but Sadala's skin had turned sickly, tenebrous. And his foot; it was swollen—rotting even. The two friends had been dining at an old colonial-style house where Sadala was living alone, and speaking under his breath, Sadala had told Matthieu he wasn't well. He said he thought he'd been poisoned.

Of course, he wasn't poisoned.

Mamy was the first one to write. She said: *Jennifer, Sadala Shabani is gone. He died last Tuesday. My condolences.*

It was the condolences part that got me, her acknowledgement that all along she'd seen what I'd hidden from myself. At the time, I'd told myself that maintaining a certain healthy distance from my colleagues was good for our work, so good for them. But that wasn't it. That wasn't why I'd allowed myself to dance and sing—teach, and be cute about it—but never engage my dear friends in conversations about the things they'd seen, loved and reviled, and how that had left them frightened or bitter or hopeful or resolute. I hadn't been dumb, or too overwhelmed. I'd been scared. And selfish. I was protecting myself. From exactly the kind of pain I was feeling right now. All that time in the Congo working for Radio Okapi, preaching about the importance of information and connectivity, and I never made the connections that truly mattered.

I vowed then and there to fix that. It became my new mission.

RADIO OKAPI KINDU, DECEMBER 2002

The RCD assault on Rigobert hadn't been the last attack against Radio Okapi—far from it. At the same time, the radio's resources continued to grow. A local technician (former RTNC) and an expatriate station manager (a certain Malick Faye) were hired, putting Radio Okapi Kindu in the enviable position of being able to break away from national programming. Mamy and Gabriel's UN contracts came through. Tumba's would follow shortly thereafter.

On Christmas Eve 2002, Mamy was in a courtroom, of all places, where all around her fidgeting military men would stand up and stride over to a junior, looking to be saluted for all to see.

Mamy tried to remember all the practical things Rigobert had taught her (like how to take a voice level, how to get good sound or record without hiss, and how to decide which stories to pitch and which interlocutors to approach). Because, of all her colleagues who'd been trained to teach, Rigobert ended up being the one to mentor her. He taught her how to turn her curiosity into questions—and told her, "Act smart. Don't go swinging around your microphone aiming for a fight." And she was never to risk her self-respect: a "brown envelope" in exchange for favourable news coverage might buy you lunch but would ensure your last supper in the longer run. "In the end, all a man has is his integrity," he'd said.

"What time's the verdict supposed to be?" said Mwinyi, loudly in her ear. She and Mwinyi had come to the tribunal together, he to record the judgement handed down. Mamy could've managed herself, and maybe just as well. But here he was, their new technician, doing what he was paid to do.

On the face of it, today's case would be open and shut. *Guilty!* had long been the default ruling. Plus, the prosecutor himself had been the one to invite the radio, suggesting he was certain things would go his way. Still, Mamy was curious to see what the judge would make of it all: RCD commanders accused of ordering Mai-Mais shot and killed. Nothing strange there—only by some adrenaline-rushed error, some flight of fancy, some random people just minding their own business had wound up bulleted to death.

Mamy checked her watch. These things were notoriously late so that to talk of delays in days was typical.

"Just start recording now," said Mamy shortly. "Or at least get set up for it."

Kasmu Mwinyi Ramzani was a weedy, impish man with a concave stomach that looked like someone's punching bag. His skin had greened like a potato, his high-bridged nose worn down to be indistinct. So he had a pliable look that wasn't entirely incongruent with his tendency to languish pending instruction.

"If I start recording now and it doesn't start for hours, we'll waste time back in the studio feeding it all in."

Mamy inhaled shallowly and thought to herself: *This Ramzani guy has an answer for everything.* She opened her mouth, just as someone cried out behind her.

"What are you doing?"

Mwinyi's black eyes cast wide over Mamy's shoulder. She turned around and looked.

"You're from the radio! You're journalists!"

A court official. Another was approaching.

Fortunately, Mamy had come prepared. She slid her hand down the smoothness of her purse to feel for a sheet of folded paper. The invitation would set things straight.

Regrettably, these men weren't at all interested in reading anything fancy. One began to yell. Then both were yelling. Then, once they'd tired themselves of that, they kicked up a real fuss and bound her in their arms.

Mwinyi ran back to alert la Monique. With his small croaky voice he cried: "Mamy's in jail!"

Would Mamy's father have a strong case now! At least, he *would have had* a strong case, had he been a different kind of man, the kind to say I told you so, or the kind less willing to be wrong—or worse, the kind of man who feared the dreaded words, "Where were the parents?" But Papa Tshibangu wasn't that man. He just wanted to see his daughter successful, and happy. And yes, safe.

Immediately, Eliane, Ulli and the others went down to the jail to negotiate Mamy's release. Her prospects looked good, though the nature of the haggle required things to stall. Eliane left and came back with a mattress when it became clear that Mamy would have to spend the night. The prison director offered up his office.

On Christmas morning, the RCD's Secretary-General, Azarias Ruberwa, himself a trained lawyer, authorized Mamy's unconditional release. Once out, Mamy shook her head and laughed. It hadn't been so bad, she said. The best part of it was she'd left with a ton of stories. She first quipped to her father, then later to Rigobert: "They really hadn't been thinking, putting a journalist on the inside like that!"

Epilogue

I DID NOT SPEND my fortieth birthday in Africa. I was only slightly disappointed, because, first, I had just been. I went back to Kindu. I had to. Mamy, Rigobert and Tumba met me at the airport, which had been turned green and, more than that, felt all turned around. And I cried when Rigobert touched my head with his and said of all the foreign *chefs d'antenne* they'd had, never once had anyone come back to see them. They threw me a party at Mamy's massive A-frame house, with its glorious giraffe-spotted brick (by now, Mamy had divorced her husband and had their house signed over in her name) and sprawling front yard enclosed by a bamboo gate. And Mamy gave up her bed for me, with its crisp new sheets and bedside fan. She had three beautiful boys, plus Esther, and another little niece was always around.

After being threatened that time, Gabriel was transferred to Radio Okapi Goma. Not long afterwards, Jean-Serge's contract with Fondation Hirondelle ran out and wasn't renewed. Rigobert said at first Jean-Serge would come to the newsroom from time to time and whoever was there would give him food. They later managed to get him an MOP to Kinshasa where he said he had family. But as it turned out, he only sort of knew a handful of people, the kind who'd put him up for a day or two. Eventually, he went south to Kikwit, an administrative centre known for its stadium, traditional Pende dance and raffia figurines.

Sadala was gone; and now Matthieu's health had taken a turn for the worse. This was why I met with Matthieu and his wife not in Kindu but in Kinshasa. He had just been released from hospital. He explained to me what the problem was, but I didn't really understand. Could it have been hepatitis? It didn't matter, because the doctors managed to fix whatever had gone wrong. Thank God.

Today, Matthieu is the only person working at Radio Okapi Kindu. There is a long drawn-out story behind that. The short story is, after years of flux, a decision was made to convert Radio Okapi Kindu from a regional station into a feeder hub. This meant an end to Kindu's *décrochage* — so no technician — plus the elimination of two journalist posts, subjecting Mamy, Rigobert, Matthieu and Tumba to a competitive recruitment process. When Mamy emailed to tell me the news, I didn't believe her. In the end, Rigobert and Matthieu were retained, and Mamy and Tumba were handed separation letters delivered all the way from New York.

Rigobert recently retired. José, who replaced Kasmu, was granted asylum in Belgium for reasons I never did get. I lost touch with Kasmu. Gabriel is still in Goma, and last I heard, Jean-Serge was still in Kikwit. Mamy had planned to run for office, but the rules disqualified her; they said she was from Kasai. She's now looking for work; Tumba I believe is not. Roger used to serve tables at Kindu's new luxury hotel, Jay Hôtel, but is once again out of a job. Cat lives in Canada with my parents. My mother renamed her L'il Kitty.

As for the Congo itself, *brassage* never worked. Too much treason and disloyalty, said Mamy. So within the framework of the Belgian-Congolese Military Partnership Programme, the Belgians drilled the Congolese army's 321st Battalion commando of the rapid reaction forces, then the 322nd, so that the Congo possessed two elite forces comprised of proper, out-of-the-box soldiers too young to have been formerly anything other than the hope of a peace-aspiring generation. Of course, such a novel approach to security sector reform could only be flanked at a soft bend in the Lualaba, in a place with real experience and success in such things.

By the end of 2013, these two elite, professionally trained units had played a vital role in putting down the M23 rebellion, which had been yet another incarnation of foreign-backed mutineers in the Congo. The Belgians later drilled a third battalion, the 323rd, after which followed a remittance of certificates and ceremonial *cordelettes*. At the time, Radio Okapi Kindu broadcast the words of then Congolese defence minister Alexandre Luba Ntambo, who told them: "Never betray the Congo." It was the battalion's new motto. Ntambo said, "The nation awaits exemplary behaviour from you."

The Congo is still fraught with problems. But there have been improvements: Take Kindu's university, Uni-Kin, for instance. Kabila had a new campus constructed. A site was chosen some distance from the city centre, accessible by a new wide, straight road, and a garage built to store people's motorcycles. Work was done to beautify a nearby lily pond; students could either study there in peace or hunker down on the campus's lush lawns, reading among the egrets. There was a football field, too—and this was not Kindu's only one, because at some point someone had the brilliant idea of transforming the old tennis court into something people could relate to, and thus would use.

I said there were two reasons why I was only slightly disappointed not to spend my fortieth birthday in Africa. You see, my husband and I had just become parents. We adopted a beautiful baby girl. The day we brought her home, she was nine months old. Nine months. It isn't long in a lifetime. But it is a period of time long enough to birth a course of love and security and, as such, deserves honour; and may I never forget it.

One final word on Radio Okapi: when recognizing the network with its Free Media Pioneer Award, the International Press Institute lauded its professionalism and success in drawing in a full third of the country every day, calling it a shining example, not only for media in other conflict or post-conflict areas but for radio stations around the world.

Radio Okapi remains the Congo's number one news and information station.

List of Abbreviations

A4 Letter paper size most commonly used outside North America

ADF Alliance of Democratic Forces (partly Islamist rebel group of Ugandan origin)

AK-47 Selective-fire assault rifle of Soviet origin (Kalashnikov family)

ANC Armée nationale congolaise (Congolese army post-independence until 1997 and the name of the armed forces of the RCD-Goma)

BBC British Broadcasting Corporation

CBC Canadian Broadcasting Corporation

CONADER Congolese government body responsible for the disarmament process

CNN Cable News Network (U.S. news channel)

CRS Catholic Relief Services (humanitarian aid organization of U.S. origin)

Chapter VI Part of the United Nations Charter that deals with the peaceful settlement of disputes

DDR Disarmament, demobilization and reintegration

DDRRR Disarmament, demobilization, repatriation, reintegration and resettlement

DEET Diethyltoluamide (most common active ingredient in insect repellents)

DRC Democratic Republic of the Congo

FARDC Forces armées de la République démocratique du Congo (Congolese army)

FDLR Democratic Forces for the Liberation of Rwanda (mostly Hutu Rwandan rebels)

FNL National Forces of Liberation (Burundian political party and rebel group)

FTP File transfer protocol (system used to transfer computer files on a network)

GSSP Special Presidential Security Group (Congolese presidential security forces)

IEC Independent Electoral Commission

KFM Kindu-based commercial FM (frequency modulation) radio station

M16 Assault rifle of U.S. origin

M23 March 23 movement (rebel military group based in eastern DRC)

MINUSTAH United Nations Stabilization Mission in Haiti

MLC Movement for the Liberation of Congo (populist, liberalist political party)

MONUC United Nations Organization Mission in the Democratic Republic of the Congo

MONUSCO United Nations Organization Stabilization Mission in the Democratic Republic of the Congo

MOP Movement of Personnel (UN form permitting travel on UN flights)

OCHA Office for the Coordination of Humanitarian Affairs (UN)

OIC Officer in charge

ONUC United Nations Operation in the Congo

OZRT Office zaïrois de radiodiffusion et de télévision (Zairian state broadcaster)

PPRD People's Party for Reconstruction (centre-left political party)

QIP Quick Impact Project (UN community-based assistance program)

RCD Rally for Congolese Democracy (social-liberalist political party and rebel group)

RCD-Goma Rally for Congolese Democracy, Goma

RCD-KML Rally for Congolese Democracy, Kisangani

RFI Radio France Internationale (French international radio)

RTNC Radio-Télévision nationale du Congo

SAR 80 Conventional assault rifle from Singapore

UNDP United Nations Development Programme

UNV United Nations Volunteer

WHO World Health Organization